ETHICS IN CRISIS

Ethics in Crisis offers a constructive proposal for the shape of contemporary Christian ethics drawing on a new and persuasive interpretation of the ethics of Karl Barth. David Clough argues that Karl Barth's ethical thought remained defined by the theology of crisis that he set out in his 1922 commentary on *Romans*, and that his ethics must therefore be understood dialectically, caught in an unresolved tension between what theology must and cannot be. Showing that this understanding of Barth is a resource for contemporary constructive accounts of Christian ethics, Clough points to a way beyond the idolatry of ethical absolutism on the one hand, and the apostasy of ethical postmodernism on the other.

Barth Studies

Series Editors

John Webster, Professor of Theology, University of Aberdeen, UK
George Hunsinger, Director of the Center for Barth Studies,
Princeton University, USA
Hans-Anton Drewes, Director of the Karl Barth Archive, Basel, Switzerland

The work of Barth is central to the history of modern western theology and remains a major voice in contemporary constructive theology. His writings have been the subject of intensive scrutiny and re-evaluation over the past two decades, notably on the part of English-language Barth scholars who have often been at the forefront of fresh interpretation and creative appropriation of his theology. Study of Barth, both by graduate students and by established scholars, is a significant enterprise; literature on him and conferences devoted to his work abound; the Karl Barth Archive in Switzerland and the Center for Barth Studies at Princeton give institutional profile to these interests. Barth's work is also considered by many to be a significant resource for the intellectual life of the churches.

Drawing from the wide pool of Barth scholarship, and including translations of Barth's works, this series aims to function as a means by which writing on Barth, of the highest scholarly calibre, can find publication. The series builds upon and furthers the interest in Barth's work in the theological academy and the church.

Ethics in Crisis

Interpreting Barth's Ethics

DAVID CLOUGH
St John's College, Durham, UK

ASHGATE

Published by
Ashgate Publishing Limited
Gower House
Croft Road
Aldershot
Hampshire GU11 3HR
England

Ashgate Publishing Company
Suite 420
101 Cherry Street
Burlington, VT 05401-4405
USA

Ashgate website: http://www.ashgate.com

British Library Cataloguing in Publication Data
Clough, David
    Ethics in crisis : interpreting Barth's ethics. – (Barth
    studies)
    1. Barth, Karl, 1886–1968 – Ethics 2. Christian ethics
    I. Title
    241'.092

Library of Congress Cataloging-in-Publication Data
Clough, David, 1968–
        Ethics in crisis : interpreting Barth's ethics / David Clough.
            p. cm.—(Barth Studies)
        Includes bibliographical references and index.
        ISBN 0-7546-3630-5 (hardcover : alk. paper)
    1. Barth, Karl, 1886–1968. 2. Bible. N.T. Romans II—Criticism, interpretation,
etc. 3. Christian ethics. I. Title. II. Series.

        BX4827.B3C54 2005
        241'.092—dc22

                                                                2004025358

ISBN 0 7546 3630 5

Typeset in Times Roman by N²productions
Printed and bound in Great Britain by MPG Books Ltd, Bodmin, Cornwall.

For Lucy

Contents

Acknowledgements

Authorship is as dialectical a concept as any discussed in these pages: no author can reach the end of a project without a visceral sense of their role in bringing the work to fruition, yet it is no less true to say that our words and ideas come from the communities we belong to and the persons we have learned from. In the instance of the present work, this second dialectical element is very clear to me, and I am grateful to my teachers, colleagues, and friends, for the many ways in which they contributed to the realization of this work. It was Nigel Biggar whose enthusiasm for Barth first sparked mine, and Oliver O'Donovan who advised me that engaging with Barth would never prove to have been time misspent. In this judgement I still concur.

Yale was a hospitable environment for pursuing my interest in Barth, and I benefited greatly from formal and informal discussions with fellow students Chris Steck, Karen Peterson Iyer, Bill Danaher, Lauris Kaldjian, Eric Gregory, and Jennifer Beste. I owe a particular debt to Jesse Couenhoven, who faithfully read large parts of earlier drafts and provided insightful comment; to Amy Laura Hall, whose regular encouragement made writing less like a survival course; and to Brian Stiltner, who read and commented on much of the text, but also generously shepherded me through the early stages of the project. The contribution of Yale faculty was indispensable: conversations with Serene Jones and Thomas Ogletree helped me to formulate my nascent ideas about Barth, and I learned much from Margaret Farley – not least the importance of a Christian ethic that can speak beyond the Church. Gene Outka has been the greatest influence on the project. He directed me towards a fruitful and manageable angle to take on Barth's ethics, and has been a painstaking reader and constructive critic.

Beyond Yale, I have been grateful for conversation with George Hunsinger, Bruce McCormack, Michael Banner, and John Webster, which provided much needed illumination as I tried to formulate my early ideas. A research fellowship from St Chad's College, Durham, sustained me through a key lap of research and writing, and study leave from my present post at St John's College, largely spent in the wonderful Meissen Library of Durham Cathedral, brought me close to the finishing post: I am thankful to all three institutions. Robert Song and Chloe Starr have been diligent and helpful readers of recent drafts, and have saved me from many a slip as well as encouraging me towards boldness and clarity, and Sylvia Graham has kindly looked over much of my German translation. Responsibility for the remaining lapses in accuracy and clarity remains, of course, my own.

Thanks are due to Blackwell Publishers for permission to include in Chapter 5 some material originally published in '*Eros* and *Agape* in Karl Barth's *Church*

Dogmatics', *International Journal of Systematic Theology* 2:2 (2000), 189–203; and to Ashgate Publishing for permission to incorporate in Chapter 6 parts of my chapter 'Fighting at the Command of God: Assessing the Borderline Case in Karl Barth's Account of War in the *Church Dogmatics*' from *Conversing with Barth* (2004), edited by John McDowell and Mike Higton.

My thinking about and work for this book has lasted almost as long as my marriage to Lucy. The joy of the latter has sustained me through times when the former seemed less joyful. My heartfelt thanks to her.

Abbreviations

CD	Karl Barth, *Church Dogmatics*, 4 volumes, 13 part-volumes, ed. G.W. Bromiley and T.F. Torrance (Edinburgh: T. & T. Clark, 1936–77)
KD	Karl Barth, *Kirchliche Dogmatik*, 4 volumes, 13 part-volumes (Zurich: Theologischer Verlag, 1986–1993)
Römer II	Karl Barth, *Der Römerbrief (Zweite Fassung) 1922* (Zurich: Theologischer Verlag, 1989)
Romans II	Karl Barth, *The Epistle to the Romans*, trans. Edwyn C. Hoskyns (Oxford: Oxford University Press, 1968)

In references to primary texts, the page number in the English translation, where available, is followed by the page number of the German edition in parentheses. English translations are those of the published editions, where available, unless noted as revised, or as my own.

Introduction

> It is not as if I had found any way *out* of this critical situation. *Exactly not that.* But this critical situation itself became to me an explanation of the character of all theology.

Be wary of those who proclaim a crisis. They may have suspect motives: they may be seeking political support for measures that would not be countenanced in the absence of crisis, or wanting the attention that comes with crying 'Wolf!' Or their judgement may be faulty, falling into the trap of confusing a personal discovery with universal truth, believing in ahistorical ignorance that the time they live in – and especially *this* moment of crisis – is unprecedented, unique, and constitutes an emergency. And yet in spite of all this politicking, false alarms, and historical ignorance, crises do occur. If they did not, the politicians and attention seekers would have no audience. There are critical turning points in the course of events when what we decide to do, or not to do, has far-reaching consequences. And when such crises exist, it is of the utmost importance to see them for what they are and address them in action. When we hear someone announcing that we are in crisis, therefore, we are faced with a task of discernment and decision. Is this instance one of the many when a crisis is named for ulterior motives or out of ignorance, or is it one of those rare moments when the crisis is significant, immediate, and requiring our attention?

This book proclaims not one crisis, but three, so should be treated especially warily. The first is the crisis of German theology at the beginning of the twentieth century in the face of the rise of Nazism, as identified by Karl Barth. The second is the crisis of theological ethics at the beginning of the twenty-first century in the face of postmodern uncertainty and fundamentalist certainty, as identified by Zygmunt Bauman. The third is the crisis of the possibility of theology in the face of a God who cannot be comprehended by us. For Barth, this third crisis was the root of the first, and dialectical theology was his response. My argument is that this third crisis also underlies the second, and that Barth's response is illuminating for how we respond to this second crisis.

Karl Barth proclaimed the first crisis with the publication in 1922 of the second edition of his commentary on Paul's Letter to the Romans. In it his readers found a strident and uncompromising announcement of a crisis in theology, and in God's dealings with the world. Following the end of the Great War of 1914–18, and the Bolshevik revolution in Russia, Barth pictured the world as a scarred battlefield in which God was evident only in the craters God's past actions had left. Faced with this 'theology of crisis', many were sceptical of the challenge Barth posed, and denied both the existence of the crisis he identified, and the dialectical theology Barth proposed as a response. Others – about whom Barth was even more worried – saw in this crisis something that accorded with their own experience, and became enthusiastic followers of the new movement.

There are good reasons one might find the crisis Barth announced in 1922 of little interest. First, the signalling of a crisis must be timely to be of use. Close to a century on surely the emergency, if it existed at all, has now passed? We might seek to glean some historical lessons from whether the crisis was genuine, and how people responded to it, but in the absence of immediacy this would sustain the interest only of the devoted specialist. Second, and more seriously, Barth himself sought to play down the significance of this period of his work. In the preface to the fifth edition of 1926, Barth wrote that he often wished he had not written the book, and in the preface to the next edition two years later, he said that much of the book 'was due to my own particular situation at the time, and also to the general situation'.[1] Barth's theology developed beyond the second edition of *Romans*, and one feature of this development was his discovery of the absence of crisis in the work of Anselm. If Barth, therefore, was content to leave this work behind in pursuit of a new theological project, it would seem to be a good reason for us to do likewise.

My argument in this book shows that neither of these reasons is good enough to justify setting aside consideration of Barth's theology of crisis. In response to the point that Barth left his theology of crisis behind, I claim that Barth's ethical thought cannot be understood adequately without the concepts of crisis and dialectic that he developed in the 1922 *Romans*.[2] Barth's ethics has been found wanting by virtually all those who have engaged with it. Most have complained at his resistance to the idea that we can know God's will for a situation in advance, claiming that his emphasis on the divine command leads to a problematic occasionalism. Others have sought to defend Barth by noting the many aspects of his thought that stress the unity of God's willing and the continuity of God's commanding, but have thereby come close to making Barth into one of the proponents of system in ethics he criticized so directly. More recently others have claimed him as a postmodern theologian, and revelled in the 'contentless norm' of his ethics in *Romans* II.[3] All of these positions miss a crucial feature in Barth's ethical thought: in consequence of the crisis proclaimed in 1922 we can neither claim to be in full possession of God's will for humankind – which would be idolatry – nor give up on the attempt to discover it – which would be apostasy. Instead we must recognize this crisis that confronts us and recognize the need to speak dialectically, affirming the necessity of ethical reflection in congruence with God's

---

1 *Romans* II, 25 (XXXVII).

2 Barth was unhappy with any kind of separation between theology and ethics, since theology properly begins and ends with human action, a vision that I share. I use phrases like 'Barth's ethical thought' or 'Barth's ethics' as shorthand for those aspects of this theology that bear most directly on the question how the life of the church and the world may best be shaped in response to the grace of God.

3 See, for example, William Stacy Johnson, *The Mystery of God: Karl Barth and the Postmodern Foundations of Theology* (Louisville, Kentucky: Westminster John Knox Press, 1997), 161.

will to guide our action, the impossibility of attaining it, and the danger of the attempt. A good reason that we should take an interest in the ethical aspects of Barth's theology of crisis, therefore, is that we cannot interpret Barth's ethical thought properly without recognizing that it is an ethics in crisis.

If my claim is right, that crisis and dialectic remain a crucial feature of Barth's ethical thought throughout his life, it should be clear that the fact that he first proclaimed this crisis nearly a century ago does not weaken its claim on our attention. The fundamental crisis is not particular to German theology coming to terms with its nineteenth-century legacy after the First World War. It cannot be set aside as the product of a personal or global situation – despite Barth's occasional attempts to do so. Instead, it expresses an inescapable feature of God's relationship with the world and the place of human beings in it. God's self-revelation in Jesus Christ puts all that we think we know in question. In particular, it reminds us both of our freedom and responsibility to attend to God's will for us, and of the limitations on our ability to exercise this freedom and responsibility. If 'crisis theology' is to be an accurate description of Barth's theology, we must recognize that the crisis to which it refers is not a brief and local phenomenon in German theology at the beginning of the twentieth century, but the ongoing crisis of how we understand and speak of our relationship with the God we encounter in the person of Jesus Christ. Once we have recognized this, it becomes clear that crisis theology is a valid description of Barth's theology in its entirety. In Barth's own words, 'It is not as if I had found any way *out* of this critical situation. *Exactly not that.* But this critical situation itself became to me an explanation of the character of all theology.'[4] His work, from 1922 to its end and despite his own erratic depiction of it, represents a sustained attempt to respond to this crisis, and the fundamental structure that permits a response without dulling the sharp edges of the problem is dialectic. Barth's ethics in crisis is not merely of historical interest, therefore, and is not only of interest to those seeking a better understanding of his ethical thought as a whole. The crisis he proclaimed is one under which we also stand, and we need theological accounts that do justice to it and attempt to respond to it. This book argues that Barth's dialectical theological ethics, first developed in response to a crisis in theology at the beginning of the twentieth century, is a resource for constructive accounts of theology and ethics facing crises of their own at the beginning of the twenty-first.

Just as the significance of Barth's theology of crisis for his ethical thought has not been adequately appreciated, so it is also the case that the importance of ethics in this aspect of Barth's theology has not been recognized. Ethics is never, for Barth, a secondary discipline, the mere application of theology that is naturally theoretical, but is a fundamental part of the concerns that theology addresses and is addressed by. This is especially clear in *Romans* II, where Barth cites the ethical question 'What

---

4   Karl Barth, *The Word of God and the Word of Man*, trans. Douglas Horton (London: Hodder & Stoughton, 1929), 101 (Karl Barth, *Das Wort Gottes und die Theologie* (Munich: Chr. Kaiser Verlag, 1929), 102).

shall I do?' as a key reason for embarking on theology, claims Paul's theology is oriented towards practice throughout, and argues that theology has failed in its task if it does not lead to new knowledge about how to engage the world. Yet beyond the recognition of the integral place of ethics in theology, ethics has a particular significance in two aspects of Barth's crisis theology. First, Barth sees ethics as provoking the crisis. Its power lies in the way it generates innumerable questions which only God can answer, in its persistent asking of questions that it refuses to answer, in its questioning of all human activity and pretensions. But second, ethics is a key reason that Barth's theology, even in *Romans* II, remains genuinely dialectical, rather than resting content with a thoroughgoing proclamation of God's 'No!' and God's otherness from us. Ethics is the reason we cannot finally opt for the luxury of such consistent formulations, because alongside putting everything in question, it also reminds us of the need to decide what we are to do. For today, and tomorrow, we must choose how to spend our time, what we will do, and what we will fail to do. If these choices, and therefore the actions that follow them, are not to be meaningless, there must be some way in which, however provisionally and tentatively, we can gain an understanding of how we are to make them. Barth could not simply throw up his hands in denial of the possibility of human knowledge and ethical action because he was too well aware of the urgent needs in the world to which he and others were called to respond. The significance of ethics for Barth's theology, therefore, is not just in his judgement that the two could not be separated, but also in the way that ethics both provokes the crisis for theology, and sets parameters for responding to it.

The thesis that Barth's theological strategy for living with the crisis in construing our relationship with God might be of use in a constructive account of theological ethics is threatened from at least two sides. First, there are many who believe that Barth's theology does not speak to the challenges that face contemporary theology: he is too conservative, too orthodox, too misogynist, too much concerned with divine sovereignty and too little concerned with creation in its human and non-human forms. To these readers, I can only recommend becoming better acquainted with Barth, and hope that this book may encourage such an improving of relations. To take one example, Barth is well known for using the uncompromising language of divine command in describing the way human beings should discern right and wrong, yet in order to understand what he means by it, we must set aside almost everything we associate with divine command ethics. In particular, while sometimes God's will may seem heteronomous, Barth insists that God's command distinguishes itself from all others in setting us free, being always 'the granting of a freedom', which does not compel, but 'bursts open the door of the compulsion' under which we live. God's command frees us from being dominated by forces beyond ourselves. It is the word of 'our true, best friend' that 'sets us on our feet' and is against us 'only insofar as we are against ourselves'.[5] As so often, the account Barth gives of divine command is a

---

5   *CD* II/2, 585–95 (648–61).

wholesale revision of the tradition, but only a close acquaintance with his thought makes this clear.

Barth has not always been well served by his interpreters: his theology and ethics have been badly misrepresented both by ardent enthusiasts and by committed critics. To be sure, there are occasions when one wishes he had said more, occasions when one wishes he had said less, and occasions when one wishes he had said something different – I am not recommending any form of uncritical 'Barthianism'. Barth would have been the last to believe his theological work was self-sufficient or in any sense complete, and it is clear that his thought requires correction as well as supplement in a number of areas. My modest proposal is that Barth is worth attending to on this issue, and that we find in Barth's theology resources that current accounts of theological ethics stand sorely in need of, and that we are therefore ill-advised to ignore.

A second group who will be initially sceptical of the thesis that Barth's account of, and response to, this ongoing crisis may be useful are those who doubt that there is any ongoing sense of crisis in Barth's theology at all. There was once a consensus that the crisis, complexity, and dialectic of Barth's 1922 *Romans* were happily resolved by 1931 in his discovery of Anselm, and that his major work, the *Church Dogmatics*, has moved beyond such problems. McCormack and others have recently disturbed this tidy narrative, but the argument in this book that crisis and dialectic remain crucial for interpreting Barth's ethical thought in *Church Dogmatics* is a new one. The parallel readings I present of the ethical components of *Romans* II and corresponding sections of *Church Dogmatics* show not only the continuing importance of crisis and dialectic in the ethics of the latter, but also how recognition of this feature of Barth's ethics solves problems in interpreting his ethical thought. On the one hand, this means that those who welcomed Barth's supposed conversion by Anselm to orthodox, non-dialectical theology need to come to terms with a Barth for whom ethics remains in crisis, as a problematic and perilous enterprise. We cannot discover in Barth the stable and secure foundation for ethics that many seek: the claim to possess such a foundation is the blasphemy of claiming to know the mind of God. On the other hand, the disruption of the narrative of Barth's development from dialectical to non-dialectical theologian means that those who celebrate Barth's *Romans* as precursor to a postmodern, contentless ethic, while lamenting his later turn to 'logocentrism' must also rethink their position. Just as God's 'Yes' to humankind cannot be separated from God's 'No' in the dialectic of *Church Dogmatics,* so God's 'No' cannot be seen without God's 'Yes' in his 1922 commentary on Romans. Instead, the two stand in tension in both works: in both works Barth saw theological ethics as a profoundly problematic but nonetheless inescapable enterprise.

There may be some who are surprised by my claim that there is a twenty-first-century crisis in theological ethics, quite apart from the question of whether Barth could be of help in overcoming it. I find one representation of the challenge that we face in a passage from a novel at the beginning of the last century: Ford Maddox Ford's *The Good Soldier*. At the beginning of the book its narrator, John Dowell, looks back at the disastrous history in which adultery and the threat of it have led to the suicides of both his wife and his best friend, and to the insanity of the woman he loves. Surveying the wreckage, he is left bemused:

> At what, then, does it all work out? Is the whole thing a folly and a mockery? Am I no better than a eunuch or is the proper man – the man with the right to existence – a raging stallion forever neighing after his neighbour's womankind?
> I don't know. And there is nothing to guide us. And if everything is so nebulous about a matter so elementary as the morals of sex, what is there to guide us in the more subtle morality of all other personal contacts, associations, and activities? Or are we meant to act on impulse alone? It is all a darkness.[6]

Eighty years on, Zymunt Bauman gives a more prosaic expression to a similar sentiment:

> Ours are the times of *strongly felt moral ambiguity*. These times offer us freedom of choice never before enjoyed, but also cast us into a state of uncertainty never before so agonizing. We yearn for guidance we can trust and rely upon, so that some of the haunting responsibility for our choices could be lifted from our shoulders. But the authorities we may entrust are all contested, and none seems to be powerful enough to give us the degree of reassurance we seek. In the end, we trust no authority, at least, we trust none fully, and none for long: we cannot help being suspicious about any claim to infallibility. This is the most acute and prominent practical aspect of what is justly described as the 'postmodern ethical crisis'.[7]

The crisis in theological ethics is that we are not sure how to begin illuminating the darkness to which Dowell bears witness, or how to resolve the ambiguity and distrust of authority that Bauman describes. Frequently theologians have denied the existence of such uncertainty with the claim that those who see nothing to guide them are simply in bad faith, shutting their eyes to the obvious moral realities that surround them. Another version of this response is to claim that true believers have ready access to moral certainty, so that it is only the unbeliever who is left mired in indeterminacy. The implausibility of either of these positions is clear to most people within and without the church. With regard to the first, Dowell's problem is not that he is wilfully in bad faith, but that he is adrift, out of sight of any moral landmark. With regard to the second, it is not necessary to have a wide acquaintance of church members to know that moral confusion exists among those who believe, and in any case Barth reminds us that to assert possession of certain knowledge of God's will is to forget our place.

Other theologians have been impressed by the novel features of the postmodern landscape, and have not wanted to deny or diminish them. They look for a new way of doing theology in this new environment, revelling in the ambiguity the conservatives

---

6   Ford Maddox Ford, *The Good Soldier* (1915; London: Penguin Books, 1946), 19.
7   Zygmunt Bauman, *Postmodern Ethics* (Oxford: Blackwell, 1993), 21.

reject and setting aside the normative aspirations of theological ethics. Such postmodern ethical theologizing is as implausible as its reactionary counterpart: the task of ethics is to provide guidance to those asking urgently what they should do, and a response that refuses the possibility of such an answer is not an alternative way of doing ethics but the renunciation of it. It is obvious that what we need is to chart a path that recognizes on one hand the experience of being without a moral compass and finding traditional authorities deficient, while on the other hand not giving up on the attempt to provide meaningful ethical guidance. It is less obvious, however, how this is to be done. That is my characterization of the crisis that confronts theological ethics at the beginning of the twenty-first century, the crisis I believe Barth's dialectical theology can help us address.

It may seem odd to respond to a contemporary ethical crisis with the suggestion that we recognize that theologically ethics is inescapably bound up with crisis. It may also seem a suggestion with exhausting implications: to be in a constant state of crisis does not recommend itself as a pleasant prospect. I would say two things in response. First, I do not think that a proper understanding of theological ethics can aspire to get beyond crisis as a recurrent feature. This is partly because we do not hold the will of God in our hands, and so must continually seek after it in new times and places. It is also partly that the nature of ethics is that we are confronted by situations, and must decide how to respond to them. Such moments of judgement often cannot be postponed: they are crises in which we must decide what path to take, and in doing so choose the persons we will become. There is no escape from the need to ensure that the shape of our living fits our calling as children of God. Second, recognizing that crisis is a recurrent feature of theological ethics does not mean that we are faced with continuous revolution in our ethical thinking or in our lives. The God we have come to know in Jesus Christ is faithful, and knows our nature as creatures with a past and future, as well as a present. Our lives are historically extended, and while there are times when we are called to sudden new realizations of ourselves and our responsibilities, there are many vocations in which we must remain true to commitments we have made. In our existence over time, therefore, there is both continuity and discontinuity. Few crises force us back to square one – though we cannot exclude this possibility – some will leave us concluding we are already heading in the right direction, and most will cause a reorientation of some degree.

It may be helpful at the outset to clarify one of the key terms I will be discussing, since its meaning has been many and varied in its journey from classical Greece to the present via the Stoics, Kant, Hegel, and Marx. In the context of the dialogues of Socrates related by Plato, dialectic is a means of interrogating beliefs in order to show their inconsistencies. Kant used dialectic to describe the contradictory relationship of scientific principles to concepts such as the soul. For Hegel, dialectic is a historic process by which thesis and the corresponding antithesis are finally unified in a synthesis. None of these captures the meaning of dialectic in the present context. Throughout this work I use 'dialectic' to denote an unresolved tension between two poles in which neither pole is adequate by itself to characterize fully the concept under discussion: in Barth's words, two poles 'as irreconcilable as inseparable'. To take an example from physics, light can be described either as a wave or as a stream of photons. In certain contexts it makes more sense to treat light as one or the other of these two models, but neither wave nor photon stream adequately accounts for the full range of its behaviour, and the two models are genuine alternatives: there is a contradiction involved in saying light is both a wave and a stream of photons. There is a dialectical relationship between the nature of light as wave and photon stream in the sense I am using 'dialectic'. The relationship between the divinity and humanity of Christ is a more theological example: if we want to affirm both that Jesus Christ was divine and that he was human, and if we accept that there is a contradiction in affirming both at the same time, then the divine/human nature of Christ is dialectical as I am using the term. Indeed, as we shall see, for Barth the dialectic between Christ's divinity and humanity is one key reason why all theology must bear a dialectical shape.[8]

This book is in the first place an argument that Barth's ethical thought is best understood when we recognize that it remained structured by the crisis first evident in *Romans* II, and in the second place an argument that contemporary theological ethics needs to recognize the significance of Barth's response to this crisis in order to overcome its own. The core of the first argument is a textual comparison between the ethics of *Romans* II and the ethics of the *Church Dogmatics*. While I chart the main features of the development of Barth's dialectic between the two texts in Chapter 4, my primary focus is a close reading of the two texts in parallel, rather than an attempt to map to development of Barth's theology during the intervening years. This approach has the advantage of illuminating striking continuities between the texts, as well as some contrasts. Since the 1922 edition of *Romans* is the most thoroughgoing statement of Barth's theology of crisis, this methodology has the virtue of attempting to make the case for continuity in Barth's ethical thought at potentially the hardest point. The weakness of the approach is that it is poorly suited to giving reasons for changes in emphasis in Barth's theology in comparison to a more

---

8   McCormack cites the distinction Michael Beintker makes between two types of dialectic. In a 'supplementary' dialectic, the stronger member overcomes the weaker, and there is movement from opposition to reconciliation. In a 'complementary' dialectic, in contrast, the members stand over against each other in opposition, and the only movement is back and forth between them without progress (Michael Beintker, *Die Dialektik in der 'Dialektischen Theologie' Karl Barths* (Munich: Chr. Kaiser Verlag, 1987), 38–9, cited in Bruce L McCormack, *Karl Barth's Critically Realistic Dialectical Theology: Its Genesis and Development, 1909–1936* (Oxford: Clarendon Press, 1995), 162–3). According to Beintker, supplementary dialectic characterizes the 1919 *Romans* and complementary dialectic the 1922 edition. This accords with the results of my survey: the dialectical elements I have found in the second edition of *Romans* and in the *Dogmatics* are oppositional and thus fall into Beintker's 'complementary' category. Beintker's term 'complementary', however, fails to do justice to the oppositional tension in the relationship between the two poles of the dialectic. See also Leonardo Boff, *Ecology and Liberation: A New Paradigm*, Ecology and Justice Series (Maryknoll, New York: Orbis Books, 1995).

historically based account. There is a wide range of studies with this emphasis, however,[9] and my primary interest is describing and evaluating Barth's theological ethics, rather than attempting to explain its origins.

Part I of this book treats the ethics of *Romans* II. In the first chapter, I set the book in context, and explore Barth's vision of the place of ethics in the midst of crisis. Chapter 2 examines Barth's treatment of particular ethical issues in *Romans* II, under the headings of love and community, and war, peace, and revolution. In Chapter 3, I examine some of the critical responses to the ethics of *Romans* II, and argue that they miss crucial features of Barth's dialectical account.

Part II looks beyond *Romans* II to the *Church Dogmatics*. In Chapter 4, I summarize the way Barth discusses the themes of crisis and dialectic between *Romans* II and the *Church Dogmatics*, before proceeding in Chapter 5 to examine the place of ethics in the *Dogmatics* in the light of *Romans*. Chapters 6 and 7 compare Barth's treatment of the themes of love and community, and war, peace and revolution in the *Dogmatics* with the results of Chapter 2.

Part III looks at the implications of appreciating the structural continuities between the ethics of *Romans* II and the *Dogmatics*. Chapter 8 draws out the results of the comparative survey of Part II, and sets out the framework for a new reading of Barth's ethical thought as inescapably dialectical. I conclude by arguing in Chapter 9, that this interpretation of Barth's ethics is a significant resource for contemporary constructive accounts of Christian ethics.

---

9 See, for example, Henri Bouillard, *Genèse et Evolution de la Théologie Dialectique* (Paris: Aubier, 1957); Eberhard Busch, *Karl Barth: His Life from Letters and Autobiographical Texts*, trans. John Bowden (Philadelphia: Fortress Press, 1976); John Cullberg, *Das Problem der Ethik in der Dialektischen Theologie*, vol. 1 (Uppsala: A.-B. Lundequistska Bokhandeln, 1938); Theodore Alexander Gill, *Protestant Political Theory: The Political Problem in Some New Reformation Theology* (Zurich: University of Zurich, 1953); George Hunsinger, 'Toward a Radical Barth', in *Karl Barth and Radical Politics*, ed. George Hunsinger (Philadelphia: Westminster Press, 1976); McCormack, *Karl Barth's Theology*; Friedrich-Wilhelm Marquardt, 'Socialism in the Theology of Karl Barth', in *Karl Barth and Radical Politics*, ed. George Hunsinger (Philadelphia: Westminster Press, 1976); Robert E. Willis, *The Ethics of Karl Barth* (Leiden: E.J. Brill, 1971).

I
THE *ROMANS* II CRISIS

CHAPTER 1

Ethics in Crisis

Between the publication of the first edition of Karl Barth's commentary on Romans in 1919, and the second edition in 1922, Barth saw the need for a complete rewriting of his project. He believed the first edition had retained too much that was nebulous, and gave the dangerous impression of pantheistic relations between God and the world. In the second edition, such passages were expunged, and the text reshaped to enable the sharp proclamation of an uncompromised message:

> Our relation to God is *ungodly*. We suppose that we know what we are saying when we say 'God'. We assign to himself the highest place in our world: and in so doing we place Him fundamentally on one line with ourselves and with things. We assume that He *needs something*: and so we assume that we are able to arrange our relation to Him as we arrange our other relationships. We press ourselves into proximity with Him: and so, all unthinking, we make Him nigh unto ourselves. We allow ourselves an ordinary communication with Him as though this were not extraordinary behaviour on our part. We dare to deck ourselves out as His companions, patrons, advisers, and commissioners. We confound time with eternity. This is the *ungodliness* of our relation to God.[1]

In the face of such ungodliness, God's self-revelation brings not cosy reassurances, but is the event in which human beings are faced with the extent of their presumption and betrayal. They have been worshipping 'No-God', an idol born of their own futile hopes with no power to redeem them. In this crisis, everything is put into question by the Gospel that is not one truth among many, but causes the dissolution and establishment of the whole concrete world. This event is the crisis of Barth's 'crisis theology'. In this chapter I briefly survey some of the encounters that led Barth to the declaration of this crisis, before turning to an exploration of its ethical aspects.

Signposts on the Way to a Theology of Crisis

Karl Barth was born in Basel, Switzerland, in 1886, but spent his childhood in Bern.[2] His father was a pastor, and his mother the daughter of a pastor, and after being inspired by his confirmation classes Barth chose to study theology first in Bern, and then in Berlin, where he was enthusiastic about the teaching he received from Adolf

---

1   *Romans* II, 45 (20–21).
2   For a detailed account of Barth's life, see Eberhard Busch, *Karl Barth: His Life from Letters and Autobiographical Texts*, trans. John Bowden (Philadelphia: Fortress Press, 1976).

Harnack, and came across the work of Herrmann for the first time. After six months in Tübingen, his father agreed to let him move to Marburg to study with Wilhelm Herrmann, whom Barth called '*the* theological teacher of my student years'[3] and who introduced him to the work of Friedrich Schleiermacher. After being ordained by his father in 1908, Barth began working on the theological journal *Christliche Welt* under the leading liberal theologian Martin Rade, while continuing to study in Marburg. In 1909 he became assistant pastor to a German-speaking church in Geneva where he spent two years, before moving in 1911 to become pastor of a church in Safenwil, in the Aargau. Barth was to spend ten years here, until the publication of the first edition of his Romans commentary led to the beginning of his academic career as a professor in Göttingen in 1921.

The Safenwil pastorate was an eventful time for Barth. He spent a great deal of time preparing sermons and confirmation classes, but church attendance was low. After a time, however, he achieved a local notoriety by taking up the cause of the low-paid industrial workers who made up the majority of the wage earners in the village. This led to great concern in Barth's church committee, and to the owners of the factories and mills resigning from Barth's church and beginning their own worship associations, but he was undaunted, stating: 'I regard socialist demands as an important part of the application of the gospel, though I also believe that they cannot be realized without the gospel.'[4] It was also in Safenwil that Barth met Eduard Thurneysen, with whom he began the biblical studies that led to the commentary on Romans. Through Thurneysen, Barth came into contact with many other theologians and socialist thinkers, and was soon actively involved in meetings and conferences. In the midst of all this activity came the outbreak of the First World War. Barth was disappointed not to be called up to defend the Swiss border, as some of his parishioners were, though he did join the 'home guard' and took his turn on duty at night, armed with a rifle. He spoke a great deal about the war in his sermons, until he reports 'finally a woman came up to me and asked me for once to talk about something else'.[5] According to Barth, the outbreak of war was a significant moment in the break with his theological past. In 1968 he wrote that it

> brought something which for me was almost even worse than the violation of Belgian neutrality – the horrible manifesto of the ninety-three German intellectuals who identified themselves before all the world with the war policy of Kaiser Wilhelm II and Chancellor Bethmann-Hollweg. And to my dismay, among the signatories I discovered the names of almost all my German teachers (with the honorable exception of Martin Rade). An entire world of theological exegesis, ethics, dogmatics, and preaching, which up to that point I had accepted as basically credible, was thereby shaken to the foundations.[6]

---

3   Ibid., 44.
4   Ibid., 70.
5   Ibid., 81.
6   Karl Barth, 'Concluding Unscientific Postscript on Schleiermacher', in *The Theology of*

As a result of coming to see this profound problem with the theology Barth received, he began to cast about for a new approach. He observed that 'the area from which I draw resources for inner concentration and upon which I would gladly rely in working and speaking must be widened and deepened – otherwise I am in danger of coming to a dead end'. Thurneysen suggested they needed a 'wholly other' theological foundation, and the next day Barth reports 'I sat under an apple tree and began to apply myself to Romans with all the resources that were available to me at the time'.[7] The discoveries he made are reflected in an address he gave in February 1917, 'The Strange New World within the Bible'[8] in which he emphasizes that the Bible is not a place to look for human history, morality, or religion, or anything else from a human standpoint. It is God's word to us: 'God's sovereignty, God's glory, God's incomprehensible love.'[9] Alongside political activity in Safenwil in the year that followed, Barth continued to work on Romans, and completed it in August 1918, a few months before the end of the war and the beginning of a general strike in Switzerland. Following the publication of *Romans* at the beginning of 1919, Barth continued his studies and lectures, and in September of that year gave the lecture 'The Christian's Place in Society' at Tambach in Thuringia, Germany. With the unfolding consequences of the 1917 revolutions in Russia clearly in mind, he pointed to the kingdom of God as 'the revolution which is before all revolutions'[10] and set out a dialectic of an affirmation and denial of life as thesis and antithesis, to which the synthesis can be found only in God. The lecture made Barth more widely known in Germany, and the copies of *Romans* that remained – 700 of the original 1,000 – were sold through the German publisher Christian Kaiser Verlag.

In the preface to the second edition of *Romans* Barth cites the reviews he received in response to this exposure in Germany as one of four reasons for the developments in his position following the first edition. The three others he lists are, first, further study of Paul, second, the work of Franz Overbeck, and third, closer acquaintance with Plato and Kant through the work of his brother, Heinrich, together with attention to Kierkegaard and Dostoevsky.[11] In relation to Overbeck, Barth refers to an article he wrote with Thurneysen in response to Overbeck's posthumous publication

---

Schleiermacher, ed. Dietrich Ritschl, trans. G.W. Bromiley (Edinburgh: T. & T. Clark, 1982), 264–5. Bruce McCormack notes that the letter was published in October, rather than August as Barth recalled, and that the development of the break with the theology of his teachers is evident over a longer period (Bruce L. McCormack, *Karl Barth's Critically Realistic Dialectical Theology: Its Genesis and Development, 1909–1936* (Oxford: Clarendon Press, 1995), 112).

7   Busch, *Karl Barth*, 97.

8   Published in Karl Barth, *The Word of God and the Word of Man*, trans. Douglas Horton (London: Hodder & Stoughton, 1929), 28–50 (Karl Barth, *Das Wort Gottes und die Theologie* (Munich: Chr. Kaiser Verlag, 1929), 18–32).

9   Ibid., 45 (29).

10   Ibid., 299 (51).

11   *Romans* II, 3–4 (XIII–XIV).

Christentum und Kultur,[12] entitled 'Unsettled Questions for Theology Today'.[13] Franz Overbeck (1837–1905) had been a figure on the margins of Christianity: although he was a theology professor in Basel he was a friend of Nietzsche and harshly critical of contemporary theology. He saw Christianity as fundamentally eschatological, and believed that theology, the 'Satan of religion', had betrayed Christianity by its inveterate tendency to become apologetics in order to shine in the eyes of the world. Theology is parasitic on other schools of thought, according to Overbeck, offering as a religious insight that which can be found more successfully elsewhere, and he prophetically railed against theology exploiting Christianity by rushing into opportunistic political alliances with nationalist movements. Schleiermacher is Overbeck's prime example of a theologian who justifies religion as it is, rather than asking whether it is true. Barth notes that the editor of *Christentum und Kultur*, Carl Albrecht Bernoulli, chooses to term Overbeck a 'sceptic', but Barth and Thurneysen prefer 'inspired critic'[14] and see his work as dangerous, but also as 'an inconceivably impressive sharpening of the commandment "Thou shalt not take the name of the Lord thy God in vain"'.[15]

The influence of Overbeck is clear throughout *Romans* II: Barth responds to Overbeck's fierce critique with an approach to theology that is a radical departure from the established positions of his teachers. The impact of Kierkegaard is also evident, most obviously in the 'infinite qualititative distinction' between God and humankind, which Barth cites in the preface.[16] Barth is right to note Kant as an important conversation partner, however, which has particular significance in his ethics for the negotiation he makes between occasionalism and universalism, as we shall see.[17]

These are some of the landmarks on the journey that led Barth to realize that the theological crisis he perceived required a crisis theology in response. It is now time to engage with the 1922 edition of Barth's commentary on Romans in all its strangeness and challenge. I turn first to look at the place of ethics within this theology of crisis, and the significance of this crisis for ethics, before examining in the next chapter

---

12   Franz Overbeck, *Christentum und Kultur*, ed. Carl Albrecht Bernoulli (Basel: Benno & Schwabe & Co., 1919). See Martin Henry, *Franz Overbeck: Theologian? Religion and History in the Thought of Franz Overbeck*, European University Studies Series 23: Theology (Frankfurt: Peter Lang, 1995) for a helpful discussion of the thought of Overbeck.

13   Published in Karl Barth, *Theology and Church: Shorter Writings 1920–1928*, trans. Louise Pettibone Smith (New York and Evanston: Harper & Row, 1962), 55–73 (Karl Barth, *Die Theologie und die Kirche*, Gesammelte Vortrag, vol. 2 (Munich: Evangelischer Verlag AG, 1928), 1–25).

14   Ibid., 58 (4–5).

15   Ibid., 57 (3).

16   *Romans* II, 10 (XX).

17   Michael Beintker judges that Kierkegaard's influence on *Romans* II is limited (Michael Beintker, *Die Dialektik in der 'Dialektischen Theologie' Karl Barths* (Munich: Chr. Kaiser Verlag, 1987), 237) and McCormack agrees that Barth's engagement with Overbeck and with his brother Heinrich's work on Plato is more important (McCormack, *Karl Barth's Theology*, 217).

how Barth addresses the ethical themes of love and community, and war, peace and revolution, in his commentary.

Ethics and Crisis in *Romans* II

Barth cites the ethical question as both a key reason for doing theology, and for reading the Epistle to the Romans in particular:

> it is our pondering over the question 'What shall we do?' which compels us to undertake so much seemingly idle conversation about God. And it is precisely because our world is filled with pressing practical duties; because there is wickedness in the streets; because of the existence of the daily papers; that we are bound to encounter 'Paulinism' and the Epistle to the Romans.[18]

Elsewhere Barth notes 'our conversation about God is not undertaken for its own sake but for the sake of His will'.[19] The same concern drives us to an awareness of the world's great insoluble question and to the realization that God is its solution:

> The need of making decisions of will, the need for action, the world as it is – that it is which has compelled us to consider what the world is, how we are to live in it, and what we are to do in it. We have found the world one great, unsolved enigma; an enigma to which Christ, the mercy of God, provides the answer.[20]

When Paul turns to explicit ethical considerations in chapter 12 of the Epistle, Barth observes,

> We are not now starting a new book or even a new chapter of the same book. Paul is not here turning his attention to practical religion, as though it were a second thing side by side with the theory of religion. On the contrary, the theory, with which we have hitherto been concerned, is the theory of the practice of religion ... the ethical problem has nowhere been left out of account.[21]

Ethics is therefore part of what drives us to theology in the first place, and its concerns are fully part of both Paul's conception of theology, and Barth's own. Yet the relationship between ethics and theology is not straightforward or comfortable. The problem of ethics 'reminds us of the Truth of God', but it also threatens to undo our speech about God.

---

18   *Romans* II, 438 (461–2).
19   *Romans* II, 426 (449).
20   *Romans* II, 427 (450).
21   *Romans* II, 426–7 (450).

[It] disturbs our conversation about God in order to remind us of its proper theme; dissolves it, in order to give it its proper direction; kills it, in order to make it alive.[22]

Ethics is no secondary discipline for Barth, merely the outworking of dogmatic theology. Barth's approach to Romans is oriented by his wrestling with the question 'What shall we do?' and one of his central concerns in *Romans* II is to find what answer he can provide in the context of the crisis that overshadows all human answers.

The crisis of this disturbance and dissolution means that the Gospel is not a truth among other truths, but 'sets a question-mark against all truths'. By it 'the whole concrete world is dissolved and established'.[23] The consequences of this are severe:

The more profoundly we become aware of the limited possibilities open to us here and now, the more clear it is that we are farther from God, that our desertion of Him is more complete … and the consequences of that desertion more vast … than we had ever dreamed … [People's] sin is their guilt; their death is their destiny; their world is formless and tumultuous chaos, a chaos of the forces of nature and of the human soul; their life is illusion.[24]

From this stark and terrifying human predicament there is no easy religious escape. Barth rejects the cosy and sentimental formulations that make God the ultimate comfort blanket, the answer to all our fears and insecurities. God is the Unknown God, and our belief that Jesus is the Christ is an assumption, 'devoid of any content'.[25] We go badly wrong in referring to God if we ignore God's hiddenness.

What men on this side of the resurrection name 'God' is most characteristically not God. Their 'God' does not redeem his creation, but allows free course to the unrighteousness of men; does not declare himself to be God, but is the complete affirmation of the course of the world and of men as it is. This is intolerable, for, in spite of the highest honours we offer him for his adornment, he is, in fact, 'No-God'. The cry of revolt against such a god is nearer the truth than is the sophistry with which men attempt to justify him. Only because they have nothing better, only because they lack the courage of despair, do the generality of men on this side of resurrection avoid falling into blatant atheism.[26]

Our relation to God is ungodly, giving God the highest place in our world, and thus placing God 'fundamentally on a line with ourselves and with things'. Our relation to God is unrighteous, since secretly 'we are the masters in this relationship'. Our

---

22 *Romans* II, 426 (449).
23 *Romans* II, 35 (11–12).
24 *Romans* II, 37 (13–14).
25 *Romans* II, 36 (12).
26 *Romans* II, 40 (17). I have not, for the most part, amended the exclusive language in Hoskyns's translation.

devotion 'consists in a solemn affirmation of ourselves'.[27] We cannot be excused from this accusation, because the 'No' of the true God 'lies as in a text-book open before us' and '[b]y calm, veritable, unprejudiced religious contemplation the divine "No" can be established and apprehended'.[28]

Our wish-fulfilling dreams about God fail to appreciate that encounter with God means radical questioning and undermining of all that we thought we were. God is pleased when 'all human righteousness is gone, irretrievably gone, when men are uncertain and lost, when they have abandoned all ethical and religious illusions, and when they have renounced every hope in this world and in this heaven'.[29] Grace 'is and remains in this world negative, invisible, hidden; the mark of its operation is the declaration of the passing of the world and of the end of all things'.[30] We cannot continue the style of thinking to which we are accustomed in this context, since 'when our thought remains direct and unbroken, it is quite certain that we are not thinking about life, about the crisis in which human life is being lived'.[31] Barth therefore calls us to

> break off your thinking that it may be a thinking about God; break off your dialectic, that it may indeed be dialectic; break off your knowledge of God, that it may be what, in fact, it is, the wholesome disturbance and interruption which God in Christ prepares, in order that He may call men home to the peace of His Kingdom.[32]

God is gracious towards us, but to creatures in our parlous state encounter with this grace is interruption and threat to the life that we have been living. No calm, reasoned and consistent thinking can survive this encounter, because these unbroken formulations are what have made us comfortable with life in denial of the grace God offers to us. What we need from God, and what God offers us, is a 'wholesome crisis' that promises to brings us back to our senses, and back to God.

The world bears the marks of this crisis. At several points Barth uses the image of the crater left by a shell to describe what we see of God's action in the world, and how the activity of the Christian community, human action generally, and the law, each witnesses to God's action. Barth compares religion to holy men sitting around a burnt-out crater.[33] The message that we have experience of God only after the fact, in negative form, is reiterated in a collection of other metaphors. The point of intersection of God's action with history is a void; the apostle is a void made visible; experience of religion must not be more than a void; genuine faith is a void. Both the

---

27 *Romans* II, 44 (21).
28 *Romans* II, 46 (23).
29 *Romans* II, 68 (47).
30 *Romans* II, 103 (85).
31 *Romans* II, 425 (448).
32 *Romans* II, 426 (449).
33 *Romans* II, 74 (53–4).

law and faith are dry canals speaking of the water that does not pass through them. Communion with God, the law, the world, faith, and ethical action are all likened to sign-posts, pointing to a destination 'which is precisely where the sign-post is not'.[34] The world shows the impress of revelation, as the impress of a signet ring speaks of the absent signet. The world is the footprint of the wrath of God. The law is 'a heap of clinkers marking a fiery miracle which has taken place'.[35] Human action is the cloud of dust that shows where an army is marching, or the shaft of a mine allowing us to conceive of part of the mountain where none is. The Unknown God is like the cavity at the centre of the cartwheel, without which the wheel could not turn. By deploying these images frequently, Barth disallows any sense of human possession of revelation or experience of God: what we find left in our hands is only the mark of where God has been, or an indication of another place where God may be found.

While ethics plays a part in alerting us to this crisis, as we have already seen, it is by no means immune from its effects. Amidst the disturbance that ethics provokes, ethics itself takes on a different character:

> The absolute character of Christian ethics lies in the fact that they are altogether problematical. [Its] evolution consists simply in the fecundity with which it puts forth questions only God can answer. Once apprehend this, and it becomes obvious, terribly obvious, that human ethical behaviour can only demonstrate, only signify, only offer a sacrifice ... The power and earnestness of Christian ethics lie in its persistent asking of questions and in its steady refusal to provide answers to these questions. Christian ethics only demonstrate, only bear witness that there is an answer ... By putting an end to all absolute ethics, Christianity finally puts an end to all the triumph and sorrow that accompanies the occupation of any human eminence.[36]

Therefore,

> [t]he question What shall I do? is capable of no material answer. It simply raises the question of the ground and purpose of all human action, and then the question, What shall I do? is transformed into a question to which the action of God Himself provides the only answer.[37]

Barth claims that human passions for ethics are as suspicious as passions for aesthetics. Passions for ethics are simply a longing for infinity, for transcending ourselves, and there is no clear boundary between this longing, and our hunger, thirst, or lust. In his commentary on Romans 7:14–17, he shares Paul's lament of being unable to do what he wills to do, but also links it with the difficulty of doing theology in the crisis:

---

34   *Romans* II, 88 (68).
35   *Romans* II, 65 (44).
36   *Romans* II, 465–6 (489–91).
37   *Romans* II, 475 (500).

The more luminously clear it becomes that the demand requires my actual obedience to the will of God, and that His commandments are not grievous, the more luminously clear it becomes to me that, even in the simplest occurrences of my life, His will has not been done, is not done, and never will be done. For not even at the most exalted moments of my life do I fulfil His commands. Does any single thought of mine express the all-compelling power of the Spirit? Does one single word of mine formulate the Word after which I am striving and which I long to utter in my great misery and hope? Does not each sentence I frame require another to dissolve its meaning? And are my actions any better?[38]

This heartfelt cry makes clear that for Barth this crisis is not merely a theological trope, or something that happens to other people. He lives and acts – and writes – from within the crisis, and is struggling even within the text with how to give expression to the inbreaking of divine grace he has discovered in Paul.

If, despite all this difficulty, human action is to be ethical, it is only in its relationship to God: all human possibilities 'are ethical possibilities only because they are ... related to their primal origin. Destroy this relationship, seek their essential nature in what they are in themselves or what they contain in themselves, and their ethical character is done away.'[39] This origin is the sole basis for all ethical reflection – or any other kind:

God is God: this is the presupposition of ethics. Ethical propositions are only ethical as expositions of this presupposition, which may never be regarded as a thing already known, or treated as a basis of future routine operations, or as something from which it is possible to hurry on to a new position.[40]

There are no moral actions that have rid themselves of the form of this world, but human action can have the status of a token, parable or demonstration of the action of God. Everything is at stake, however, in our recalling this status:

All human duties and virtues and good deeds are set upon the edge of a knife. They hang on a single thread. Is the man who practises them and cherishes them really prepared to sacrifice them; really prepared to see in them no more than demonstrations, and thus to give glory to God? What is more than this is of the evil one, even if it be the holiness and purity of a martyred virgin.[41]

The existence of Christian ethics is therefore imperilled by the crisis of God's judgement on human affairs. There is no longer any stable position from which we can evaluate actions or make choices ourselves. The very desire for such a position is an indication of how far we are from appreciating the depths of our predicament before God and the import of the statement that 'God is God': there is nothing beyond

---

38   *Romans* II, 260–61 (265).
39   *Romans* II, 461 (486).
40   *Romans* II, 439 (463).
41   *Romans* II, 433 (456).

this proposition that we can establish as a guide. All we can properly hope for in our actions is that they may witness to the One who is other than we are. These are the implications of the crisis Barth proclaims in *Romans* II for ethics.

And this is where most reflection on Barth's ethics in *Romans* has ceased. Critics have come across Barth's destabilizing of ethics and swiftly concluded that he is a misguided and irresponsible theologian of little interest to those seeking to do serious work in theological ethics. Others have enthusiastically taken up this denial of ethical knowledge and celebrated the postmodern contentless norms they find in Barth's early work.[42] What both groups of commentators miss is the dialectical character of *Romans* II. In wrestling with these disturbing texts undermining the possibility of ethics, we have only heard half of what Barth wants us to hear, because alongside the profound difficulties the crisis causes for Christian ethics, there are also striking positive possibilities in the ethics of *Romans* II.

The first example of what remains for human beings following this crisis is that there remains the possibility of responsible human ethical action. God's 'No' does not mean we are abandoned to in morass of ethical ambiguity. Already we have seen that Barth allows human actions to have the status of parables of God's action. God is not so other from us that God does not have a will for how we live our lives, and God speaks of this will to us: 'Our lack of humility, our lack of recollection, our lack of fear in the presence of God, are not in our present condition inevitable, however natural they may seem to us ... The speech of God can always be heard out of the whirlwind.'[43] Barth elsewhere returns to this theme:

> Is it possible to remove the guilt of the Church by saying that it did not hear, that is has not yet heard? The *word of Christ* would then be a new thing which some men have heard and some have not. It would then be a gift bestowed upon those who dwell in some particular corner of the world, in some other street. There would then be some further knowledge which we do not as yet possess. There would then be something more which we could know, if an angel descended from heaven to-day, and smote upon the table, and uttered the new thing with a voice of thunder. But no, this is not so. Whoever we are we have heard the word of Christ and we are within the picture. It is an objective impossibility for us to discover that we have not heard.[44]

---

42 Robert Willis and John Cullberg are among those dubious about whether Barth can provide an adequate account of moral responsibility (see Robert E. Willis, *The Ethics of Karl Barth* (Leiden: E.J. Brill, 1971), 37; John Cullberg, *Das Problem der Ethik in der Dialektischen Theologie*, vol. 1, (Uppsala: A.-B. Lundequistska Bokhandeln, 1938), 45); Stephen Webb is one of those who revels in the problematic character of Barth's theology: 'a discourse deprived of its subject matter' (Stephen H. Webb, *Refiguring Theology* (New York: State University of New York Press, 1991)).

43 *Romans* II, 46 (23).

44 *Romans* II, 389 (407). Cf. 'The objection is obviously futile that God has not really given, and does not and will not give, His command with such wholeness, clarity and definiteness that it only remains for us to be obedient or disobedient, and not to try to discover what the divine command really is ... We are able to hear it, as surely as we belong to Him and no one else. The question cannot be whether He speaks, but only whether we listen' (*CD* II/2, 669–70 (746–7)). I have amended the translation

While the tone here is harsh – Barth seems to refer to God's word to us only to convict us of dishonesty in denying our ability to hear it – it is nonetheless clear that we are not dealing with a God who in judgement of the world has deserted it, or who has set up insuperable barriers to our discernment of God's will for our lives. God's word to us is gracious: it allows the positive possibility of faithful human discipleship even in the midst of the crisis, if we will but listen to what God wants of us. Barth elsewhere makes this connection between God's grace and human action:

> Grace is the power of obedience; it is theory and practice, conception and birth; it is the indicative which carries with it a categorical imperative; it is the call, the command, the order, which cannot be disobeyed. Grace has the force of a downright conclusion; it is knowledge that needs no will to translate it into action, as though will were something alongside knowledge. Grace is knowledge of the will of God and as such it is the willing of the will of God.[45]

Again, Barth's polemic emphasis here can mislead us: certainly the idea that God determines human action is not immediately recognizable as a positive ethical possibility, and critics have questioned whether Barth can give any account of genuine human action. I discuss this among other interpretative issues in Chapter 3: suffice it here to say that this passage represents one side of a more complex dialectic, and Barth, even in *Romans* II, recognizes the importance of human action being properly human. Barth's depiction of God's grace as forceful and authoritative may also be uncongenial and grounds for dismissing Barth, but again this represents only one side of the picture he is trying to paint. He is commenting here on Romans 6:12–14, where Paul calls the members of the church in Rome not to let sin exercise dominion in their bodies, and proclaims that they are released from sin because they stand under grace. Barth's concern here, therefore, is to emphasize the power of grace to free Christians from slavery to sin. To anticipate his treatment of this theme in the *Dogmatics*, Barth is here describing the way in which God's command is a gracious permission to live differently, to escape those actions that represent our domination by sin. To enable this new life at odds with the power of sin that has determined our lives to this point, grace must be sufficiently powerful to defeat the forces that oppose it.

Continuing to follow Barth's commentary on this passage makes clear that God's grace in freeing human beings from the power of sin is indeed the most hopeful of possibilities:

---

here: at this point Harold Knight translated 'hear' in place of listen. '*Hören*' can mean either, but Barth means to contrast our ability to hear and willingness to listen. *Romans* II clearly anticipates the *Dogmatics* here.

45   *Romans* II, 207 (205). This is one of the few times Barth uses the concept of command in *Romans* II, which he uses to characterize his account of ethics in the *Dogmatics*. Barth also refers to the commandments of God in a passage cited at p.11 above, 260–61 (265). Robert Willis identifies Barth's movement to the language of command with his work subsequent to *Romans* II (Willis, *Ethics*, 41).

Grace is the power of the Resurrection: the knowledge that men are known of God, the consciousness that their existence is begotten of God, that it moves and rests in Him, and that it is beyond all concrete things, beyond the being and course of this world. Inasmuch as men have discovered it, Grace is the existence begotten of God, the new man, created and redeemed by God, the man who is righteous before Him and in whom He is well pleased, the man in whom God again discovers Himself, as a father discovers himself in his child. Of supreme significance, then, is the demand that I, the new man in the power of the resurrection and within the crisis of the transition from death to life, should by faith and under grace – will the will of God. As the man under grace, I am in a position to hear and understand this demand, for existentially and assuredly I live from God and am what He desires. By this demand, moreover, I am reminded of that primal origin by which my existence is under grace, and I perceive that *I* – and yet not I – *am*. As the man under grace, I am created and quickened and awakened. But I am also disturbed, for the demand bids me take up arms against the world of men and against the men of the world.[46]

Alongside the language of grace having the force of a downright conclusion, then, we must place the altogether gentler image of God discovering Godself in human beings as a father discovers himself in his child. Through God's gracious crisis we are roused from our slumber and quickened to the new existence that is the discovery of our true selfhood.

We are now a long way from the conception of God's crisis as a tumultuous chaos in which God is hidden from us and the only true faith is a void. Clearly, we now have reason to doubt perspectives on Barth's ethics in *Romans* II that either bemoan or celebrate his exclusively negative characterization of human possibilities within God's crisis, for the simple reason that Barth's characterization of human possibilities is not exclusively negative. Barth resoundingly echoes God's 'No' to human presumption in *Romans* II, but not to the exclusion of God's 'Yes'. Attentive readers of the commentary find that together with the loud and fearsome declarations of the destructive consequences of God's judgement on a world gone astray, we find – even in *Romans* II – the proclamation of positive human possibilities lived in accordance with God's 'Yes' to humankind. This does not mean that we can set aside the dark and forbidding passages: this would be to replace a one-sided reading emphasizing the chaos of God's crisis with an equally one-sided reading focusing on the positive possibilities that remain. God's 'No' is not superseded or overcome by the possibilities of grace: they exist together. Their relationship is complex: on the one hand even the aspects of the crisis that seem most disorientating and destructive are examples of God's gracious decision to challenge, rather than abandon, the morass of human sin; on the other hand the possibility of human ethical action is precarious at best – set on the edge of a knife, hanging by a single thread – in the context of the crisis of God's judgement. In other words, the ethics of *Romans* II is *dialectical*, not in a Hegelian sense where thesis and antithesis lead inevitably to synthesis, but

---

46   *Romans* II, 207–8 (205).

where thesis and antithesis remain in unresolved mutual tension. The brokenness of the relationship between God and humankind and our predicament resulting from it can only be expressed in the brokenness of the language of dialectical theology.

CHAPTER 2

Ethics Within the Crisis

Barth does not confine his discussion of ethics in *Romans* II to the questions of its possibility and nature, which I discussed in the previous chapter. Barth claims that Paul's is a practical theology, concerned with practical questions, and Barth's own interest in the epistle arises 'because our world is filled with pressing practical duties; because there is wickedness in the streets; because of the existence of the daily papers'.[1] Barth, therefore, cannot avoid consideration of particular ethical questions in his commentary, and his choice of topics is clearly informed by the context in which he wrote.[2] In this chapter I group the ethical issues Barth examines in *Romans* II under two headings: love and community; and war, peace and revolution. Barth's engagement with these topics makes clear once more that he is not content with throwing up his hands in the face of the crisis in which God confronts humanity: even within the crisis there are decisions to be made and pressing duties to be performed. Yet, within the crisis, our ethical reflection cannot proceed as if nothing has happened, and the way Barth employs dialectic in his approach to these issues makes this clear.

Love and Community

Divine activity initially seems to overpower and preclude human action in the act of love. Human love for God 'knows itself to be altogether the gift and operation of God, altogether the calling which is grounded upon the purpose comprehended in God before all time and before every moment in time'.[3] It is not a property that humankind may possess or deserve and it will never be self-evident or certain:

> Predestination means the recognition that love towards God is an occurrence, a being and having and doing of men, which takes place in no moment of time, which is beyond time, which has its origin at every moment in God Himself, and which must therefore be sought and found only in Him.[4]

Human love for God is God's recognition of humanity and can be apprehended 'not by experience, nor by argument, nor by the assertion of assurance, but only by God

---

1 *Romans* II, 438 (461–2).
2 Barth's distance from the ethical concerns that the modern church looks to Romans for help with is evident from the fact that he makes no mention of homosexuality in his commentary.
3 *Romans* II, 322 (334).
4 *Romans* II, 324 (336).

Himself'.[5] It 'is not a particular form of behaviour within the sphere of human competence', but

> the power and significance which God can bestow upon this or that form of human behaviour through its relationship with Him. The love of God, contrasted with the questionableness of our life, is its deepest reality. Men love God, whatever their visible behaviour may be, when, veritably and existentially, quite clearly and once for all, without possibility of avoidance or escape, they encounter the question: 'Who then am I?'[6]

Love for God is intelligible only as the 'more excellent way ... wrought by God'. It is a 'humiliation, so well aware of its intention that it excludes confident questionings and no longer claims its rights'.[7] Barth identifies love for God as agape, and makes clear its distinction from eros:

> Love towards God – agape – is separated from all religious or other forms of eros by the flaming sword of death and eternity. Love proclaims that the new man stands before God, and that He cannot be wooed by any love-song as Baal and his like are wooed.[8]

Alongside this negative assessment of human possibilities, we again find a positive counterpoint standing in dialectical tension to it. Barth identifies subjection to the powers as the great negative ethical possibility. Subjection is negative not in the context of the dialectical polarity I am discussing here, but, according to Barth, because Romans 12:21–13:7 is an assault on the pride of humankind, and requires negative behaviour, 'a human not-doing'.[9] Yet subjection has a positive counterpart, which Barth identifies as agape. This is positive in the context of the dialectic I am describing because it demands action initiated by human agency rather than divine. It is positive in Barth's sense because it demands human activity rather than passivity. There is a further level of complexity in the negative/positive polarity here, though: Barth plays with the negative/positive distinction in identifying the positive possibility of agape as a breaking-up of the existing order:

> We define *love* as the 'great positive possibility' for the same reason as we have previously defined *subjection* as the 'great negative possibility'. We are not now thinking of a single act, but of the combination of all positive – that is to say, protesting – possibilities; we are thinking of a general ethical manner of behaving. We define *love* as the 'great positive possibility', because in it there is brought to

---

5   *Romans* II, 325 (338).
6   *Romans* II, 318–19 (329–30).
7   *Romans* II, 320 (331).
8   *Romans* II, 320 (331).
9   *Romans* II, 477 (502).

light the revolutionary aspect of all ethical behaviour, and because it is veritably concerned with the denial and breaking up of the existing order.[10]

Barth argues that we cannot excuse ourselves from loving by claiming that we live in the 'shadowy region of evil' and can only bear witness by 'not-doing'. Love 'does not stand under the law of evil' and must be enacted as 'protest'.[11] This love encompasses both love for God and for the neighbour:

> Next to eros stands the greatest positive ethical possibility, the epitome of the commandments of the second table, the epitome of those actions foreign to the form of this world: agape, love, as love of humankind for one another. As human love for God, agape is the great unobservable work of the first table, the existential act of humankind under grace (5:5; 8:28–9), represented in the primary ethical action of worship.[12]

This primary action 'must be extended, or rather translated, into the secondary action of love' towards our fellows and it is 'precisely by this extension or translation of worship that the honour of God is demonstrated'. Worship 'can represent existential love only in so far as it is significantly engaged in the corresponding love of men which is the parable of love towards God'.[13] If this 'honour we pay to another' is to be ethical, it must be 'unconditional, genuine preference, which expects nothing in return'.[14]

The first level of the dialectic is clear, then: this exposition of love as the great human ethical possibility, the 'existential act of humankind', and the earlier account of love as altogether the gift of God, stand in juxtaposition as the thesis and antithesis of a dialectic that appears both to require and rule out human agency in love for God and for the neighbour. As Barth continues his exposition of love, it becomes clear that there is a second level of dialectic in operation here, since the great positive possibility of agape is not simple or unitary. There is a worship expressed in terms other than those of love for our fellows, Barth maintains, and cites Luther's commentary on Romans 12:14 that cursing is an 'operation of the Holy Spirit'. Therefore, '[t]here can be … no absolute exhortation to love, any more than there had been (xii. 3–8) to fellowship, or to prophecy, or to theology &c'.[15] Love of the neighbour, then, is no absolute for the Christian: loving does not exhaust what we are called to do. Yet even when we are called to love our fellows, it will not be an easy or sentimental love, but may be harsh and conflictual:

---

10   *Romans* II, 493 (519).
11   *Romans* II, 492 (518).
12   *Romans* II, (476); my translation. Hoskyns's translation here (451–2) portrays Barth as confusingly defining agape first as love of humankind for one another and then as love for God. Barth's intention is that agape encompasses both.
13   *Romans* II, 452 (476).
14   *Romans* II, 455 (479).
15   *Romans* II, 453 (477).

Agape is the crisis in which the others stand. Agape can never be the simple, direct, unmistakable thing which sentimentalists yearn after – because it is indissolubly linked with the agape which is directed towards God. Love is therefore both sweet and bitter. It can yield; but is can also be harsh. It can preserve peace; but it can also engage in conflict.

Barth cites Luther again here:

All the good works and love that I might perform on behalf of my neighbour and all the love that I might display towards him ought to be governed by the will of God. Should I be able to make the whole world happy for one day, nevertheless I must not do so – if it be not God's will.[16]

Only love strong enough to abhor evil can cleave to the good: 'Love forgets – and knows; forgives – and punishes; freely receives – and utterly rejects.'[17] Barth's depiction of the positive possibility of love has an internal dialectic: sweet and bitter, yielding and harsh, forgetting and knowing, forgiving and punishing, receiving and rejecting.

With respect to the first level of the polarities operational here, between divine and human agency, Barth takes a step beyond the dialectical tension we saw in the previous chapter. He affirms the possibility of something beyond the to and fro between negative and positive poles:

All things work together for good to them that love God ... Everything must work together, in order that the man whom God loves may be fitted to participate in that good thing. Everything: the wholly unedifying visibility of the world, as well as the equally unedifying invisibility of God; the misery of our createdness, as well as the darkness of the divine wrath; the incurable ambiguity of time, as well as the constrasted ambiguity of eternity. For God, as the God of love, stands where the two negations are first manifested in sharp antagonism and are then seen to meet and dissolve one another. The Love of God stands where there is disclosed, beyond and above and in the twofold negation, the pre-eminent affirmation – Jesus Christ, the Resurrection and the Life.[18]

This is not an isolated claim. Love of God is 'the unobservable place where the consummation of all things has already been completed' and 'human duality' finds its unity in God.[19]

Elsewhere Barth makes it even clearer that if God is with us, paradoxes can be overcome. In a passage which is an important step beyond the emphasis on God's 'No' that is the sum of what many commentators find in *Romans* II, Barth anticipates

---

16   *Romans* II, 454 (478). I have dropped Hoskyns's use of capitals to emphasize 'agape', 'eros', and 'crisis'.

17   *Romans* II, 454 (478).

18   *Romans* II, 320–21 (332).

19   *Romans* II, 320 (331), 322 (334).

the unambiguous confidence in God's goodness towards humankind that he develops in his later work:

> 'God for us' – that means, however, the unheard-of: that the realm of opposites lies behind us, that the duality has been overcome, the duality in which we see everything here and now and for all time, the world from God's point of view and God in darkness from the world's point of view. This duality is indeed the duality of humankind, knowing and desiring their otherness and individuality in the face of God, detached from God, plunged into relativity, and finally and at last still religious. They have 'imprisoned the truth in unrighteousness' (1:18). They have against them God and the world, death and sin. They can only think in contrasts, in antimonies, in tensions. They are the unredeemed, who know no unity. Those whom God is with, however, and who therefore by virtue of divine initiative stand on God's side, know of no duality, do not think in antimonies, have no one and nothing against them. Here corruption has put on incorruption, and mortality immortality. Here the word is fulfilled: 'Death is swallowed up in victory!' (1 Cor. 15:54). With this 'If God is for us!' is said what can be said about fulfilment, redemption, perfection, splendour, and about the unclear centre: what *must* be said is that the beginning and the end is 'God may be all in all' (1 Cor. 15:28). We do not have to have words and ideas for that, as if otherwise it would not be what it is. We content ourselves with the discovery that all signs point in that direction, and break off.
>
> We break off deliberately, however, not because we have been dreaming, but because we have seen the final unforgettable truth: 'He that spared not his own Son, but delivered him up for us all, how shall he not also with him freely give us all things?'[20]

The proximity of the crisis causes Barth to break off his reflection here: in the *Dogmatics*, as we shall see, he is prepared to go further. Barth concludes his commentary on Chapter 8 of the epistle with the claim that in the love of Jesus Christ, the 'unattainable identity has been attained' – the love of God for humankind and the love of humankind for God is made one.[21]

In his discussion of love of the neighbour, Barth calls love the 'human religious impossibility' because it is a possibility of God, and cites the text that love is the 'fulfilling of the law.' He then recalls his earlier contentions that our reflections are always 'disturbed by their relation to the concrete world in which we live' and our conversations about God are 'always interrupted conversations; for He withdraws Himself from us and opposes Himself to us when we are confronted by the question, What shall we do?' Yet in this context he is prepared to hazard an answer to the ethical question: 'To this question we now answer "Thou shalt love thy neighbour as thyself".'[22] Clearly, this is not the material answer to the ethical question that Barth has ruled out: it does not provide us with concrete ethical rules for our behaviour. Equally clearly, however, the introduction of love of the neighbour as a paradigm

---

20   *Romans* II, 326–7 (338–9); my translation.
21   *Romans* II, 329 (342).
22   *Romans* II, 493–4 (520).

within which we will find the answer to the ethical question moves beyond his previous position that judged it impossible to provide any answer.

In these passages, Barth is driven beyond a simple thesis and antithesis by the Pauline texts that portray love as the consummation of all things. To be sure, this escape from paradox and duality is an eschatological reality, rather than a present one. We can hope for this consummation, however, rather than remaining agnostic as to whether God's 'Yes' or 'No' will be finally determinative. The hope of this realm beyond the dialectical tension of the crisis is the most positive possibility we have yet seen in *Romans* II.

For Barth much is at stake in the question of whether we can solve the riddle of how it is that in our neighbour 'we encounter, finally and supremely, the ambiguity of our existence, since in the particularity of others we are reminded of our own particularity, of our own createdness, our own lost state, our own sin, and our own death'. The solution to this riddle, he suggests, must also be the solution to 'those perpetually recurring interruptions of our conversation about God'. Here we must make a decision

> as to whether the impossible possibility of God – which lies beyond all human possibility – is or is not a mere phantom of metaphysics; whether, when we speak of the pre-supposition behind all things that are capable of analysis and description, when we speak of the outpouring of the Spirit in our hearts, we are or are not merely dreaming; whether our apprehension of the final 'Yes' in the final 'No' is or is not merely a wild guess; whether our knowledge of God is or is not simply the 'renunciation of knowledge' (Kierkegaard); whether the Unknown God has spoken to us in Jesus Christ; whether our being touched by the freedom of God, the establishing of our personalities, our proceeding along the still more excellent way, are existential events.

Barth claims that all this depends on whether we find God in our neighbour:

> The decision lies in our answer to the question – Do we in the unknowable *neighbour* apprehend the Unknown God? Do we in the Otherness of *the other* – in whom the whole riddle of existence is summed up in such a manner as to require its solution in an action on our part – hear the voice of the One?

His conclusion is that if we 'hear in the *neighbour* only the voice of *the other* and not also the voice of the One ... then, quite certainly, the voice of the One is nowhere to be heard'.[23]

Here we see once again the pivotal role ethics plays in *Romans* II. The question of whether in our neighbour we encounter God and hear God's voice determines whether the chaos of the crisis is the final truth of our existence, or whether there is instead a final 'Yes' in the final 'No'. It is the search for an answer to the ethical question 'What shall I do' that motivates Barth to study Romans, and it is his

---

23 *Romans* II, 494–5 (520–21).

commitment to ethics that drives him to retain his belief in the positive pole of the dialectic, and helps him to see into a realm beyond that duality.

The dialectical theme is also present in Barth's discussion of community. In comment on 'All have sinned, and fall short of the glory of God' (3:22), Barth expounds on the 'remarkable union' brought about by the 'dissolution of every distinction':

> There is no positive possession of men which is sufficient to provide a foundation for human solidarity; for every positive possession – religious temperament, moral consciousness, humanitarianism – already contains within itself the seed of the disruption of society. These positive factors are productive of difference, since they distinguish men from one another. Genuine fellowship is grounded upon a negative: it is grounded upon what men lack. Precisely when we recognize that we are sinners do we perceive that we are brothers.[24]

Barth extends this account of community when he comments on Paul's metaphor of the body. He rejects what he terms the 'conservative' interpretation of the parable, which pictures 'individuals as "partial" things comprehended in a larger whole' as cells in an organism. This would lead to a view proper to sociology or biology, Barth suggests, rather than a depiction of the Kingdom of God, which we must expect Paul to be describing. He emphasizes that he is departing from the first edition of *Romans II* in rejecting the view 'that the Christian "corporation" is competent to represent to the individual the claim of God, or that the totality of the community – the mass of the faithful – is competent to judge between God and man'.[25] Barth identifies this view of Paul's metaphor with 'natural philosophy'. He claims instead that the parable reminds the individual of 'the fact of community' and that the ethical problem itself – 'What shall we do?' – 'appears at the point where the existence of these "others" emerges as a problem'.[26] Fellowship means 'an encountering of the other in the full existentiality of his utter otherness' and rather than blurring the 'otherness' of each individual, it 'both requires the "otherness" of each individual and makes sense of it'.

Barth advances a concept of the individual in which the believers are 'in their full-grown and in no way attenuated individuality, one body, one individual in Christ'.[27] He sees this conception of the individual as critical for the presupposition of ethics:

> If the crucified Christ is *the measure* of faith which God hath dealt to each man ... if each single one of us must, in his particularity, *put on the Lord Jesus* Christ ... if the 'other' – the neighbour – who stands at the side of each one of us is the uplifted finger which by its 'otherness' reminds us of the *wholly* other; if the community is that fellowship that reminds us of the Fellowship which is the oneness of every

---

24 *Romans* II, 100–101 (82).
25 *Romans* II, 441 (465).
26 *Romans* II, 442 (465–6).
27 *Romans* II, 443 (467).

man and of all mankind in the unsearchableness of God – then for each one of us who is thus reminded of his 'individuality', all Titanism, all mounting of high places is excluded; and to think soberly – that is to say, to recollect that God alone occupies the High Place – is set forth as *the* ethical action.[28]

We saw above that Barth ascribes the utmost importance to whether we hear the voice of the One in the other. Here we see a movement from the 'otherness' of our neighbour to the Wholly Other, and its ethical significance. Barth emphasizes elsewhere the way in which the other points us to the Other: 'The discovery of the One in the other can occur only as each single individual is confronted by particular concrete others.'[29] Love in the form of charity also witnesses to the relationship between the One and others: Barth states that charity both overcomes the tension between the self and others, and demonstrates the recognition of the 'One' in the others.[30] In a confirmation of the importance Barth ascribes to love in the Christian community here, we find his interpretation that Paul's metaphor of the church as body means that the foundation of ethics is to be found 'in the constitution of the Community as Fellowship'.[31]

War, Peace, and Revolution

The second cluster of ethical topics Barth considers in *Romans* II is of a very different kind. His reflection on warfare has an immediate context: in the preface to the English edition, he begs his readers to remember that at the time he wrote the book 'it required only a little imagination for me to hear the sound of the guns booming away in the north'.[32] His first move is to show how human the motives for war are. The current situation 'is so confused and unpeaceable that it requires a distribution of blows to right and left'. Our fellows clearly have no right to peace: they are 'unattractive, crotchety, impenitent' and they irritate us. Why should we not engage in conflict with others? Barth asks, and 'What is more natural than war?'[33] We see this endorsement of Hobbes's account of the state of nature to be ironic when Barth continues that war is indeed a natural human activity: the natural activity 'of men engaged in making themselves God by making of their attitude to their fellow men an absolute moral attitude'.[34] It is the recognition that war represents the usurpation of God's place, Barth argues, that encourages us to preserve peace with our fellows at all costs.

---

28   *Romans* II, 444 (467–8).
29   *Romans* II, 476 (501).
30   *Romans* II, 459 (483). Comparison with the work of Emmanuel Levinas is inescapable here. See Steven G. Smith, *The Argument to the Other: Reason Beyond Reason in the Thought of Karl Barth and Emmanuel Levinas* (Chico, California: Scholars Press, 1983), for one attempt at this.
31   *Romans* II, 449 (473).
32   *Romans* II, v.
33   *Romans* II, 469 (494).
34   *Romans* II, 470 (495).

Barth notes, however, that Paul's injunction is to be at peace 'as much as in you lieth'. We are fully aware why Paul cannot say more than this, Barth comments, since 'God is the boundary of human possibility'. God 'is not known: He will be known', so the possibility that we must engage in conflict with our fellows remains. There remains a reservation that God may 'forbid us to see Jesus Christ' in another person.[35] Barth emphasizes that this is God's reservation, not ours, so we are not free to apply it 'under the pressure of peculiarly difficult circumstances'. It cannot lead us to believe that we can go to war in 'good conscience', since there is no such thing as a good conscience, whether in war or peace. The knowledge of God 'directs us to God; it does not direct us to some human position or to some human course of action either in time of war or peace'. We must descend from every warlike 'high place' in recognition that we do not have knowledge of God, but we may not then ascend some 'high place of peace'. Therefore, '[a] Church which knows its business well will, it is true, with a strong hand keep itself free from militarism; but it will also with a friendly gesture rebuff the attentions of pacifism'. Paul's command to be at peace is not absolute and 'has no final accuracy': it is a broken command bearing witness to 'the peace of the Coming World'.[36]

In comment on Paul's instruction to feed and give water to the enemy, Barth depicts the enemy as 'the other in his extreme unknowableness', who 'displays clearly what we ought not to do', and 'incites me to render evil for evil'.[37] The enemy 'opens my eyes to what it really is that I find so strangely irritating in my fellow men' and shows me 'evil freely running its course' without obstacle. He 'lets loose in me a tempestuous, yearning cry for a higher – non-existent – compensating, avenging righteousness, and for a higher – non-existent – judge between me and him'. What can I do, Barth asks, when everything I can do against the enemy is evil?

> But can it be evil to bring into operation against the enemy that higher righteousness for which I so earnestly yearn? Then it is that the last, supreme temptation to Titanism lies so strangely near at hand. Shall I take the matter into my own hands? Shall I undertake to battle for the right? Shall I myself become the invisible God? Shall I, as an enemy, set myself against the enemy? Shall I, as a Titan, war against the Titan? Who will pronounce judgement upon me, if I do this?[38]

Barth rejects this path of reasoning:

> Once it is granted that men can and ought to perform objective righteousness, this whole forceful procedure on behalf of right is clearly inevitable ... But it is precisely this presupposition, the presupposition that men can and ought to do

---

35   *Romans* II, 470 (495).
36   *Romans* II, 471 (496).
37   *Romans* II, 471–2 (496).
38   *Romans* II, 472 (496).

what is objectively right, which the disturbance of men by God renders altogether questionable.[39]

We cannot claim to be doing what is objectively right 'without seizing the sceptre of God'; precisely in the intention to do what is objectively right, I do objective unrighteousness. The wrath of God 'is revealed against human ungodliness in doing evil and in doing good', which is a criticism of both militarism and pacifism, Barth argues. He suggests that we fail to 'leave room' for the wrath of God and do not 'seriously reckon with the fact that human action will ... be driven off the field by the pre-eminent action of God'.[40]

Refraining from the attempt to perform objective righteousness, however, seems to leave me with no action but withdrawal in relation to my enemy. Barth finds an alternative in Paul: to 'do the irrational, impossible, and altogether impractical thing: If thine enemy hunger, feed him! If he thirst, give him to drink!' These actions 'draw attention to the fact that the enemy has presented us with a problem that presses upon us too hardly for us to regard him as some one who can be attacked whilst we ourselves remain unbroken'.[41] Yet we must be careful here, Barth warns, not to make these actions a viable human ethical possibility. Love of the enemy can only be a response to 'the ethical paradox of the One in the other', a means of recognizing the One in the other even when this is my enemy. Barth claims that Christian ethics has taken a particular interest in love of the enemy because it is a signifying action that 'announces the Coming World'.[42]

This reflection on appropriate responses to the actions of our enemies provides our first opportunity to see the application of the ethics of *Romans* II to a concrete issue. We see that its first impact is critical, questioning the legitimacy of acting on the basis of 'natural' human emotions or from a belief that we are enacting objective righteousness. We note that the theological insight that we are not justified in seizing the sceptre of God has an immediate ethical relevance here. It suggests that we can neither go to war in confidence of being in the right, nor believe that forswearing violence is the ethical high road. We are called to be more humble in our aspirations for our actions and for our ethics: the most we can hope is that our action may signify God's own action, that we may act in accordance with God's righteousness. Barth does not provide us with further guidance here regarding when we will signify God's action by engaging in conflict. Providing this guidance would obviously be problematic, since to begin to specify when we could be sure we were acting in accordance with God would be to begin the specification of objective righteousness

---

39 *Romans* II, 472–3 (497).
40 *Romans* II, 473 (497–8).
41 *Romans* II, 474 (499).
42 *Romans* II, 475 (500). Hoskyns terms love towards the enemy a 'significant' action in this passage, which is easily taken to mean that the action is important in its own right. Barth is making the opposite point here: that love of the enemy only has meaning insofar as it *signifies* God's action. 'Significant' can clearly take this latter meaning, but is too ambiguous to be used in this context.

that Barth has firmly rejected. The impact of *Romans* II on the ethics of war and peace is not to provide us with just another answer: we already have answers encompassing every possible position on the question, and giving one more answer would be to leave us exactly where we were. Instead, Barth makes us rethink our relationship to these answers: is our first allegiance to just war theory, or pacifism, or to the unknown God? If we take his interpretation of Paul seriously, we will recognize the uncertain and provisional nature of the results of our reflections on these issues, and will act not with self-righteous zeal, but in hope that this is how we may signify God's action. In the *Dogmatics*, as we will see, Barth does attempt to go further than this in offering an answer.

Many of Barth's readers in the early 1920s must have turned first to see what he would say in relation to the beginning of Romans 13, Paul's treatment of how Christians should behave in relation to secular government. Barth includes a warning at this point that those who do not understand the book as a whole 'will be puzzled as to why we say what we do say, why we do not say more, and why we do not say less'.[43] Barth introduces the powers of 'church and state, of law and society' and poses the question in terms of whether we consider them authoritative:

> If we admit their authority, we concede quite clearly the principle of legitimism; if, on the other hand, we reject it, we are bound to accept the principle of revolution. Being, however, concerned to demonstrate the honour of God, we do not – as the impatient reader desires, or rather, since every one is as a matter of course a party man, as the opponent of revolution quite naturally desires – concede the principle of legitimism. But, on the other hand, neither do we – as so many readers of the Epistle secretly hope – concede the principle of revolution.[44]

Barth claims he finds 'a direct denial of revolution' in Paul's letter, but also a denial of legitimism. He is more anxious about the forces of revolution, however, than about the forces of conservatism:

> because it is most improbable that any one will be won over to the cause of reaction – as a result of reading the Epistle to the Romans! On the other hand, it is not unlikely that its reading may foster a contempt for the present order and an attitude of negation towards it. The disquiet, the questioning, the negation, the emphatic insistence upon the parable of death, to which Christianity is definitely committed ... may be so misunderstood as to be transformed into a positive method of human behaviour, into a means of justification, indeed, into the Titanism of revolt and upheaval and renovation. The revolutionary Titan is far more godless, far more dangerous, than his reactionary counterpart – because he is so much nearer the truth.[45]

---

43 *Romans* II, 476 (501).
44 *Romans* II, 477 (502).
45 *Romans* II, 478 (502–3).

Barth next comments on Paul's command to 'Be not overcome with evil, but overcome evil with good'. Revolutionaries do not err in their estimation of the evil of secular government, according to Barth. He notes that the invectives hurled against governments 'from the Revelation of John to the fulminations of Nietzsche' are not against defects in governments but against their right to exist at all, and argues with characteristic vigour that the state is incurably presumptuous:

> That men should, as a matter of course, claim to possess a higher right over their fellow men, that they should, as a matter of course, dare to regulate and predetermine almost all their conduct, that those who put forward such a manifestly fraudulent claim should be crowned with a halo of real power and should be capable of requiring obedience and sacrifice as though they had been invested with the authority of God, that the many should conspire to speak as though they were the One, that a minority or a majority, even the supreme democratic majority of all against one – should assume that they are the community, that a quite fortuitous contract or arrangement should be regarded as superior to the solid organization of the struggle for existence and should proclaim itself to be the peace which all men yearn after and which all should respect; the whole pseudo-transcendence of an altogether immanent order is the wound that is inflicted by every existing government – even by the best – upon those who are most delicately conscious of what is good and right.[46]

There is no legality that is not fundamentally illegal; no authority that is not tyrannical. The revolutionary sees this evil and undertakes to battle with the existing order and replace it with a new just one. The plan is cogent and understandable, just as conflict with the enemy and with our fellows is understandable. But the revolutionary cannot avoid being overcome with evil; he 'forgets he is not the One' and emulates the state by usurping an authority that is not his. He is not Christ before the Grand Inquisitor, but the Grand Inquisitor encountering Christ.[47] The revolutionary is overcome with evil, 'because with his "No" he stands so strangely near to God'.[48] In place of the revolution that is the 'impossible possibility' of the forgiveness of sins and the resurrection of the dead, the revolutionary

> has adopted the possible possibility of discontent and hatred and insubordination, of rebellion and demolition. And this choice is not better, but much worse than choosing the possible possibility of contentment and satisfaction, of security and usurpation; for by it God is far better understood, but far more deeply outraged.[49]

---

46   *Romans* II, 479 (503–4).
47   *Romans* II, 480 (505). The fable of the Grand Inquisitor from *The Brothers Karamazov* is one example of the impact of Barth's attention to Dostoevsky, which he acknowledges in the preface to the second edition, 4 (XIV).
48   *Romans* II, 480 (505–6).
49   *Romans* II, 481 (506).

The revolutionary aims at revolution, but succeeds only in reaction; the legitimist aims at legitimism, but maintains what is actually revolt. There is no more radical action, Barth claims, than to turn back and 'not be angry, not engage in an assault, and not demolish,' and this turning back 'is the ethical factor in the command Overcome evil with good'. Barth finds in Paul 'no approval of the existing order', but 'endless disapproval of every enemy of it'.[50] The most radical revolution 'can do no more than set what exists against what exists' and thus justify and confirm the existing order, forcing it to adapt and therefore become more dangerous.[51] Barth pictures the 'Primal Order of God' as a minus sign outside the bracketed sum of (state + church + law + society), representing their dissolution by God. Revolution within history can only change the signs inside the brackets to negative ones, which, when combined with the negative sign outside the brackets, has the effect of making them positive terms, turning the existing order into a new and more powerful form.[52]

Charles Villa-Vicencio characterizes the difficulty of interpreting Barth here as a choice between quietism and anarchism.[53] On one hand, Barth seems to deny legitimacy to the defender of the existing order and the revolutionary, leaving the student of Barth 'paralyzed by the realization that tyranny warrants destruction, while the revolutionary in turn needs to have "wrest from his hands the principle of revolution"'.[54] On the other, Barth heralds the great revolution of God, bringing the dissolution of all existing orders and the end of all hierarchy and authority. The interpretative task becomes harder when we appreciate that the commentary on Romans 13 is one of the sections Barth revised most comprehensively between the first and second edition. The first edition focuses on the criticism of the role of the state, the necessity for Christians to have nothing to do with the state, and for them to prepare for its dissolution by God: the changes in the second edition are striking, with Barth's concerns about the revolutionary receiving the most attention, as we have seen.[55] Clearly, Barth aims in the second edition to distance himself from a naïve

50   *Romans* II, 481 (506).
51   *Romans* II, 482 (507).
52   *Romans* II, 482–3 (508).
53   Charles Villa-Vicencio, 'Karl Barth's "Revolution of God": Quietism or Anarchy?' in *On Reading Karl Barth in South Africa*, ed. Charles Villa-Vicencio (Grand Rapids, Michigan: Eerdmans, 1988), 45.
54   Ibid.
55   For a comparison of the two versions on this issue, see Robert E. Hood, *Contemporary Political Orders and Christ* (Allison Park, Pennsylvania: Pickwick Publications, 1985), 45–61; George Hunsinger, 'Toward a Radical Barth', in *Karl Barth and Radical Politics*, ed. George Hunsinger (Philadelphia: Westminster Press, 1976), 203–11; and C.A. Wanamaker, 'Romans 13: A Hermeneutic for Church and State', in *On Reading Karl Barth in South Africa*, ed. Charles Villa-Vicencio (Grand Rapids, Michigan: William B. Eerdmanns, 1988). Friedrich-Wilhelm Marquardt argues that Bultmann's rejection of the first edition 'meant in effect the banning of social consciousness from modern German theology' and that the second edition 'was a public success in Germany because of its supposedly antirevolutionary tendency' (Friedrich-Wilhelm Marquardt, 'Socialism in the Theology of Karl Barth', in *Karl Barth and Radical Politics*, ed. George Hunsinger

endorsement of revolution. Equally clearly, he retains a comprehensive attack on the legitimacy of the state, and a strong commitment to the truly radical revolution that God brings.

The key to interpreting Barth's treatment of the question of revolution is not in the section headed 'The Great Negative Possibility', that I have discussed above. There his focus is on revolution, but he maintains the position that pronounces both the state and revolution to be illegitimate, and leaves us with the great negative possibility of subjection and 'not-doing'. The section that follows is 'The Great Positive Possibility' of love. Here his first word, which I have already cited above, is that in love 'there is brought to light the revolutionary aspect of all ethical behaviour', because it is 'veritably concerned with the denial and breaking up of the existing order'. Barth continues:

> It is love that places the reactionary also finally in the wrong, despite the wrongness of the revolutionary. Inasmuch as we love one another we cannot wish to uphold the present order as such, for by love we do the 'new' by which the 'old' is overthrown. And so, in speaking of the breach in the wall of the incomprehensible 'not-doing', we have to speak now of the much more incomprehensible action of love.[56]

Here the warning remains that the revolutionaries are also in the wrong when they take on the mantle of the Chosen One and believe that an earthly revolution could stand in for the true revolution that belongs only to God. Yet we see here more than a finely balanced judgement leading to the quietist alternative Villa-Vicencio identified. We see Barth's concerns regarding revolution as qualifications and stipulations for the interpretation of the core message here, which is radically revolutionary. He has told us that he considers it most improbable that anyone could be won over to the cause of reaction by Paul's letter to the Romans. The revolutionary position is particularly dangerous 'because it is so much nearer the truth', and here we discover that the wall of not-doing can be breached by love, the great positive possibility that demonstrates 'the revolutionary aspect of all ethical behaviour'. This is no quietism, but a call to action qualified by an insistence that we recognize that

---

(Philadelphia: Westminster Press, 1976), 51). Marquardt's argument that Barth's socialist commitments were central to his theology throughout his career are developed in Friedrich-Wilhelm Marquardt, *Theologie und Sozialismus: Das Beispiel Karl Barths* (Munich: Chr. Kaiser Verlag, 1972). Hunsinger and Villa-Vicencio concur that it was Barth's disillusion with the Weimar Republic and the Russian revolution that lead to the wholesale revision of this section; Hunsinger agrees with Marquardt that this was a major impetus for the publication of the second edition as a whole (Villa-Vicencio, 'Revolution of God', 48; Hunsinger, 'Toward a Radical Barth', 210; Marquardt, 'Socialism', 57). See also McCormack's critique of Marquardt's assertion that Barth underwent a 'sensational antirevolutionary turn' between the two versions of *Romans* (Bruce L. McCormack, *Karl Barth's Critically Realistic Dialectical Theology: Its Genesis and Development, 1909–1936* (Oxford: Clarendon Press, 1995), 282).

56   *Romans* II, 493 (519).

our action is human, and that it is significant only insofar as it signifies the action of God.[57]

Barth's Treatment of Ethical Themes in *Romans* II

This examination of Barth's treatment of ethical themes in *Romans* II shows that when he moves from metaethics to ethics his thought retains its dialectical shape. Human agency in loving the neighbour is at once rejected and required; love itself must be harsh as well as sweet; community is founded upon absence; individuality is properly understood as communal; we must not play God in resisting the enemy but must also reject pacifism; and we must side neither with legitimism nor with revolution. This approach is valuable in illustrating the problematic nature of ethical action: there is no simple recipe for doing the right thing, since even the aspiration to enact what is objectively right betrays our Titanism. We cannot claim God's blessing by adopting militarism or pacifism, legitimism or anarchism. None of these human categories has the power to put us in the right: righteousness belongs to God alone.

The survey in this chapter has also shown that there are elements in Barth's treatment of the issues of love and community, and war, peace, and revolution, that go beyond the dialectical polarities I have identified. He is frequently not content to rest at the apparent impasse of the tension between God's 'No' and God's 'Yes'. In his account of agape he expresses a deep yearning and hope for an existence free from the contrasts, antinomies, tensions and dualities of earthly life, and for the consummation Paul promises in which God becomes all in all. In his treatment of revolution, we have seen that we must reject the interpretation of his dialectic as a recommendation to quietism, and recognize that Barth is calling us to action, albeit to action that continues to recall its status as human rather than divine. These moves require a refinement of the characterization of Barth's dialectical ethics I set out at the end of the previous chapter. When Barth confronts particular ethical questions he does not simply juxtapose God's 'Yes' and 'No' as thesis and antithesis in a tensive and unresolved relationship. First, he often looks ahead in eschatological hope to an

---

57   Villa-Vicencio concludes that Barth's emphasis on God's revolution, 'which at first sight seems to negate all human responsibility', in fact 'makes Barth's theology an inspirational source for sustained human participation in a continuing quest for something more than any particular society can deliver'. He claims Barth's 'deabsolutizing of the revolution and his relativizing of impetuous activism are shaped by his commitment to ensure that political action remains human in what is all too often a dehumanizing struggle'. I suggest that the overriding opposition here is not human/inhuman but human/divine – Barth defuses the hubris of human actions that claim to be divine. This delimitation of human aspirations, however, certainly has the effect of guarding against the dehumanization of the struggle that Villa-Vicencio sees. He adds that 'Barth makes a profound theological contribution to the Marxist distinction between thoughtless practice and critical praxis', which 'both radicalizes and deabsolutizes Marx's revolutionary theory' (Villa-Vicencio, 'Revolution of God', 56).

existence that will be beyond paradox, ambiguity, and complexity, when all things will become clear. The duality of God's 'No' and 'Yes' to us determines our lives in these days, but it will not always be this way, and we can properly look forward to a time when this fragmentation will become whole. Second, even while we live in the midst of paradox and ambiguity, we cannot excuse ourselves from the requirement to act by claiming ourselves to be paralysed by the dialectical tension that we exist in. Genuine theology begins and ends in action, and we can no more escape the requirement to act in the world than we can the complexity of the reality we act within.

These first two chapters have shown that the ethics of *Romans* II exist in a dynamic tension between two poles, each of which express partial truths about theological ethics, yet which are mutually exclusive. Barth's recognition of the necessity to find immediate answers to the question 'What shall we do?' means that he cannot be satisfied with a purely formal ethic. It is the 'wickedness in the streets', the 'daily papers', and 'the need for action' that motivates his study of Romans: an account of ethics that remained above the fray might be theoretically satisfying, but would fail to respond to these concerns. Ethics must speak, therefore – it cannot avoid the responsibility of providing a guide to making decisions about what to do. On the other hand, there is no shortage of ethical systems that provide detailed day-to-day guidance, but which become ends in themselves, self-important structures with no sense of the questionable status of all human endeavour aspiring to be significant beyond signifying the action of God. The impact of the crisis of God on ethics is to make us realize that we cannot speak: we cannot substitute our judgement for the judgement of God, nor can we believe we can capture the will of God in our own ethical constructs. Barth's dialectical account of ethics in *Romans* II is an attempt to give expression to a Christian ethics that seeks to embody the truth of these incompatible extremes in an energetic and unstable juxtaposition. Construing Christian ethics in this way enables him to retain a balance between recognition of the limitations and pitfalls of human action, and the need to find immediate answers to the question 'What shall we do?' In the next chapter, I review and assess the merits of the critiques the ethics of *Romans* II provoked.

CHAPTER 3

Response to the *Romans* II Crisis

In the face of the stark diagnosis of the human predicament in relation to God presented in the second edition of Barth's commentary on Romans, and the strange shape Barth announces that theology and ethics must take as a result, it is not surprising that few theologians have taken much account of his ethics of crisis. Those who have engaged with it have usually found the ethics of *Romans* II wanting. In this chapter, I examine these critiques in order to sift the many based on partial and one-sided readings from those that raise genuine problems with Barth's approach.

An Irresponsible Ethic?

In one of the few book-length studies of Barth's ethics in *Romans* II, Robert Willis's assessment of the ethics of *Romans* II is uncompromising. He argues that, although it does not necessarily follow 'that emphasizing eschatological realities diminishes the importance of concrete situations and possibilities within the world', Barth makes it clear that the action of God impinges directly on the world, which 'appears to leave no room for establishing any sort of independent status for the world or human action'. Willis concludes that either the impact of revelation results in the 'total elimination of the world, including human action' or 'the world and the human are somehow absorbed into the being of God'.[1] The latter is not a possibility for Barth, Willis notes, whereas the former is suggested in two ways. First, the dialectic between God's 'Yes' and 'No' is not equally balanced: the 'Yes' emerges only within the 'No'. Willis claims this leaves humanity in a 'perilous' situation of attempting 'responsible, ethically meaningful decisions remembering that these are already under judgement so that there is no way of guaranteeing that the possibilities open in the sphere of human decision and action can emerge as significant actualities'.[2] Second, Willis argues that while Barth makes use of existentialist categories in *Romans* II, he does not embrace Kierkegaard's exploration of human subjectivity in relation to God. For Barth, Willis suggests, human existentiality lies in one's transcendent identity in relationship with Christ rather than in one's givenness as acting subject, making the reality of the self as ethical agent problematic. Willis judges that Barth does not deal successfully with 'serious questions about the existential identity of man in his historicity, and thus about the possibility for there being meaningful ethical actions

---

1   Robert E. Willis, *The Ethics of Karl Barth* (Leiden: E.J. Brill, 1971), 36.
2   Ibid., 37.

which move beyond the primary action of repentance'.[3] As he moves to Barth's work beyond *Romans* II, Willis comments that somehow Barth 'will need to find a way to give the human its due without diminishing the significance of the covering action of God'.[4]

Willis is not alone in considering that there are difficulties with Barth's ethics in *Romans* II, and cites John Cullberg and Henri Bouillard to support his view. Cullberg is concerned that Barth's concept of predestination disallows any possibility of responsible action, and claims that the ethics of *Romans* II are not only an absolute attack on all persons as they are plunged into the crisis in which moral goodness seems an impossibility, which Barth maintains, but are also an absolute attack on all ethics:

> Predestination in this heightened metaphysical sense allows, or in fact implies, that the ethical question 'What should I do' is exchanged for another: 'What will I do?' or, better, 'What will happen to me?' With this change to the future tense, every ethos is killed. Responsible human action in the real sense is completely out of the question. Therefore it may be said with every right that the 'ethics' of *Romans* II means the 'absolute attack on all ethics'.[5]

Cullberg introduces his consideration of the problem of ethics in dialectical theology by quoting Willhelm Link. Link observes that '[t]he question of ethics is willingly asked by dialectical theology and is unwillingly answered by most dialecticians' and asks, '[h]ow can the affirmation of the ethical act come from the negation of everything human? Can that negation and this affirmation coexist?'[6] It is Barth's insistence that Christian ethics must persistently ask questions but refuse to answer them that most concerns Bouillard:

> Certainly, Christianity inclines more towards the negation than the affirmation of life. But, like the thesis, the antithesis is relative, relative to the Origin, to the synthesis that is only found in God. Christian ethics is not only a question: God alone is the answer.[7]

While John Webster is generally far more appreciative of Barth's early ethical thought, he cites the following passage as 'the point at which Barth's handling of divine transcendence seems least satisfactory, above all because of its apparent

---

3 Ibid., 38.
4 Ibid., 39. Willis's concerns here are not specific to *Romans* II. Two of the questions he identifies in his conclusion with respect to Barth's work as a whole are the threatened status of the person as subject and agent (433) and the way that creation as the external basis of the covenant 'obscures' the independence of the created order (437).
5 John Cullberg, *Das Problem der Ethik in der Dialektischen Theologie*, vol. 1 (Uppsala: A.-B. Lundequistska Bokhandeln, 1938), 45.
6 Wilhelm Link, '"Christliche Ethik" und "Dialektische Theologie"', in *Theologische Aufsätze. Karl Barth Zum 50. Geburtstag*, ed. E. Wolf (Munich: Chr. Kaiser Verlag, 1936), 262.
7 Henri Bouillard, *Genèse et Evolution de la Théologie Dialectique* (Paris: Aubier, 1957), 70.

subversion of any sense in which the world of human selfhood and agency could be given a positive appraisal':[8]

> We come from the all-embracing dissolution of every predicate of our known existence, and we advance to meet the equally comprehensive, but *totaliter* aliter, predication of our unknown existence in God, the predication of the new man, which I am not, but which, nevertheless, dwells in me, and which is, undeniably, my existential ego.[9]

Webster notes that Barth even here says 'Nevertheless ...' and that this qualification 'will become an increasing preoccupation' but he maintains that 'for the present, man as subject and agent of his own history almost, if not quite, vanishes'.[10]

The overriding theme of these criticisms is the absence of genuine and responsible human agency; the two other problems raised are the refusal of ethics to provide answers, and the overwhelming of the 'Yes' of the dialectic by the 'No'. I will respond to these three criticisms in turn.

Regarding the question of whether Barth can allow for real human action, there is clearly a case to answer. As we have seen in the previous chapter, he is concerned to emphasize the power of grace in relation to human will. Obedience is 'claimed from the standpoint of grace as the only possibility', which is awaited by God 'with passionate impatience and zealous longing'.[11] Grace 'is the call, the command, the order, which cannot be disobeyed', with 'the force of a downright conclusion'.[12] Barth is aware of the issue such language raises, however, and in a passage that none of the critics cites, he addresses the question of the relationship between human and divine action directly:

> Human conduct is related to the will of God neither as cause nor as effect. Between human responsibility and the freedom of God there is no direct observable relation, but only the indirect, underivable, unexecutable relation between time and eternity, between the creature and the Creator.[13]

Human action is not overwhelmed by God here, but stands only in an indirect relationship to God's action. We are not automatons, but live in relation to God as responsible creatures. This text makes clear that Barth intends human responsibility and divine freedom to coexist. He means neither the dependency of the created order on God, nor his account of predestination, nor his depiction of the dissolution

---

8   John Webster, 'On the Frontiers of What Is Observable', *Downside Review*, 105 (1987) 175.

9   *Romans* II, 291 (299).

10   Webster, 'Frontiers', 175. Webster also discusses human agency in his essay '"Life from the Third Dimension": Human Action in Barth's Early Ethics', in *Barth's Moral Theology* (Edinburgh: T. & T. Clark, 1998), 11–39.

11   *Romans* II, 223 (223).

12   *Romans* II, 207 (205).

13   *Romans* II, 355 (371).

of our existence in the face of the wholly other God, to deny the reality of human action. In order to decide whether responsible human action is possible in the ethics of *Romans* II, it is clearly not sufficient to quote the passages in which Barth undermines and deconstructs the independent human subject. His intention at these points in the commentary is to cause the disorientation we see in his critics: to push the reader towards the realization that the crisis leaves us with nothing we can clutch hold of for safety, not even our own subjectivity. Once he has forced us to recognize the perilousness of our situation, he is prepared to introduce the other half of the dialectic, in which responsible human action is not only possible, but required. To decide whether his account can do justice to human ethical action, we must look at both sides of the dialectic and weigh whether the resulting tension is one we can accept.

Barth considers the relationship between divine and human action again in his discussion of grace:

> If grace means that, because God does everything, men ought to do nothing, there are but three alternatives. Either, with the scarcely-veiled approval of the men of the world, we 'do nothing', with the result that the body of sin is for the first time firmly set upon the throne. Or, rejecting this 'do nothing' policy, and adopting the grim earnestness of the religious moralist, we 'do' what we can and battle with sin, with the result that it – more exceedingly abounds (v. 20). Or – and this is the course more safely and normally selected – without genuine conviction we swing hither and thither between quietism and activism. The utterly human consequences which result from the acceptance or rejection of grace when it is defined as a human possibility make it quite obvious that this is not what we mean by grace ... Grace, then, means neither that men can or ought to do something, nor that they can or ought to do nothing. Grace means that God does something. Nor does grace mean that God does 'everything'. Grace means that God does some quite definite thing ... Grace means that God forgives men their sins.[14]

Grace is God's action, but there can be no mistaking in this passage that Barth sees human beings as called to action, too: doing nothing is how the world would have us live. He defuses his claim that human action is only a parable of divine action, by suggesting that this is no mean calling:

> Human action is therefore in itself only – but why should we say 'only'? – a parable, a token, of the action of God; and the action of God cannot occur in time; it can occur only – and again, why should we say 'only'? – in eternity. Is 'only' a relevant description of a cloud of dust, if that cloud of dust betrays the whereabouts of a column on the march? Is a shell-hole 'only' a shell-hole, if it marks the spot where an explosion has taken place? Is the shaft of a mine sunk into the side of a mountain 'only' a shaft, if it enables us to conceive of a part of the mountain where no mountain is? So it is that every human position, every far-reaching, deeply penetrating human achievement, is to be sought out and recommended, for it is an urgent testimony to the power of the Spirit.[15]

---

14   *Romans* II, 214–15 (213–14).
15   *Romans* II, 435 (458).

Note that it is great *human* achievements that are tokens of the action of God, and that Barth recommends here. All these human acts, however, cannot escape the form of this world, and Barth questions how the 'gravity and power of ethics' and of the great disturbance can lie in the Promethean and egoistic acts of humankind. He answers that

> [n]evertheless, there are actions from which the light of sacrifice shines, actions where men are offered up, not in order that a new human achievement, positive or negative, may be brought to view, but that the peculiarity of God, His particular will and power and might, may be disclosed, and that He may be known as – Lord.[16]

Although there is 'no human action which is not in itself fashioned according to the form of this world', yet 'there are actions which seem almost to bear in themselves the mark of the divine protest against the great error' and 'actions which seem so transparent that the light of the coming Day is almost visible in them'.[17] Human conduct 'is positively ethical when it is not conformed to this world ... when, within the framework of this world and in complete secrecy, it bears witness to the strangeness of God'.[18]

The evidence in these texts that Barth intends his ethical thought in *Romans* II to include responsible human agency is supported by the attention he pays to specific ethical issues, which I discuss in the next chapter. Barth, then, clearly has a twofold objective in his ethics here. With the negative pole of his dialectic, he aims to undermine and destabilize human confidence in our knowledge of God, our knowledge of right and wrong, and our ability to engage in responsible action. Within the crisis, all this is rendered profoundly uncertain. We are left adrift in uncharted and turbulent waters, without bearings, with no familiar landmarks by which to orient ourselves: our very ability to stay above water seems a fragile, mysterious and precarious thing. The positive pole of the dialectic does not deny that this is our situation. It does not provide us with charts and instruments that would allow us to turn this insecure existence into something known and within our control. It tells us that our ability to act virtuously is balanced on a knife-edge, or hangs from a single thread. But it tells us that if we can accept this instability, if we can embrace an existence in which we are not in charge of our destiny and do not make the rules, if we can repent of our desire to eat the fruit of the tree in the middle of the garden and be like gods, then we can perform responsible, significant, genuinely human actions.

This tension between the negative and positive sides of the dialectic may not provide sufficient scope to human agency to satisfy the critics cited above. To be sure, Willis will never find in Barth the 'independent' creation he seeks. One of Barth's central commitments from *Romans* II to the *Dogmatics* is that creation itself is

---

16   *Romans* II, 435 (459).
17   *Romans* II, 434–5 (458).
18   *Romans* II, 493 (518–19).

secondary to the relationship between God and creation.[19] There is more instability and less emphasis on human creativity in *Romans* II than in Barth's later work. Human agency here is precarious, threatened on all sides and dependent on God for its realization. However, the commentators who say that *Romans* II has no place for genuine human action are taking no account of the positive pole of the dialectic I have described. They may choose to conclude that this depiction of human agency on a knife-edge is finally too uncertain to be satisfactory. They cannot claim simply that for the early Barth there remains no human subjectivity, or that everything is absorbed into the being of God, or that responsible action is out of the question.

Beyond the main criticism that *Romans* II disallows human agency, I noted two other concerns: Bouillard's contention that ethics must provide answers as well as provoke questions, and the judgement he and Willis share that the 'Yes' in Barth's dialectic is overwhelmed by the 'No'. With regard to the first, Barth clearly does provide specific ethical answers in *Romans* II. He concludes, for example, that the church should be neither militarist nor pacifist, and that revolution is a questionable response to unjust regimes.[20] Barth also repeatedly asserts what Bouillard claims as his correction to Barth: that God is the answer to the questions Christian ethics must continue to press.[21] What Barth opposes is the human attempt to lay claim to this divine answer: if God is the answer to the ethical question, the answer is no human possession. We cannot remove it from its origin and examine, comprehend, systematize, rationalize, and apply it. When we try to do so, we hold in our hands at the end only the dust and ashes of our own answer, which is no answer at all. Christian ethics steadfastly refuses to provide a systematic answer to the ethical question, but continually struggles to find the specific answers it needs to guide the decisions that confront Christians from day to day.

Bouillard's second concern is that the 'Yes' of the dialectic is overwhelmed by the 'No'. The passages I have cited in this chapter indicate that this criticism is mistaken. The 'No' is certainly Barth's first word in this work, and was the prophetic word he felt the need to proclaim with most intensity. The 'Yes' is certainly threatened at all times by the 'No' and can never be claimed as a human possession. If the 'No' truly overwhelmed the 'Yes', however, *Romans* II would be finally nihilistic, and it is clear that this is not the case. We have seen that Barth speaks of human actions that bear the glory of God, of human duties and virtues and good deeds that are unstable, but not inconceivable. In fact, it seems that the 'Yes' is heard most clearly in the ethical sections of *Romans* II. The 'great positive possibility' is the possibility of Christians showing agape to the other.[22] We saw at the outset that Barth cites the myriad pressing practical duties as the reason for studying Paul at all. It is plausible that it is the

---

19 In the *Dogmatics* he claims that we are created for covenant with God and that creation is the external basis of the covenant (see *CD* III/1).

20 *Romans* II, 471 (496), 477 (502).

21 See, for example, *Romans* II, 46 (23), 465 (489), 475 (500).

22 *Romans* II, 518–29 (492–502).

immediate demands of these duties that force him to maintain that the 'Yes' cannot finally be negated by the 'No'.[23]

When we look at the full range of Barth's treatment of ethics in *Romans* II, we see that the passages cited by those who accuse him of allowing no meaningful human action are held in tension by other texts that emphasize the possibility of responsible ethical action. To state that Barth's ethical thought here is dialectical in this way is widely recognized, but, as we have seen, critics have listened to the bold and striking notes of the threats to human agency without attending to the counter-melody in which genuine human action has its place.

A Contentless Ethic?

A second kind of misreading of Barth's ethics in *Romans* II results from a similarly one-sided focus on God's 'No' to the exclusion of God's 'Yes', but this time evaluates the resulting interpretation positively. William Stacy Johnson, for example, recognizes the crucial place of ethics in Barth's theology. He observes that Barth's ethics are 'open-ended', a view for which we have already seen some evidence, but goes on to claim that they are akin to Kant in their categorical imposition of 'a radical and purely formal regard for the other'.[24] While others might bemoan this emptying out of ethics, Johnson celebrates it, and believes that Barth's ethics can be used as a pivotal tool to prise open an otherwise 'narrowly confessional theology'.[25] Walter Lowe similarly celebrates Barth's account of ethics in *Romans* II as a persistent asking of questions, and proposes that Barth's affirmation of the radical otherness of God is a strategy for defending the difference and richness of creation.[26] Stephen Webb is a third voice in this mode. He offers a rhetorical analysis of Barth and is struck by his use of hyperbole and irony, though considers it a further lamentable irony that 'Barth's irony failed, and his vision of the failure of our knowledge of God was turned into still one more positive theological program'.[27]

One critical point at which the open-endedness of Barth's ethics can be tested is in relation to the Decalogue. Are there any fixed moral norms that we can count on as

---

23   Further support for this reading is provided by Webster, who notes that 'even the Barth of the 1920s can insist that the negatives of *Romans* II are only a ground-clearing exercise, subservient to a more central positive purpose'. He cites a 1923 letter to Tillich in which Barth wrote that 'Nothing less than all depends on the exact and thorough determination of the positive point which is here in question', and identified Luther's 'deep secret YES under and above the No' with 'the Kingdom and Dominion of God' (Webster, 'Frontiers', 178).

24   William Stacy Johnson, *The Mystery of God: Karl Barth and the Postmodern Foundations of Theology* (Louisville, Kentucky: Westminster John Knox Press, 1997), 161.

25   Johnson, *Mystery*, 156.

26   Walter Lowe, *Theology and Difference: The Wound of Reason* (Bloomington: Indiana University Press, 1993), 127, 137.

27   Stephen H. Webb, *Refiguring Theology* (New York: State University of New York Press, 1991), 18.

inviolable, or are even the Ten Commandments open to revision? Barth's answer is clear, and seems to confirm Johnson's view of radical open-endedness. He affirms that 'God may be honoured in behaviour that contradicts the commandments of the second table'.[28] But having allowed this, Barth is aware of the problems that allowing this indeterminacy causes, and he introduces criteria for such 'irregular' human action. Commenting on Romans 12:17b ('Take thought for the things honourable in the sight of all') Barth claims that here again his ethics 'have affinities with the ethics of Kant'[29] in that an action is ethical if it is 'approved by the invisible One in All'. Ethical action is always to some extent a protest, but it is the 'One in All' that provides the standard for the protest:

> Even if an action genuinely represents the disturbance of persons by God, and not merely the arbitrary and unauthorized disturbance of persons by their fellows, it cannot escape the criterion of universal validity. It may not avoid the light of publicity. It may not be based on or referred to a private paradox or a forgetting of the One in the Individual; therefore the ethical paradox consists exactly in the recollection of this invisible One, and there can be no second paradox next to this one (here Kierkegaard needs occasionally to be corrected with Kant). It can certainly not have some secret happiness or unhappiness as its goal.[30]

The Kierkegaardian paradox is that the individual is higher than the universal;[31] the Kantian correction is that the individual must only act in accordance with universal law.[32] Barth makes clear that this 'disturbance' of a person by God cannot be finally incomprehensible to others, as the actions of Kierkegaard's knight of faith are. He continues:

> Just as the relationship between the individual and the historical reality of human society often must be disordered (such as the Apostlic call in 1:1!), so the relationship between the individual and the established truth of society must be in order. Order must be the reason behind any prophetic disorder. We can justifiably refrain from appealing to the judgement of the Many, but not for a moment can we refrain from appealing to the judgement of the All. This is the criterion by which all apparently irregular action must be measured.[33]

---

28   *Romans* II, 451 (475).
29   Earlier, he noted that he was in agreement with Kant that in the sphere of morals 'there should be no mixing of heaven and earth' (*Romans* II, 432 (455)).
30   *Römer* II, 493, my translation. Hoskyns's translation (468) is misleading here, obscuring the fact that each of these sentences places a limit on how a genuine disturbance of a person by God may appear.
31   'For faith is just this paradox, that the single individual is higher than the universal, though in such a way, be it noted, that the movement is repeated, that is, that, having been in the universal, the single individual now sets himself apart as the particular above the universal' (Søren Kierkegaard, *Fear and Trembling*, trans. Alasdair Hannay (London: Penguin Books, 1985), 84).
32   This is clearest in the first formulation of Kant's categorical imperative: 'Act on the maxim which can at the same time be made a universal law' (Immanuel Kant, *Groundwork of the Metaphysic of Morals*, ed. H.J. Paton (London: Hutchinson & Co. Ltd, 1948), 98).
33   Barth, *Römer* II, 493; my translation.

Barth attempts to retain both the possibility of genuinely prophetic action that can only be received by society as a protest, and the possibility of giving reasons why particular 'irregular' actions are unlikely to originate from disturbance by God. He is clearly not adopting a Kantian criterion of universality – the goodness of human action is dependent on God, not on its conformity with any human system of thought – but it is clear that, even amidst this crisis, God's disturbance of human persons will reflect a final order, and will not be arbitrary, or even finally incomprehensible.[34] Clearly, then, Barth is not content with a Kierkegaardian incomprehensibility in the actions of ethical agents, and equally clearly the criteria he sketches for determining ethical actions are not purely formal. While he does acknowledge the possibility of exceptions to the second table of the Decalogue, he steers very wide of the radical contentless openness that Johnson claims to find.[35]

The difficulty with the postmodern revelling in the negative components of Barth's dialectic in *Romans* II is the same as that with the readings that lament the lack of human agency. Both interpretations depend on pouncing on the passages where Barth sets out the consequences of God's 'No' and ignoring the passages in which he describes the life of human beings under grace. It is abundantly clear from the passages I have cited that Barth is not content with Johnson's purely formal regard for the other, with Lowe's defending of difference, or with Webb's rhetorical tropes. Barth does not believe the reader of Romans is simply adrift in contingency and ambiguity as these accounts suggest: she is called to action that is a practical engagement with the world, just as Paul was. Barth forbids the church from excusing its guilty inaction with the claim that it is unable to hear the Word of God in the midst of all this dialectical complexity: 'we have heard the word of Christ and we are within the picture. It is an objective impossibility for us to discover that we have not heard.'[36] Where postmodern appropriations of the ethics of *Romans* II threaten to mire us in a morass of complacent indeterminacy, Barth pictures human existence under God as at once hope and challenge: 'As the man under grace, I am created and quickened and awakened. But I am also disturbed, for

---

34 One other potential example of Barth's openness to criteria for ethical action is misleadingly suggested by Hoskyns's translation. At the end of Barth's commentary on the sixth chapter, we read that persons under grace 'are again and again compelled to draw up a list of sinners and righteous men and to make a catalogue of what is permitted and what is forbidden ... They are bound to attempt a system of ethics' (*Romans* II, 228 (229)). This recommendation to create a system of ethics would be a marked departure from Barth's position in this work and elsewhere. In fact, Barth says that it is ordinary persons, who live in a 'twilight world' where they cannot see the chasm between good and evil, who are condemned to this unrelenting search for an ethical system. Those under grace rely instead on the 'power of obedience', which is the 'power of the resurrection'.

35 Johnson admits at the outset that his book is more about what he thinks Barth should have said, rather than what Barth actually said (Johnson, *Mystery*, 9), but this is not an excuse for making no distinction between the two.

36 *Romans* II, 389 (407).

the demand bids me take up arms against the world of men and against the men of the world.'[37]

We have, then, two groups of theologians who share a mistakenly one-sided reading of Barth's ethics in *Romans* II, but evaluate it in opposite ways, either lamenting the absence of a stable foundation for theological ethics, or rejoicing in the absence of foundation and content they claim to find. Both groups fail to appreciate that what is of value in Barth's account of ethics results from the tension he maintains between the negative and positive aspects of the dialectic he describes. Only in this tension can he do justice to the reality of God's confrontation and engagement with the world and humanity: neglect of either side of the dialectic collapses a complex, dynamic, and compelling account into montononous univocity. This dialectic is reducible neither to the absence of responsible action the critics fear, nor to the refusal to engage in constructive ethics from which the postmoderns derive inspiration. Nor, clearly, is it an unnuanced constructive project that gives rise to an uncritical and self-assured ethical system. In the account of ethics Barth presents in *Romans* II he is both committed to the struggle for a constructive account of ethics in order to guide faithful action and well aware of the pitfalls of the attempt, and the tentative character of the result.

An Irrelevant Ethic?

The responses to the 1922 edition of Barth's Romans commentary I have surveyed to this point have focused on the merits or demerits of what theological ethics looks like in the midst of the crisis of God's judgement. Before concluding this chapter, however, I want to note one other critique of Barth's project from an entirely different angle: not debating the adequacy of Barth's account of ethics, but questioning the need for any new account of ethics at all. If there is no crisis, after all, there is no need for a crisis theology or an ethics that responds to it. In his discussion of the controversy between Barth and Brunner concerning natural theology, Alan Richardson attempts to put distance between himself and contemporary German theology in this way:

> We in Britain find it hard to understand the dialectical theology of Barth and Brunner because we live in a very different spiritual and mental climate from theirs. We do not feel their problems as our problems or their burdens as our burdens. The whole pattern of our civilization has not been shattered, as theirs has, by war and economic upheaval. Post-Kantian philosophy has not under-mined our belief in reason and conscience, and we have not been driven to choose between nihilism and some form of existentialism. We were not brought up on a theology dominated by Schleiermacher and 'the consciousness of religion'; if Feuerbach laughs, we do not feel he is laughing at us. If Barth and Brunner

---

37   *Romans* II, 207–8 (205).

disagree with each other about the details of their erroneous view of the *imago Dei*, we do not get excited. We are insular, we live in a different world ... We cannot see through the dialectical spectacles. Consequently we dismiss Barthianism or existentialism with a remark about passing post-war neurosis, and our complacency is undisturbed.[38]

Despite Richardson's light-hearted style, he means what he says, and I take this to be a more serious argument for dismissing Barth's ethics of crisis than any of the others discussed in this chapter. Ethics would be a much more straightforward exercise if we could rely on the kind of stable foundation Barth rejects, and could build on it a reliable system for telling right from wrong: to this extent the ethicists that find Barth's ethics in *Romans* II unsatisfactory are right. If we are to give up on this dream of a systematic ethics and find a way to live with a reality in which ethics is a precarious activity in which we can never be quite sure we are getting it right, we need a good reason. Barth believed that the crisis of God's judgement is the reason why ethics cannot attain the determinacy to which it aspires: what we make of his ethics depends on whether we agree.

It is easy to find points to criticize in Richardson's view here. The world is a smaller place 50 years on, so Richardson's confidence in remaining unmoved by the currents that move his theological neighbours is less plausible – we cannot see ourselves at such a remove from the German philosophical and theological tradition, from existentialism and nihilism; and war and economic turmoil are ever-present global realities. But this does not detract from the crux of Richardson's argument: if he is right, the crisis to which Barth was responding is distant from us, there is no crisis as far as we are concerned, and therefore no reason to resign ourselves to the circumscribed and unstable role Barth gives to ethical reflection.

The remainder of this book is an attempt to answer the question of whether the crisis that Barth announced was a local or temporary phenomenon, which can be safely set aside as a historical curiosity, or whether it bears on us too, so that we must also wrestle with what kind of theology and ethics can sustain life within the crisis. In this first part, I have set out Barth's ethics of crisis and responded to critiques of it. Many have suggested that Barth himself found that the crisis could be overcome, so the second part of the book briefly traces Barth's development between *Romans* and the beginning of the *Church Dogmatics*, and then compares the ethics of the *Dogmatics* to those of *Romans* II. Part III puts Barth's ethics of crisis in the context of the questions theological ethics faces at the beginning of the twenty-first century. My aim is to show that Barth's theology and ethics never escaped from the crisis he proclaimed in 1922, and that in our theology and ethics we must face the reality that there is no escape for us either.

---

38   Alan Richardson, 'Review of Cornelius Van Til, *The New Foundations of Modernism*', *Theology*, 51:331 (1948), 30.

II
CRISIS BEYOND *ROMANS* II

CHAPTER 4

From *Romans* to the *Dogmatics*

Barth completed the second edition of his commentary on Romans at the end of 1921. He began work on the *Church Dogmatics* in 1932. According to his own account, and the accounts of many commentators, Barth's theology underwent a revolution in the intervening ten years. The chapters following this one compare the ethics we have surveyed from *Romans* II with the view of ethics Barth sets out in the *Church Dogmatics*, and show that – at least in relation to his ethics – the thesis that Barth made a decisive break in this period from the crisis theology of *Romans* II is mistaken. In this chapter, I look at some of Barth's writings between 1922 and 1932, to demonstrate that dialectical language – the strategy Barth developed for doing theology in the context of the crisis of God's judgement – remains an important characteristic of his theology between *Romans* II and the *Dogmatics*. Barth moves away from frequent reference to 'crisis' or 'crisis theology', which may be because he found that the terms had lost their usefulness. There is no escape, however, from the reality of the crisis, or from its consequences.[1]

The Dialectical Word of God, 1922

In July 1922 Barth gave an address to a meeting of ministers in Schulpforta, Germany, called 'The Need and Promise of Christian Preaching'.[2] Already here he is concerned to chart the development of this theology, and to give his audience a sense of how he sees his work:

> Do not think that I make my contribution to theological discussion, today or any day, in rivalry with the fundamentalist, liberal, Ritschlian, or history-of-religion type of theology. Take it rather as a kind of marginal note, a gloss which in its way

---

1 In *Karl Barth's Critically Realistic Dialectical Theology: Its Genesis and Development, 1909–1936* (Oxford: Clarendon Press, 1995), Bruce McCormack argues persuasively that the thesis that Barth's theology underwent a radical change in this period – and with his work on Anselm in particular – needs rethinking. Building on the work of Ingrid Spieckermann and Michael Beintker he shows that the story Hans Urs von Balthasar told of Barth's development from dialectic to analogy is problematic in many respects, since Barth's theology continues to be dialectical up until 1936. My focus on the ethical aspects of Barth's theology in this book both supports McCormack's thesis in the period he studies and demonstrates the significance of dialectic for Barth's theology well beyond 1936.

2 Schulpforta was a leading Protestant boarding school, which Friedrich Nietzsche attended between 1858 and 1864.

agrees and yet does not agree with all these types – and which, I am convinced, loses its meaning the moment it becomes more than a note and takes up space as a new theology next to the others.[3]

He claims that his perception of the problem of finding a way between the problem of human life on one hand and the content of the Bible on the other lead him to his study of Romans and his commentary:

> It is not as if I had found any way *out* of this critical situation. *Exactly not that.* But this critical situation itself became to me an explanation of the character of all theology. What else can theology be but the truest possible expression of this quest and questioning on the part of the minister, the description of this embarrassment into which a man falls when he ventures upon this task and out of which he cannot find a way – a cry for rescue arising from great need and great hope?[4]

Given the temporal proximity of the address to *Romans* II, it is of little surprise to find the familiar language of contradiction here. As preachers, he told his audience,

> [w]e are *worthy* of being believed only as we are aware of our unworthiness. There is no such thing as *convincing* utterance about God except as Christian preaching feels its *need*, takes up its *cross*, and asks the *question* which God demands in order to be able to answer it. From this need we may not hope to flee.[5]

Yet this contradiction does not lead merely to a void: from the dialectical tensions can come an appreciation of what can be affirmed by Christians:

> The person who says that the Bible leads us to where finally we hear only a great No or see a great void, proves only that he has not yet been led thither. *This* No is really Yes. *This* judgment is grace. *This* condemnation is forgiveness. *This* death is life. *This* hell is heaven. *This* fearful God a loving father who takes the prodigal in his arms. The crucified is the one raised from the dead. And the explanation of the cross as such is eternal life. No other additional thing needs to be joined to the question. The question is the answer.[6]

Barth argues that Luther's charge against Catholicism was that it wanted to be free from this need. Luther's commentaries on Psalms and Romans show his concern with the scholastic and mystic cultivation of

> a *theologia gloriae*, a naïve religious will to be edified, a *flight* from the question which God demands in order to be able to give his answer. *Here* he entrenched

---

3   Karl Barth, *The Word of God and the Word of Man*, trans. Douglas Horton (London: Hodder & Stoughton, 1929), 98 (Karl Barth, *Das Wort Gottes und die Theologie* (Munich: Chr. Kaiser Verlag, 1929), 99–100).

4   Ibid., 101 (102).

5   Ibid., 129 (120).

6   Ibid., 120 (114).

himself; and this theology, which became that of the Reformation and which we claim as the basis of our own, he defined as a *theologia crucis*.[7]

Barth is concerned to press this Reformation challenge on his contemporaries, and asks of the church whether its theology is a *theologia gloriae* or a *theologia crucis*. The former is a theology that flees from the crisis of God's questioning of women and men; the latter is a theology that recognizes this crisis and responds to it. Clearly, Barth sees a link here between his theology of crisis and Luther's theology of the cross.

By September of 1922, Barth became more self-conscious in his use of the language of dialectic, paradox, and contradiction. In 'The Problem of Ethics Today' he acknowledges that it would be contradictory to claim that dialectical theology could play some unique role in mediating between God and humankind. Dialectic cannot function as a refuge from theological problems that would otherwise be too hard to face, and we cannot assume that the contradiction of thesis and antithesis will be resolved in a transformational synthesis.[8] Dialectical language may appear to be a mere word-game, a playing with words, but it is a way of resisting the desire for direct knowledge of God that Kierkegaard identified. We are tempted 'in Fichtean ignorance to grasp what does not belong to us'; dialectical theology is a way of doing theology once we have given up on such attempts: 'There is no way from us to God – not even a *via negativa* – not even a *via dialectia* nor *paradoxa*. The god who stood at the end of some human way – even of this way – would not be God'.[9]

Barth's concern to put his dialectical method in perspective is also evident in a lecture he gave the following month. In 'The Word of God and the Task of the Ministry' he begins by depicting the problematic situation of the minister:

> Our difficulty lies in the content of our task. How far this is is felt by this man or that is a question which we should not need to raise; for here we are discussing our common situation. This situation I will characterize in the three following sentences:– *As ministers we ought to speak of God. We are human, however, and so cannot speak of God. We ought therefore to recognize both* our obligation and our inability *and by that very recognition give God the glory*. This is our perplexity. The rest of our task fades into insignificance in comparison.[10]

---

7   Ibid., 129–30 (120–21).

8   Ibid., 151 (135).

9   Ibid., 177 (153).

10 Ibid., 186 (158). In commentary on this passage in his review of Graham Ward's *Barth, Derrida, and the Language of Theology*, McCormack argues that Barth's purpose is to indicate ironically that theology is a human impossibility made possible by God, rather than a frank impossibility (Bruce L. McCormack, 'Graham Ward's *Barth, Derrida and the Language of Theology*', *Scottish Journal of Theology*, 49:1 (1996), 105). In clarifying this, however, it is important not to revert to a simple affirmation that, with God, all theological difficulties are overcome. Of course that is the case, but we must not miss the difficulty and peril of those little words 'with God': resting on them comfortably is a large part of what Barth is railing against. The ongoing significance of dialectic for Barth that McCormack has identified means that here, as everywhere else, we need to retain an appreciation both of what makes theology possible and what threatens to make it impossible.

Barth also treats the position of theology faculties in universities in this address, and finds their position similarly perplexing:

> It is the paradoxical but undeniable truth that as a science like other sciences theology has *no* right to its place; for it becomes then a wholly unnecessary duplication of disciplines belonging to the other faculties. Only when a *theological* faculty undertakes to say, or at least points out the need for saying, what the others *rebus sic stantibus* dare not say, or dare not say out loud, only when it keeps reminding them that a chaos, though wonderful, is not therefore a cosmos, only when it is a question mark and an exclamation point on the farthest rim of scientific possibility – or rather, in contradistinction to the philosophical faculty, beyond the farthest rim – only then is there a reason for it.[11]

Again here, however, as in *Romans* II, the dialectical paradoxes are not hopeless and nihilistic, but point to a possibility beyond the human:

> Man is a riddle and nothing else, and his universe, be it ever so vividly seen and felt, is a question. God stands in contrast to man as the *impossible* in contrast to the possible, as *death* in contrast to life, as *eternity* in contrast to time. The solution of the riddle, the answer to the question, the satisfaction of our need is the absolutely new event whereby the impossible becomes *of itself* possible, *death* becomes life, *eternity* time, and *God* man. There is *no* way which leads to this event; there is *no* faculty in man for apprehending it; for the way and the faculty are themselves new, being the revelation and faith, the knowing and being known enjoyed by the new man.[12]

In response to the problem of how ministers might speak of God, Barth sets out three approaches to theology: dogmatism, self-criticism, and dialectic. While dogmatism 'surpasses many of the schools that oppose it' in its appreciation for what is important, its weakness is that it simply quashes the human question about God. Instead of acknowledging, considering, and responding to our questioning, dogmatism gives an answer in place of the question, leaving the inescapable question in place.[13] By self-criticism, Barth means mystical or negative theological approaches that deny that anything can be attributed to God. The strength of these strategies is that they do not underestimate the degree to which human existence is put in question by God, but there is no answer: '*God* has not become man. *Man* has become man with a vengeance, but there is no salvation in that'. The way of self-criticism is therefore unable to speak of the incarnate God.[14]

The way of dialectic is better than these two, because '[t]he great truths of dogmatism and self-criticism are presupposed by it, but so also is their

---

11   Barth, *Word of God*, 193 (163).
12   Ibid., 197 (165).
13   Ibid., 200–202 (167–9).
14   Ibid., 203–6 (169–71).

fragmentariness, their merely relative nature'.[15] 'Flatlanders' who do not understand the aims of dialectical theology will be merely confused by its method: reacting first against the positive position, then against the negative, then against the contradiction between the two. In response, the dialectical theologian must say:

> My friend, you must understand that if you ask about *God* and if I am really to tell about *him*, dialectic is all that can be expected from me. I have done what I could to make you see that neither my affirmation nor my denial lays claim to being God's truth. Neither one is more than a witness to that truth, which stands in the center, between every Yes and No. And therefore I have never affirmed without denying and never denied without affirming, for neither affirmation nor denial can be final.[16]

Again here, however, Barth recognizes the limitations of the way of dialectic: '[t]here is no reason why the dialectical theology should be *specially* capable of leading one up *to* a gate which can be opened only from within'.[17] The dialectical approach to theology has a particular weakness:

> the possibility that God *himself* speaks when he is spoken of, is not part of the dialectical way as such: it arises rather at the point where this way *comes to an end* ... The real weakness of the dogmatician and the self-critic, their inability really to speak of *God*, the necessity which is upon them always to speak of something else, appears to be raised to a higher power in the dialectician. For the very reason that he refers *everything* to the living truth itself, the inevitable *absence* of that living truth must be only the more painfully evident.[18]

It is clear that for Barth this weakness is inescapable, and the way dogmatism and self-criticism obscure it merely makes the situation a great deal worse.

The *Göttingen Dogmatics*, 1924–25

In 1924, Barth gave his first series of lectures on dogmatics in his post as Professor of Reformed Dogmatics at Göttingen. Dialectical theology remains a strong emphasis throughout, but he is playfully ironic as he introduces his students to it:

> This is where the famous dialectic comes in. Do not let yourselves be bedazzled by the word. Above all do not use it too often. Learn to be relaxed when you come across it, for it is absolutely unavoidable. You will see from the context in which I refer to it that for me it is in fact only one of my tools, number 11 of the twelve relativities that I regard as indispensable for an understanding of the relation

---

15   Ibid., 206 (171).
16   Ibid., 209 (173).
17   Ibid., 212 (175).
18   Ibid., 211 (174–5).

between scripture and preaching, among which, for good or ill, there is also number 11. There can be no question of the dialectic being itself revelation or the Spirit or the good Lord himself. But since we have to bear in mind most emphatically the early character of our dogmatics as distinct from the blessed in heaven or of God himself, there can also be no question of not needing to take it seriously, of imagining that we can think nondialectically. This will not work, it is completely forbidden, not because we can and should delight in this disruptive factor, but because of the object of dogmatic thinking.[19]

Barth talks of dialectic in the sense of a conversation with others, and of thinking in such a way that there is a dialogue. In a passage deleted from the manuscript, he stresses the importance of letting the other speak in this dialogue:

> Dogmatic dialectic is nothing other than genuine, open, honest dialogue, with no confusion between me and the other, between this side and that, between object and subject. The aim is a purification of what I think and speak about God by what God thinks and speaks.[20]

In a significant phrase for an understanding of the meaning of dialectic in his theology, Barth characterizes the relationship between the sides of this dialogue as 'incompatible but inseparable' (*'unversöhnliche, aber auch unzertrennliche'*): 'There must be two incompatible but inseparable partners in my thinking: a word and a counter-word, for example, faith and obedience, authority and freedom, God and man, grace and sin, inside and outside, etc.'[21]

Barth explains to his students that dialectic is essential to theology because we cannot succeed in talking about God with non-dialectical words:

> For every time, on the one side, when I believe that I have a thought about God, I must remember that God is subject, not object. I have to turn around, then, and think radically, on the other side, whence I came to in order to be able to do this. When this situation is seen again at any point there arises the dialectical relation of two concepts. Dialogue takes place in this relation, and to that extent, like all dogmatic thinking, it is a dialectical dialogue. Thinking nondialectically would mean in principle not thinking before God. Before God human thoughts *become* dialectical.[22]

In the *Göttingen Dogmatics*, then, it is clear that dialectical language in theology continues to be a vehicle for continuing to speak of God in the midst of the crisis of contradiction:

---

19   Karl Barth, *The Göttingen Dogmatics: Instruction in the Christian Religion*, trans. Geoffrey W. Bromiley, ed. Hannelotte Reiffen, vol. I (Grand Rapids, Michigan: Eerdmans, 1991), 309 (Karl Barth, *Unterricht in der Christlichen Religion, Erster Band: Prolegomena, 1924*, ed. Hannelotte Reiffen, Karl Barth-Gesamtausgabe (Zurich: Theologischer Verlag, 1985), 373–4).

20   Ibid., 310n. (374–5n.).

21   Ibid., 309–10 (374–5).

22   Ibid., 311 (375–6).

To think dialectically is to acknowledge that we are in contradiction, that we are sinful and fallen, that we are people who, not on our own inquisitive initiative, but because of the Word of God that is spoken to us, cannot escape giving God the glory and confessing that we are only human with our questions, but also – and here already is the dialectic – confessing God and God alone with his answer even as we confess ourselves. The dialogue with which this twofold confession begins in our thinking; the unheard-of movement, not between two poles – God is not the one pole and we the other – but between us in our totality and God in his; the dynamic which grips every word because in this dialectic it is either the divine norm or the human relation to this norm; the world of doubtful but promising, or promising but doubtful relativities that open up here, encircled both above and below by the sole deity of God – this is dogmatic dialectic.[23]

It will not be needed in heaven, but for now we need it and should be thankful for it as one of God's gifts. Barth again rejects the idea of dialectic as mere word-play:

Let us see to it that we use it to God's glory, not as a game, but as the serious work of the catharsis of our pious words. How are these words to be purified for the purpose that they should serve if we do not think them together with the Word of God that is to be proclaimed through them, if we do not think dialectically?[24]

Serious Theology, 1925

Later in 1925, Erik Peterson, a Roman Catholic theologian, published a critique of Barth called *Was Ist Theologie?* In it he accused Barth of not being serious in his approach to theology:

And yet the seriousness that is found in this form of dialectic is only sham seriousness. It is just as much sham as the dialectical questioning is sham and the dialectician's answer is a sham, and as God Himself in this dialectic is only a dialectical possibility. All dialectic attains no higher seriousness than that of a dialectical seriousness, than that of a possible 'taking seriously' (*Ernstnehmen*). It is a dialectical possibility to take God seriously in such a way that one is prepared, like Abraham, to sacrifice Isaac, but it is only a dialectical – a mythical – possibility, beside which at the same level of seriousness that other possibility exists: to write the diary of a seducer. *That is the nemesis which comes upon the dialectician, that for all their 'taking seriously' they do not attain seriousness.* Would that all readers of Kierkegaard's religious speeches would think over this sentence. All dialectic can therefore lead to no higher seriousness than to a possible 'taking seriously'. Just as dialectic cannot meaningfully attain even a real *human* seriousness, so how much less can it reach the seriousness of God in its dialectic?[25]

---

23   Ibid., 311–12 (376–7).
24   Ibid., 312 (377).
25   Erik Peterson, *Was Ist Theologie?* (Bonn: Friedrich Cohen, 1925), 7.

In October 1925, Barth twice gave an address 'Church and Theology' responding to Peterson's attack on his dialectical theology.[26] He rejects the possibility that theology can achieve the kind of seriousness Peterson demands:

> If Peterson now says to us that theology under such conditions does not with its statements attain to 'the seriousness of God' (p. 7), then we must answer that it can never have been intended to reach the seriousness of the knowledge with which God himself speaks. 'It did not please God to save his people by dialectic', Peterson quotes from Ambrose. Certainly! But it must be said that what God does and what the theologians do ought to be quite different things. Their more modest part – I do not see what this has to be said as disparagement – is in fact 'taking' the *revelation* seriously (p. 7).
>
> To take the revelation seriously in the sphere of conceptual thinking means to walk with entire definiteness and determination on the double path marked out for us by the necessity we are under to speak as *men*, but about *God*.[27]

Taking revelation seriously, Barth comments, means taking it dialectically.

Barth contrasts ectypal theology – 'a theology of wayfarers', *theologia viatorum* – with archetypal theology – the theology of God himself, the *theologia comprehensorum* of the angels and the saints in heaven. The human activity of theology must recognize itself as the former. 'For theology as for the Church, it must be granted and recognized actually as essential that it is always an earthly activity in a definite "here and now" (*hic et nunc*). It is an activity carried on by man, as man is defined by Adam, a wayfarer (*viator*) journeying towards his country, but not possessing (*comprehensor*) any country.'[28] This is not the only reason why theology must be dialectical, however:

> Theology is not only ectypal (ἔκτυπος) and the theology of wayfarers (*viatorum*); it is also, according to the further analysis of our elders, theology after the fall (*theologia post lapsum*). And that means that it is conditioned in its basic assumptions by human misery. And such conditioning involves the impossibility (in spite of all the energy that Peterson expends) of rejecting with a gesture of irritation the dialectical character of theology. The fragmentariness, the paradox, the continual radical need of completion, the essential open-endedness of all its assertions are not to be denied.[29]

Barth agrees with Peterson that the revelation of which theology speaks is not dialectical:

---

26   The address is published in Karl Barth, *Theology and Church: Shorter Writings 1920–1928*, trans. Louise Pettibone Smith (New York and Evanston: Harper & Row, 1962), 286–306 (Karl Barth, *Die Theologie und die Kirche*, Gesammelte Vortrag, vol. 2 (Munich: Evangelischer Verlag AG, Zollikon-Zürich, 1928), 302–28).

27   Ibid., 300 (319–20).

28   Ibid., 298 (318).

29   Ibid., 299 (319); translation revised.

That hardly needs to be said. But when theology begins, when we men think, speak, or write, or (if Peterson thinks it more accurate) 'argue' on the basis of this revelation, then there is dialectic ($\delta\iota\alpha\lambda\acute{\epsilon}\gamma\epsilon\sigma\theta\alpha\iota$). Then there is a stating of essentially incomplete ideas and propositions among which every answer is also again a question. All such statements together reach out beyond themselves towards the fulfillment in the inexpressible reality of the divine speaking.[30]

Barth illustrates the character of his dialectical theology with a series of antitheses: judgement and grace; creation and providence; the visibility and invisibility of the Church; justification and salvation on God's side juxtaposed with faith and obedience on the human side; Word and Spirit as the principle of Scripture; celestial and terrestrial as the nature of sacraments; eating with the mouth and eating spiritually; and the 'ought' and 'cannot' in the position of the theologian.

In all these and similar antitheses, there is no possibility of accepting both together. Such antitheses stand opposed to each other, not quantitively, not in a 'relation of tension', not to be comprehended in any *one* word; but unsubsumed by any word which we can speak, mutually exclusive. They are irreconcilable because in different ways they express the infinite qualitative distinction between God and man with which a theology of sinners (and that is *all* theology), however theocentric or Christocentric it may be or may wish to appear, has to deal in presenting the communion of God and man.[31]

Barth shows again in this address, however, that he faces a challenge in persuading others to accept his dialectical methodology:

I cannot help it if this word *dialectic*, once it is thrown into a discussion, immediately becomes a bogy with which one frightens children, as if some kind of horror of sub-Christian philosophy lurked behind it. It means really only the simple recognition that the Scriptural word, 'Except the Lord build the house, they labour in vain that build it', applies to theology at every moment.[32]

The *Christliche Dogmatik*, 1927

At the end of October 1925, Barth moved from Göttingen to Münster, replacing a poorly paid honorary professorship with limited rights, with the position of Professor of Dogmatics and New Testament Exegesis. In the new post, he continued with the dogmatics lectures he had begun at Göttingen, as well as embarking on new lectures on exegesis and the history of Protestant theology since Schleiermacher. In the summer of 1927, however, he was faced with beginning his dogmatics lectures from the beginning again. He found that he needed to rewrite his lectures completely, and

---

30   Ibid., 300 (319).
31   Ibid., 300–301 (320–21).
32   Ibid., 302 (322).

commented that, just as with *Romans* II, 'here too hardly one stone remains on another'.[33] Barth's intention was to publish this new dogmatics as *Die Christliche Dogmatik im Entwurf* (*Christian Dogmatics in Outline*). In the event, however, only the first volume – *Die Lehre vom Worte Gottes: Prolegomena zur Christlichen Dogmatik* (*Doctrine of the Word of God: Prolegomena to Christian Dogmatics*) – was published before he decided in 1931 to abandon the project and begin again with *Die Kirchliche Dogmatik* (*Church Dogmatics*).[34] Despite the revisions Barth made to the lectures between 1924 and 1925 in Göttingen and 1927 in Münster, Barth's vision of the dialectical character of theology remains significant. He emphasizes the gulf between dogma and *veritas divina*:

> Since dogma is the concept of this event, how could it not be then a completely dialectical concept, with a higher and lower, an absolute and a relative side? So that one must say: dogma is, insofar as it understands the relationship of *revelation* to the human word of the church, God's eternal, unchanging, infallible, self-contained, truth; insofar as it understands the relationship of the *human word* of the church to revelation, temporal, incomplete, changeable, fallible truth.[35]

Barth also retains the distinction he made in response to Peterson between *theologia comprehensorum* and *theologia viatorum*:

> Dogma is only apprehended as complete (*erschöpft*) and self-contained truth by God, as '*theologia ἀρχέτυπος*', as the ancients said. As a truth apprehended by us, it is either an *eschatological* concept – '*theologia comprehensorum*' or '*theologia patriae*', dogma as it is already apprehended by the angels and the saints in heaven but to be apprehended by us only in eternal salvation – or it is only '*theologica viatorum*', that is truth apprehended, believed and confessed provisionally and in an earthly, human way, an *attempt* to approach it, to approach dogma.[36]

While dogmatics cannot, therefore, avoid the task of asking about dogma,

> it can only answer this question with sentences that indicate tentative approaches towards that goal. Dogmatics occurs on earth and within time. It cannot put itself in the place of God and its sentences in the in place of His Word. It can really only attempt to do justice to Him through its service of preaching in church, and cannot look back on any of its attempts except with the recognition that it has not done Him justice. Dogmatics wants to give instruction and guidance in preaching with

---

33 Eberhard Busch, *Karl Barth: His Life from Letters and Autobiographical Texts*, trans. John Bowden, (Philadelphia: Fortress Press, 1976), 173.

34 The prolegomena section of the lectures was published as Karl Barth, *Die Christliche Dogmatik im Entwurf. 1. Bd.: Die Lehre vom Worte Gottes. Prolegomena zur Christlichen Dogmatik, München 1927*, Karl Barth-Gesamtausgabe (Zurich: Gerhard Sauter, 1982), and has not been translated into English. The further lectures on dogmatics at Münster were not published.

35 Ibid., 161.

36 Ibid., 162.

its sentences, to establish boundary markers and set aids to navigation. But *no less* than that: preaching as a human activity has need of such reminders of dogma, of the relationship therefore from which it lives, and these recollections are exactly the dogmas of the church and the principles of its dogmatic knowledge. But it is also *no more* than that: no dogma and no dogmatics has the status and power to lay dogma, the Word of God, on the lips of the preacher. That takes place through the royal Word of God itself, or it does not take place. Dogmatics can challenge and instruct us to reflect only on this royal Word. This is what it can and must do.[37]

Clearly, we stand once more in a dialectical tension here: dogmatics is necessary for the church in order to act as a reminder to preachers, but finally it can only serve as a signpost to the dogma that belongs to God alone.

In *Christliche Dogmatik* Barth also speaks of dialectic in a different and new sense. Alongside the idea of tension between irreconcilable opposites, he introduces the concept of dialectic as conversation between two parties, which is closer to the Socratic sense of dialectic:

> In view of its theme, dogmatic thought is conversational – not a monologue, but a dialogue – dialectical thought. Dialectical thinking is a thinking in speech and reply, in question and answer; so, therefore, that fundamentally the conversation does *not* break off, that the answer is always another question, which then finds its answer exactly in the precise form of the first question posed; so, therefore, that fundamentally there is *no* last word that might be drawn from this movement between question and answer. A conversation belongs to *two*. There are always two to be thought of, as adversaries just as irreconcilable as inseparable (*ebenso unversöhnliche wie unzertrennliche*), two, who wrestle with each other and just for that reason do not let go of each other, a word and its counter-word (*Gegenwort*).[38]

Barth gives examples of such irreconcilable and inseparable pairs: 'faith and obedience, heteronomy and autonomy or authority and freedom, the speaking of the Holy Spirit to us and in us, the incarnation of the Word and the outpouring of the Holy Spirit, reconciliation and sin, prehistory and history in revelation, the Word of God and human words in the Bible and similarly in preaching'.[39] Each of these pairs originates, Barth claims, from the original example that makes the whole of dogmatics dialectical: 'God and humanity in the person of the reconciler: Jesus Christ'. It is only possible to be an undialectical theologian by deleting this 'and', by replacing 'God and humanity' with 'Godhuman' and 'Jesus Christ' with a single name. Barth cites Schleiermacher here as one example of such an undialectical theology, because it refers to only a qualitative difference between God and humanity.

---

37   Ibid., 163.
38   Ibid., 579. Beintker points out this dialogic aspect to Barth's use of dialectic and compares it to Bultmann's use of dialectical theology: Michael Beintker, *Die Dialektik in der 'Dialektischen Theologie' Karl Barths* (Munich: Chr. Kaiser Verlag, 1987), 166.
39   Barth, *Christliche Dogmatik*, 580.

Barth cites 1 Corinthians 13:9 ('we know only in part and we prophesy only in part') as support for the view that our knowledge can only be a 'patchwork'.[40]

Barth sees a clear link between this dialogical view of dialectic and his view of theology as *theologia viatorum*. All dogmatic mistakes and triteness, Barth argues, arise from theology forgetting or not wanting to know that it must be the theology of wayfarers 'and instead of this imagines that it can flee from this movement from speech and reply to the safe haven of *one* word'.[41] God speaks the one undialectical word: God's theology is undialectical.

> But we are human beings ... If we are to praise God one day with all the angels and saints in heaven, to see Him face to face (see 1 Cor. 13:12), then there may also be another possibility for us. Now and here, however, we cannot even imagine this other possibility, much less that it could be given to us.[42]

In concluding his explanation of dialectic in *Die Christliche Dogmatik*, Barth develops a somewhat convoluted allegory he treated briefly in the *Göttingen Dogmatics*, comparing the methodology of dialectical theology with the Israelites crossing the Red Sea:[43]

> The people of Israel, being chased by the Egyptians, have to cross the Red Sea. The Red Sea is the mass of unqualified pious human words about God. The people of Israel are those who fear and love God, who as the people that they are, want and ought to recognize God. The Egyptians are those who do not fear or love God, who as such have every human right to take knowledge of God to be impossible. The passage is the reality of such knowledge. But how is this reality to be reached? Now Moses stretches out his hand, and the Lord makes a strong east wind to blow, which is the appearance and proclamation of revelation. 'And the children of Israel went out into the midst of the sea on dry land, and the water was as walls for them to the right and the left' (Ex. 14:22). So those who fear and love God, take a chance, because Moses stretches out his hand, because the Lord makes the east wind to blow, take a chance to go into the middle of the sea, as if there were no such thing as drowning, take a chance to take seriously the pious word without any qualification, as if it could make the knowledge of God possible. And see there: because Moses stretches out his hand, because the Lord makes the east wind to blow, the pious word breaks up into word and counter-word [*Gegenwort*], stands as walls to the right and the left, and through the middle, threatened by the impossibility of the word *and* counter-word, protected by the possibility of both, as long as Moses stretches out his hand and the Lord makes the east wind to blow (therefore by its relative possibility!), Israel moves in peace towards its destination: the knowledge of God is really for those who fear and love Him. And the warning epilogue should also not be stifled: if those who do not fear and love God, want to try to imitate the supposed 'dialectical feat' with

---

40   Ibid., 580–81.
41   Ibid., 582.
42   Ibid., 583.
43   Barth, *Göttingen Dogmatics*, 311 (376).

word and counter-word, so that they may also know God, but adopt the dialectical method without God, without knowing that the Spirit is the one who brings life, just as the flesh is also useless here (see Jn. 6:63) – indeed, they may try it, it will certainly come to pass for them, as it is written: word and counter-word will not remain standing as walls, their tensions and ambiguities will crash into each other again as *one* word, in which *no* knowledge is possible. 'And the water came back and covered chariots and riders and all the power of Pharaoh, who had followed them into the sea, so that not one of them was left' (Ex. 14:28). The question is for everyone at every time an open question, whether they belong to Israel or to the Egyptians.[44]

The moral of this tale is not hard to determine: dialectic in theology is the only way to cross the sea of 'pious words' towards the knowledge of God without being swept away by them. The threat of the towering walls is evidence that the crisis Barth identified in *Romans* has not been left behind.

Faith Seeking Understanding, 1931

Clearly, in the *Christliche Dogmatik* lectures delivered in 1927, dialectic remains a prominent theme and a key part of Barth's theological vision. Yet according to many of Barth's interpreters, the publication of his book on Anselm, *Fides Quaerens Intellectum* (*Faith Seeking Understanding*), only four years later, marked a decisive break with his use of dialectic in theology. For Hans Urs von Balthasar, *Fides Quaerens Intellectum* represented the end point of Barth's second conversion, 'his final emancipation from the shackles of philosophy, enabling him finally to arrive at a genuine, self-authenticating theology'.[45] As McCormack has noted, Barth shares responsibility for this view of the role of his Anselm book. In an observation on his own development that both von Balthasar and McCormack cite, Barth comments that between 1928 and 1938:

> I have had to rid myself of the last remnants of a philosophical, i.e., anthropological … foundation and exposition of Christian doctrine. The real document of this farewell is, in truth, not the much-read brochure *Nein!*, directed against Brunner in 1934, but rather the book about the evidence for God of Anselm of Canterbury which appeared in 1931. Among all my books I regard this as the one written with the greatest satisfaction.[46]

There is no doubt that Barth finds in Anselm a theology undertaken in a very different mood than *Romans* II. Barth is impressed by Anselm's 'provocative lack of all doubt, including all "philosophic doubt", of all anxiety, including all apologetic anxiety' and

---

44   Barth, *Christliche Dogmatik*, 584.
45   Hans Urs von Balthasar, *The Theology of Karl Barth: Exposition and Interpretation*, trans. Edward T. Oakes (San Francisco: Communio Books, Ignatius Press, 1992), 93.
46   Karl Barth, *How I Changed My Mind* (Richmond, Virginia: John Knox Press, 1966), 42–3.

by his 'no less provocative intellectual coolness'. This is theology as 'devout obedience,' Barth comments, 'assent to a decision coming from its object, the "Lord", acknowledgement and recognition of the "Lord's" own communication of himself.'[47]

Even amidst this provocative calm, however, there are aspects of Anselm's theology that are familiar from Barth's dialectic, and which tell against the interpretation of 1931 as a turning point. The 'characteristic absence of crisis' in Anselm's theologizing, Barth claims, can only be understood in the context of the Christian humility to which we are compelled before the Word of God.[48] Anselm recognizes with Barth that 'every theological statement is an inadequate expression of its object', and that 'strictly speaking, it is only God himself who has a conception of God'. 'God shatters every syllogism', and while this does not mean that no theological statement can be true, it does mean that theology should not be ashamed of always remaining 'speculative'.[49] From this Barth concludes that:

> theological statements can be made with only scientific certainty, which, on account of its relativity, has to be distinguished from the certainty of faith. Theological statements as such are contested statements – challenged by the sheer incomparability of their object. It is just this very absoluteness of the revelation to which his statements apply that isolates the theologian in his meditation.[50]

The theologian therefore can often 'work only by experiment', 'waits on the correction of others', and 'can never assume the ultimate certainty of even his best conceived statements'.[51] Wherever theological statement goes beyond quotation of the Bible, 'such a statement is not final; fundamentally it is an interim-statement, the best that knowledge and conscience can for the present construe; it awaits better instruction from God or man'.[52]

While, as McCormack notes, such passages indicating the continuing influence of dialectic in *Fides Quaerens Intellectum* are the exception rather than the rule, they decidedly weaken the argument that this book was a decisive turning point for Barth. In his analysis, McCormack observes that here, as elsewhere, Barth is not the best interpreter of his own development, that contemporaneous notes report no dramatic new insight, and that it was only in the second preface in 1958 that Barth saw the book as an influence on the 'movement of thought' leading to the *Dogmatics*. McCormack is also alert to the difficulty throughout the book of determining the relationship

---

47   Karl Barth, *Anselm: Fides Quaerens Intellectum: Anselm's Proof of the Existence of God in the Context of His Theological Scheme*, trans. Ian W. Robertson (London: SCM Press, 1960), 151 (Karl Barth, *Fides Quaerens Intellectum: Anselms Beweis der Existenz Gottes im Zusammenhang Seines Theologischen Programms*, ed. Eberhard Jüngel and Ingolf Ulrich Dalferth (Zurich: Theologischer Verlag, 1981), 153–4).
48   Ibid., 26 (25).
49   Ibid., 29–30 (28–9).
50   Ibid., 30 (29).
51   Ibid., 30 (29).
52   Ibid., 31 (30).

between Barth's own theological views and his description of Anselm's, evidenced in the preface to the first edition, in which Barth distances himself from Anselm's views, and he draws out continuities with Barth's treatment of Anselm in *Die Christliche Dogmatik*.[53] The cumulative weight of these insights makes clear that *Fides Quaerens Intellectum* cannot bear the burden of marking the significant point in Barth's development that he and others believed it to be.

In fact, it was obvious in advance of my consideration of *Fides Quaerens Intellectum* that von Balthasar's thesis that the book was the conclusion of Barth's ten-year 'second conversion' from dialectic to analogy is a mistake. This chapter has shown that dialectic remained a lively and important theme in Barth's theology from 1922 through to 1931. Michael Beintker's instructive and detailed survey of the development of Barth's theology in this period merits more attention, and identifies some changes of emphasis in this period. He shares with von Balthasar, however, a distaste for Barth's dialectical theology, and is similarly anxious to chart Barth's departure from it: 'In our sketch of the way from *Römer* II to *Christliche Dogmatik im Entwurf* we have tried to show how the dominant dialectical statements and references gradually fade away and the search for a responsible theological doctrine takes its place.'[54] Beintker's view is similar to Peterson's, that dialectical theology is 'not serious', but this is not a position that Barth came to, in the period between *Romans* II and the *Dogmatics*, or beyond. Barth was uncomfortable with the label of 'dialectical theologian', and became more circumspect in his use of the term 'dialectic' in the transition from *Die Christliche Dogmatik* (*Christian Dogmatics*) to *Die Kirchliche Dogmatik* (*Church Dogmatics*). This was a change of language and emphasis, however, rather than a fundamental change in methodology.

It is important to recognize the significance for ethics of rejecting the view that Barth moved from a dialectical to an analogical perspective. If von Balthasar were right, Barth's theology beyond 1931 would be responsible and 'self-authenticating':[55] it would have escaped from the peril of the encounter with the Word of God and could rest content with its findings. Its analogical character would mean not that it could know right from wrong as God does, but that in an analogical way it could be the possessor of knowledge appropriate to itself, as a stable foundation for action. In the period from 1922 to 1931, as I have shown in this chapter, Barth consistently rejected this view in favour of a dialectical understanding of theology and ethics that denies the possibility of such reliable knowledge of God and God's will.

The following three chapters demonstrate that this remained crucial for his theological method throughout the *Dogmatics* by tracing Barth's discussion of the ethical themes present in *Romans* II into the *Dogmatics*. The final two chapters of Part

---

53   McCormack, *Karl Barth's Critically Realistic Dialectical Theology*, 444–5.
54   Beintker, *Dialektik*, 156–7.
55   von Balthasar, *The Theology of Karl Barth: Exposition and Interpretation*, 93.

III make clear the significance of appreciating the enduring role of dialectic in Barth's theology both for the interpretation of Barth's ethical thought, and for contemporary Christian ethical reflection as a whole.

CHAPTER 5

The Place of Ethics in the *Dogmatics*

Ethics, Crisis and Command

I began my consideration of Barth's ethics in *Romans* II with a discussion of the place of ethics in relation to theology. Barth gave ethics as a key reason for doing theology and studying Romans, and claimed that the ethical problem disturbs our conversation about God in order to remind us of its true object. Turning to the *Dogmatics* on this topic, the continuity between the works is striking. Barth retains the same view of the integral relationship between ethics and dogmatics, and the role of the ethical question:

> the dogmatics of the Christian Church, and basically the Christian doctrine of God, is ethics. This doctrine is, therefore, the answer to the ethical question, the supremely critical question concerning the good in and over every so-called good in human actions and modes of action.[1]

Dogmatics 'has the problem of ethics in view from the very first, and it cannot legitimately lose sight of it'.[2]

The most striking difference between the metaethics of *Romans* II and those of the *Church Dogmatics* is their context within the respective works. In *Romans* II, we have seen that the metaphor of crisis impacts all other discussion, and that ethics in particular has its role destabilized by the uncertainty and threat of the crisis of God's 'No'. In the *Church Dogmatics*, the crisis initially seems to be absent. Barth has found a source of confidence in the object of his faith that allows him to speak clearly of God's revelation to humankind. Barth decided to place ethics within a Trinitarian framework in the *Church Dogmatics*: following an initial two part-volumes on the doctrine of the Word of God, and a consideration of the place of ethics at the end of the two part-volumes on the doctrine of God, Barth's plan was to complete volumes on creation, reconciliation, and redemption, with particular topics in ethics considered as they fell under each of these headings. In fact, only the first of these additional sections, the four part-volumes of *Church Dogmatics III: The Doctrine of Creation*, was completed. The fourth and final part-volume of *Church Dogmatics IV: The Doctrine of Reconciliation* exists only in fragmentary form, and Barth ceased working on the *Dogmatics*, largely due to ill health, before beginning the final section on redemption. While Barth's ethical thought is an integral part of his theological project as a whole in this work, his specific consideration of ethics in the *Dogmatics*

---

1   *CD* II/2, 515 (571).
2   *CD* III/4, 3 (1).

is concentrated in particular sections. Chapter 8, 'The Command of God' in volume II/2, discusses the possibility of ethics and character of Christian ethics, and its relationship with other forms of ethical enquiry. The final volume of Barth's doctrine of creation, III/4, discusses particular issues he sees as falling under this heading: the Sabbath, confession, and prayer; relationships between men and women, parents and children, and people of different nationalities; respect for life, including topics such as the treatment of the natural world, contraception, abortion, euthanasia, killing in self-defence, capital punishment and warfare. The fourth section of the *Dogmatics* has an astonishingly intricate structure. In the first part, volume IV/1, Barth treats the sin of pride, the doctrine of justification, the gathering of Christian community by the Holy Spirit, and the cardinal virtue of faith. In the second part, volume IV/2, Barth discusses the sin of sloth, the doctrine of sanctification, the building up of the church, and the virtue of love. In the third part, IV/3 – itself subdivided into two books! – Barth discusses vocation, and witness, the sending out of the church into the world, and the virtue of hope. The final part, IV/4, is a short section on baptism, which Barth controversially characterized as primarily ethical: a human response to what God has done for us.

The size and scope of the *Dogmatics* obviously allows a much more comprehensive and systematic exposition of ethical themes than a commentary on Paul's letter to the Romans and in this sense juxtaposing the two works is not comparing like with like. In response to this challenge, the approach I have adopted is to begin with the themes Barth discusses in *Romans* II and follow them into the *Church Dogmatics*, in order to trace continuities and discontinuities between his treatment of them. In this chapter, I pursue the metaethical issues raised by my discussion of Barth's crisis theology in Chapter 1: is ethics possible at all, and if so, how are we to go about it? The following two chapters continue the comparison by focusing on Barth's consideration of ethical issues under the two headings introduced in Chapter 2: love and community; and war, peace, and revolution. This approach means that large parts of the ethics of the *Dogmatics* remain unconsidered, so these three chapters do not pretend to be a comprehensive guide to the ethical issues Barth addresses in the *Dogmatics*. It does, however, serve well in illuminating striking continuities between *Romans* II and the *Dogmatics*, as well as notable contrasts.

The first consideration of ethics in the *Church Dogmatics* follows and is the consequence of Barth's doctrine of election, God's 'primal decision' to reconcile the world to Godself. Election expresses the sum of the Gospel 'because it is the good news, the best news, the wholly redemptive news, that from all eternity God has decided to be God only in this way, and in the movement towards man which takes this form'.[3] This self-election of God has its counterpart in God's determination of humankind to be the beloved of God and God's partner in the covenant. Ethics finds its role in the question of what God wants from us, how we should respond to this

---

3   *CD* II/2, 91 (98).

determination, and what sort of lives we should live as God's covenant partners.[4] The high tension, complexity, and ambiguity of *Romans* II seems to have been overcome, and the Christian life seem less perilous, more secure and stable. As a consequence of God's 'Yes' to us, we can be confident of our status as persons called to be God's covenant partners: we are commanded to be free of the anxiety that characterized *Romans* II.[5]

When Barth turns to ethics, however, we find some of the symptoms of the crisis remain. In *Romans* II, ethics played a role in provoking the crisis, undermining and destabilizing speech about God with its questions. In the *Dogmatics*, the ethical question remains unsettling to humankind:

> by revelation and the work of God's grace this question is actually put as the inescapable question of human existence which is quite incomparable with other questions in weight and urgency and which the answers to other questions are quite unable to silence. For it is as he acts that man exists as a person. Therefore the question of the goodness and value and rightness, or the genuine continuity of his activity, the ethical question, is no more and no less than the question about the goodness and value and rightness of his existence, of himself. It is his life question, the question by whose answer he stands or falls. 'To be or not to be, that is the question'. Why? Because with its answer there is put into effect the decision of the power which disposes absolutely of his existence or non-existence, the power of God.[6]

By the grace of God we are put under God's command, which, Barth claims, means that we become the answer to the ethical question. But

> man is not content simply to *be* the answer to the question of the grace of God. He wants to be like God. He wants to know of himself (as God does) what is good and evil. He therefore wants to give this answer himself and of himself. So, then, as a result and in prolongation of the fall, we have 'ethics', or, rather, the multifarious ethical systems, the attempted human answers to the ethical question.[7]

Barth's depiction of God's response to these human attempts places more emphasis on God's 'Yes' than *Romans* II would have done, but the destructive potential of God's power is still in evidence:

> The grace of God protests against all man-made ethics as such. But it protests positively. It does not only say No to man. It also says Yes. But it does so by completing its own answer to the ethical problem in active refutation, conquest, and destruction of all human answers to it.[8]

---

4   *CD* II/2, 510 (565).
5   *CD* II/2, 597 (663).
6   *CD* II/2, 516 (572).
7   *CD* II/2, 517 (573).
8   *CD* II/2, 517 (573).

Here we find ourselves back within the tension between God's 'No' and God's 'Yes', and grace has the same double role: confronting, challenging and destroying in order to claim human beings and redeem them.

Elsewhere in the *Dogmatics* Barth's attitude to human answers to the ethical question is more open. After explaining why apologetics on behalf on theological ethics are unwarranted, he adds that there is no reason that the general conception of ethics cannot be 'a witness to the ethical knowledge which has itself to present, and which is to be acquired from the divine command of God'. There is no reason why this general conception should not have a place in the discussion: theological ethics can give ear to it and 'receive instruction and correction' from it, since 'the Word of God is also objectively spoken and prevails in the midst of human perversity'. Theological ethics must not 'disarm its distinctive Whence? and Whither' – its action in relation to other ethical enquiries is annexation, not accommodation – but it 'will be absolutely open to all that it can learn from general human ethical enquiry and reply'. This openness is possible because 'it has absolutely nothing to fear from this quarter'.[9] Already it is clear that in the ethics of the *Dogmatics* Barth has not left behind the dialectical complexity that characterized *Romans* II. Grace destroys all human answers to the ethical question, yet ethical reflection of any kind may witness to the divine command.

In *Romans* II the crisis of God's judgement threatened the possibility of all human activity. Yet the promise of God's 'Yes' meant that there remained the possibility of a resurrected life quickened by grace in which human beings could bear witness in their actions to the purposes of God. In the *Dogmatics*, Barth spells out this gracious possibility further, but the dialectical tension between God's 'No' and God's 'Yes' remains. If human thought and action is not oriented according to God's grace and command, God's 'No' brings the same conquest and destruction that we found throughout *Romans* II. If our thought and activity are in accordance with the will of God, however, we can both have confidence in a relationship with God, and, grounded in this covenant partnership, we can be open to learning from all other sources of knowledge. The world is still under the judgement of God's 'No' and far distant from its redemption, but we can claim our place as covenant partners of God and be freed for life under the affirmation of God's 'Yes'. Barth has not ceased to believe in the crisis – a large part of his discussion of ethics in the *Dogmatics* is devoted to undermining and destabilizing what we understand by it – but he is now prepared to give more time to explicating how, nevertheless, ethics may be attempted.

The emphasis on the concept of command in the *Church Dogmatics* is a second apparent contrast between the two works. Barth describes the operation of grace as a command in *Romans* II, but in the *Dogmatics*, the command of God becomes the controlling metaphor for how Christians learn the will of God. Both the reason for

---

9   *CD* II/2, 523–4 (580–81).

Barth's choice of this central image for his later theological ethics, and the direction he follows in explicating the concept of command, however, are in continuity with the central ethical concerns of *Romans* II. Barth introduces the idea of command in answer to the ethical question: human action is good insofar as it is obedient to God's command, responsive and responsible to God's call, judged by God, and determined by God. Human action cannot otherwise be good because none but God is good.[10] Barth reaches this point in his account after rejecting in turn, first, any apologetic attempts by theological ethics to make itself acceptable to the general conception of ethics; second, attempts to show that ethics is a twofold enquiry in which theological and general ethics each have their place; and third, accounts of theological ethics that try to hold nature and supernature as distinct but not separate.[11] The concern behind this answer to the ethical question, and the rejection of the alternative accounts, is that theological ethics must depend solely and completely on God for its content. We cannot act as if we had to decide for ourselves, nor use our reason to decide about God's revelation. We are called to accept our role as covenant partners, a role which includes accepting the sovereignty of God. We are confronted by the reality that God gives commands; we hear them, and we are made responsible. We cannot go behind this: theological ethics is simply the theory of this practice.[12] The concern that ethics should depend solely on the Word of God is clearly continuous with the implications for ethics of the crisis of *Romans* II. In *Romans* II the possibility of good human action is set on the edge of a knife, or hangs from a single thread: its sole criterion is whether the action is recognized as a mere demonstration of the action of God. In the *Dogmatics* we now see Barth retains this commitment to human goodness being entirely dependent on the judgement of God.

The clearest indication that Barth's use of command in the *Dogmatics* is not a move away from the crisis of *Romans* II is that he links the concepts of crisis and command together. When writing about the universal character of God's commanding, he notes that in refusing to acknowledge this universality 'I can protect myself against the crisis which the existence of God's command signifies for me and brings down upon me'.[13] God's commanding, then, is not an escape from crisis, but is itself an expression of it, a means by which God confronts and reorients us.

Barth's explication of the concept of command also follows *Romans* II. It is immediately clear that this account of God's command will not be a casuistic treatment of the Decalogue, the deduction of a systematic framework with which we can decide the rightness and wrongness of all human action. Barth railed against such presumption in *Romans* II and continues to reject it strongly here. Instead, God's command is an event, which demands that we approach it with great openness:

---

10   *CD* II/2, 546–7 (607–8).
11   *CD* II/2, 520–35 (577–93).
12   *CD* II/2, 548 (609).
13   *CD* II/2, 655–6 (730).

When we honestly ask: *What* ought we to do?, we approach God as those who are ignorant in and with all that they already know, and stand in dire need of divine instruction and conversion. We are then ready, with a view to our next decision, to bracket and hold in reserve all that we know concerning the rightness and goodness of our past and present decisions, all the rules and axioms, however good, all the inner and outer laws and necessities under which we have placed ourselves and perhaps do so again. None of them is identical with the divine command.[14]

We cannot take refuge in universal rules to assure our righteousness, since

God seems hardly to be interested at all in general and universally valid rules, but properly only in certain particular actions and achievements and attitudes, and this in the extremely simple and direct way of desiring from man (as a father from his child or a master from his servant) that this or that must or must not happen.[15]

This concern that the divine command not be anticipated or forestalled echoes the call in *Romans* II that we break off our thinking so that it becomes truly a thinking about God: here the call is to break off our thinking so that we can truly hear the command of God.

The Critique of Casuistry

These common themes between *Romans* II and the *Dogmatics* are restated forcefully in Barth's severe criticism of casuistry at the beginning of III/4. Casuistry seems to be the ideal solution to the problem of special ethics, Barth notes, giving the benefits of its superior knowledge to doubtful consciences. It is right in saying that

in every moment and act of human activity the point at issue is a concrete and specific human choice and decision, in which the inner intention and external action are not to be separated from each other, but make up a whole. And this whole of human activity is undoubtedly confronted every time by a command of God which is also concrete and specific.[16]

Casuistry is also correct that the 'individual with his actions is not an atom in empty space, but a man among his fellows, not left to himself in his cases of conscience nor in a position to leave others to themselves'.[17] There is, then, a necessary 'practical casuistry', which is 'the unavoidable venture – the final judgement upon this venture

---

14   *CD* II/2, 646 (719–20).
15   *CD* II/2, 672 (750).
16   *CD* III/4, 8 (7).
17   *CD* III/4, 9 (8).

rests with God – of understanding God's concrete specific command here and now in this particular way'.[18]

What Barth rejects is not this task of understanding God's specific commands, but 'casuistical ethics', the 'fixation of the divine command' in a text of ethical law.[19] He provides three reasons for rejecting this casuistry, each of which are in continuity with the concerns of *Romans* II. First, casuistry fails to recognize the sovereignty of God:

> the moralist wishes to set himself on God's throne, to distinguish good and evil, and always to judge things as one or the other, not only in relation to others but also to himself. He makes himself lord, king and judge at the place where only God can be this.[20]

In fact, we can only confront God as recipients, beneficiaries and absolute beginners, venturing to understand what God commands in immediate encounter. Casuistry 'would like to win clear of the occurrence, the freedom and the peril of this event, to reach dry land, as it were, and to stand there like God, knowing good and evil'.[21] Barth makes the same point with another striking image:

> At a safe distance from the ethical battlefield – like a staff officer of the Lord – he maintains for himself and others a method of correct decisions – correct in the sense of the law that he has set between the divine decision and his own or that of others.[22]

This rejection of the usurpation of God's authority is clearly in accord with *Romans* II, but the evocation of the freedom and peril of the encounter with the command of God takes us even closer to the crisis-threatened atmosphere of the earlier work.

Barth's second reason for rejecting casuistry is that it 'makes the objectively untenable assumption that the command of God is a universal rule, an empty form, or rather a tissue of such rules and forms'.[23] This would imply that it needs filling out by application to concrete cases to become a command. For Barth, this would be no command at all. The divine command

> commands not only how man is to think and act here and now, but also quite specifically what is to take place inwardly in his mind and thoughts and outwardly in what he does or refrains from doing. It leaves nothing to human choice or preference. It thus requires no interpretation to come into force. To the last and smallest detail it is self-interpreted.[24]

---

18   *CD* III/4, 9 (8–9).
19   *CD* III/4, 9 (9).
20   *CD* III/4, 10 (9).
21   *CD* III/4, 11 (10).
22   *CD* III/4, 11 (10).
23   *CD* III/4, 11 (11).
24   *CD* III/4, 12 (11).

We have only ourselves to blame if we do not hear this clear and precise command clearly: 'The obscurity of God's will in a particular case always arises on man's side, not God's.'[25] These passages are arresting echoes of *Romans* II, where Barth both claimed that grace 'has the force of a downright conclusion; it is knowledge that needs no will to translate it into action, as though will were something alongside knowledge'[26] and stated that it is an 'objective impossibility for us to discover that we have not heard' the Word of God.[27]

The third reason Barth provides for the unacceptability of casuistry is that 'casuistical ethics also involves an encroachment in relation to man's action under the command of God, a destruction of the Christian freedom, in which alone this can be a good action'.[28] The command of God is an appeal to human freedom, not a choice of this or that, but a decision to live in freedom for God. Casuistry

> destroys the freedom of this obedience. It openly interposes something other and alien between the command of God and the man who is called to obey Him. It replaces the concrete and specific command of God's free grace and therefore the authentic will of God which man must freely and voluntarily choose, affirm, approve and grasp, by the interpretation and application, invented by himself or others, of a universal moral truth fixed and proclaimed with supreme arbitrariness.[29]

The problem with casuistry here, then, is that it stands in the way of a relationship between God and humankind, and encourages us to believe that we could obey God by conforming to an abstract set of rules, rather than by choosing to realize ourselves through action in response to God. We are called to freedom, to be God's confidants, to knowledge of the command in the form God gives it, and so to action with a clear conscience. Casuistry, however, calls us away from these things, conceals the character of action as our direct responsibility, and spares us what we should not be spared: the knowledge that God demands not only our external conduct, will, purpose, and intention, but ourselves.[30] Here again Barth's account of ethics is in continuity with those of *Romans* II, where he railed against all attempts to provide human answers to the ethical question, and pronounced human deeds as worthless if we are not prepared to recognize them as mere demonstrations of God's action.

---

25   *CD* III/4, 12 (11).
26   *Romans* II, 207 (205).
27   *Romans* II, 389 (407).
28   *CD* III/4, 13 (12).
29   *CD* III/4, 13 (13).
30   *CD* III/4, 14 (13–14).

Dialectic in the *Dogmatics*

The most striking attribute of the ethics of *Romans* II was its dialectical shape: caught in the powerful tension between the poles of God's 'No' and God's 'Yes'. This tension has slackened in the *Dogmatics*, but the ethics of II/2 and III/4 retain the form of an unstable oscillation between two unacceptable polarities, and Barth continues to show reluctance to demarcate the ground between them, which is part of what continues to discomfort those who seek a systematic ethic. One of Barth's images here is finding the way between Scylla and a Charybdis: '[t]rue dogmatics and true ethics steer a middle course – between what they must not be and what they cannot be'.[31] They may not offer more than guidance, but cannot fail to offer it.

In describing how we approach the event of the divine command, Barth identifies his position in relation to two poles. We cannot come to the divine command in complacency, confident of our prior actions and reflections, asking secretly 'How can I progress further on the right path which I am, of course, already treading?' Instead, we must come in 'complete openness', recognizing that 'a radical attack is already opened on our own life and understanding'. We come as those who are 'ignorant in and with all that they already know, and stand in dire need of divine instruction and conversion'. On the other side, however, Barth says he does not mean that we come as *tabula rasa*, with every answer we and others have found in the past 'dismissed and effaced'. We have not been in vain to the 'school of the divine command', he notes, but we bring and hold in reserve all our previous experience and all we think we know of rules and axioms.[32] So we approach the divine command neither with complacent confidence nor having thrown out all our previous understandings: we are both absolutely open and aware of all we have learned in the past. Barth's thought here remains dialectical: there is no resolution to the tension between these themes. The only way of generating a simple coherent methodology is to catch one of these ideas and lose the other. Thus those who seek ethical system seize upon the importance Barth ascribes to our moral learning here, but the absolute openness he enjoins escapes them. Those, on the other hand, who rejoice in the absence of structure, claim to find an ally in Barth here, and enlist him as a proponent of an ethic without content, but they pass over his assertion that forgetting all our previous hypotheses and commitments 'could not possibly be a good basis for ethical reflection'.[33] Comparison with the ethics of *Romans* II makes clear that Barth's ethics can be properly understood only as the dialectical tension between these two opposing forces.

---

31   *CD* III/4, 31 (34).
32   *CD* II/2, 645–7 (718–20).
33   *CD* II/2, 646 (719). Nigel Biggar is an example of those who emphasize the structural elements of Barth's thought; William Stacy Johnson celebrates the absence of structure. See Chapter 8 of this volume for a discussion and critique of their positions.

Another example of this dialectical structure is Barth's depiction of the divine command as both universal and particular. At the outset of describing the way of theological ethics, Barth distances himself from approaches that start with the identification of some universal to begin from: 'In the relationship between the command of God and the ethical problem, as we have defined it in its main features, there is not a universal moral element autonomously confronting the Christian.'[34] Later, when he discusses the biblical witness concerning the commanding God, he notes 'it is certainly not the case that, according to the Bible, God commands only or even primarily where these universally valid rules are thought to be discovered'. Barth adds here the comment we noted earlier, that 'God seems hardly to be interested at all in general and universally valid rules'.[35] So we receive the clear impression that whatever God's commandments will be, they will not be based on or result in standards we can recognize as universal. Yet Barth is quick to undermine this impression. In a section on the goodness of the divine command, he stresses that while 'we have now to retract nothing of what we have said concerning its particularity', this does not mean that it 'dissolves itself into a chaos of individual conflicting intimations to individual men in individual situations'. The encounter between God and humanity is not characterized by 'isolation and fortuitousness'; instead, 'the goodness of the divine command is something universal'.[36] Barth restates this point in volume III/4: 'in all the infinite diversity in which He gives and reveals His command, we do not have a disconnected multiplicity of individual demands, claims, directions and prohibitions, but a single and unitary command'.[37]

The most striking passage concerning the relationship between the universality and particularity of the divine command bears quoting at length. Barth argues the correct form of the ethical question is not 'What ought I to do?' but 'What ought we to do?'

> Even the claim which is addressed to me is not for me alone, but of universal validity. And I have to understand the universally valid claim as valid for me too and applying to me. If I refuse to do this, then from the detached standpoint of the individual and peculiar characteristics of my situation, my special case, I can protect myself against the crisis which the existence of God's command signifies for me and brings down upon me. And in the last analysis who cannot claim in every respect to be in a highly singular situation? ... That the universally valid command of God applies to me and affects me in a very definite way cannot be taken to imply that I can treat it as conditioned by the peculiar factors of my personal situation; that I can secure and fortify myself against its universal validity as it certainly applies to me too. At this point, again, we have something to learn from Kant – from his definition of the ethical as that which is adapted to be 'the principle for a universal law'.[38]

---

34   *CD* II/2, 543 (603).
35   *CD* II/2, 672 (750).
36   *CD* II/2, 711 (793–4).
37   *CD* III/4, 16 (16).
38   *CD* II/2, 655–6 (730).

There are two reasons this passage is arresting. First, we have seen that Barth uses Kant in exactly the same place in his argument in *Romans* II. Barth argued Kierkegaard must be corrected by Kant in relation to 'irregular' actions, and that the order of the judgement of 'the All' must be behind any apparent disorder. Now, in the *Dogmatics*, we find that Barth again turns to Kant to achieve the same redirection of emphasis from the individual to the universal. This is another indication of the close relationship between Barth's ethical thought in the two works.

The second reason this passage makes one pause is how strange it seems for Barth to be claiming as an ally the moral philosopher who is most stringent in requiring ethical norms to be universal, and intelligible to autonomous agents. This emphasis on the universality of the divine command is strange for a theologian whose ethics have been criticized as relying on intuition.[39] The reference in the *Dogmatics* shows that Barth's invocation of Kant in *Romans* II was not an erratic boulder in the terrain of his thought. Rather, we see that Barth has a long-standing awareness of and response to the danger of his theory becoming individualistic and antinomian. Ethics, he insists, can never be a merely individual practice, but is essentially concerned with the social and universal. God's command is universally valid, and while it will impact me in definite ways, these ways will be the expression of its universality, not exceptions to it. For Kant, whether a maxim could be applied universally was the test of whether it was part of the moral law.[40] In this passage, Barth has a form of Kant's test in mind: if I believe I have received a command of God, but cannot understand it as of universal validity, then I can be sure that it is not from God. We then have a criterion for evaluating the commands others have received, so that if a serial killer claims to have been acting on divine commands, we have grounds for rejecting the claim. The application of this criterion, however, is not straightforward even in the context of Kant's moral philosophy, let alone in Barth's ethics of divine command. It is unclear exactly which commands we would be able to allow or disallow on this basis, but there is no doubt that Barth is committed to a form of universality as a criterion for a genuine divine command.

Barth's commitment to the particularity of the divine command, however, is just as strong. If a divine command were not definite and particular, but just a universal rule, it would at best set bounds on what we decide to do for ourselves. At worst, a universal rule would merely allow us to pour 'the dictates and pronouncements of our own self-will into the empty container of a formal moral concept'.[41] There is far too much conditioning by the agent in the use of a universal rule, which does not become anything like a command

---

39   See, for example, James Gustafson's treatment of Barth's ethics in James M. Gustafson, *Ethics from a Theocentric Perspective*, vol. 2 (Chicago: University of Chicago, 1984), 31.

40   Immanuel Kant, *Groundwork of the Metaphysic of Morals*, ed. H.J. Paton (London: Hutchinson & Co. Ltd, 1948), 67.

41   *CD* II/2, 664 (740–41).

until it is first heard, and understood, and acknowledged in itself, then made a law on the basis of that perception and recognition, and then given the necessary interpretation and application to the case in hand – which is, again, of course, a matter for our own decision. In this conception far too much devolves upon those who, in relation to a real command, do not enter except as the obedient or disobedient. A command – that is, the command in the strictest sense, the command of God – is a claim addressed to man in such a way that it is given integrally, so that he cannot control its content or decide its concrete implication. A command is a demand and not merely a theoretical exposition of the form which it may take ... It does not need any interpretation for even to the smallest details it is self-interpreting.[42]

God's command, therefore, is both universal and particular: it must be seen as universally valid, but is particular and definite to the smallest detail. We are clearly still in the realm in which our speech about God and God's willing can only be expressed in broken and dialectical language.

One final example of the polarities still evident in Barth's ethical thought in the *Dogmatics* is the extent to which we can know what a divine command will be in advance. He is committed, of course, to the view that the divine command cannot be frozen in any human system: there can be 'no fixation of the divine command in a great or small text of ethical law'.[43] The command of God is an event, not an inference from known principles; no existing rule can be identical with it. Barth cites Bonhoeffer here:

> An ethic cannot be a book in which there is set out how everything in the world actually ought to be but unfortunately is not, and an ethicist cannot be a man who always knows better than others what is to be done and how it is to be done. An ethic cannot be a work of reference for moral action which is guaranteed to be unexceptionable, and the ethicist cannot be the competent critic and judge of every human activity. An ethic cannot be a retort in which ethical or Christian human beings are produced, and the ethicist cannot be the embodiment or ideal type of a life which is, on principle, moral.[44]

Ethics cannot anticipate the event of God's command, but can only provide a 'reference' to it. Yet alongside this rejection of human advance knowledge of divine commands, Barth also wants to insist that there is still a role for the ethicist, and

---

42   *CD* II/2, 665 (741). I have already cited the similar assertion Barth makes in III/4 that God's commands are self-interpreted to 'the last and smallest detail' (*CD* III/4, 12 (11)).

43   *CD* III/4, 9 (9).

44   *CD* III/4, 10 (9), citing Bonhoeffer's *Ethics* (Dietrich Bonhoeffer, *Ethics*, ed. Eberhard Bethge, trans. Neville Horton Smith (London: Collins, 1964), 269). In the paragraph following the one Barth cites, Bonhoeffer continues to emphasize the positive role of ethicists: they should help people join in life, 'not in mistrustful surveillance and appraisal of everything that is and everything that ought to be, and not in the timidly over-scrupulous subordination of the natural to the deontological, of the free to the necessary, of the concrete to the universal and of the purposeless to purpose', but 'in the abundant fullness of the concrete tasks and processes of life with all their multiplicity of motives' (269–70).

that it is possible to provide guidance to those listening for God's commands. This possibility arises because the vertical dimension of the event of God's command intersects the horizontal of the 'constancy and continuity both of the divine command and human action'.[45] We can be sure that God will always command as Creator, Reconciler and Redeemer, on the one side, and that the person commanded will always be the creature of God, the reconciled sinner, and the redeemed child of God, on the other. These horizontal continuities allow the reference to become 'formed', and make special ethics – the study of how persons are sanctified by God in their concrete action – possible. While special ethics still cannot anticipate the divine command, it can execute its task of giving 'instructional preparation for the ethical event'.[46] How detailed can this instructional approximation to the command be? Barth's answer illustrates the intricate dance between the poles of no-knowledge and knowledge of the divine command he is performing here:

> naturally it can and must happen that this approximation becomes as intensive as possible, and the directives and directions as urgent and binding as possible. If we take the ideal case of a full knowledge of definite general spheres and relationships in which the ethical event takes place, then the question whether in these spheres and relationships this or that and not something else is commanded or forbidden, and is therefore good or bad, gains a sharpness in which the question almost acquires the character of an answer. It obviously cannot pretend to be an answer. For the most concrete sphere of the individual ethical case to which an answer must relate will still have escaped ethics. Ethics will still leave the final judgment to God. And our knowledge of these general spheres and relationships will never actually be full, so that the question of what is commanded and forbidden will always necessarily retain a certain breadth and openness. On the other hand, there can be no doubt that the question gains in precision, and therefore the directives and directions to be given by ethics gain in urgency and compulsion, in proportion as the knowledge of these spheres and relationships becomes broader and deeper. And it is clear that the service which ethics should render special ethics is genuine and useful in proportion as it finds itself in this movement (though always aware of its limits), and can thus indicate with increasing urgency and compulsion the divine command and the human action corresponding to it.[47]

The tension between what the ethicist can and cannot say indicating the divine command continues throughout volume III/4 of the *Dogmatics*, the special ethics of creation. While in his treatment of most topics Barth finally leaves open what command the individual may hear, in several cases – notably his rejection of homosexuality and the proper hierarchy he sees in male–female relations[48] – he seems to assume full knowledge of the divine command. We must judge these to be

---

45   *CD* III/4, 17 (18).
46   *CD* III/4, 18 (18–19).
47   *CD* III/4, 31 (33).
48   See *CD* III/4, 166 (184–5), 170 (188).

examples of Barth saying more than he is legitimately able to given his metaethical commitments.

The comparison in this chapter of Barth's conception of ethics of the *Dogmatics* with the ethics of *Romans* II shows that the form of Barth's ethical thought in the two works remains largely unchanged. Barth still views ethics as an integral part of dogmatics and theology in the *Dogmatics*; the crisis is still evident, even on occasion in name; the new metaphor of command expresses commitments Barth set out in the earlier work; and Barth's critique of casuistry restates the central tenets of his ethics in *Romans* II. Moreover, the central characteristic of the ethics of *Romans* II – its dialectical form – is clearly evident in the *Dogmatics*, as we have seen in examining the polarities of approaching the command with openness/experience, the nature of the command as universal/particular, and the no-knowledge/knowledge possible regarding what God's command will be. Barth's approach to ethics is more systematic in the *Dogmatics*, his thought is more nuanced, more detailed (and more extensive!), and is explicated with different terminology and imagery, but the foundational and formative insights and commitments are common between the two works. The next two chapters continue this task of comparison in relation to Barth's treatment of particular ethical topics.

CHAPTER 6

Love and Community in the *Dogmatics*

In Chapter 2, I identified two groups of ethical topics that Barth addressed in *Romans* II: love and community; and war, peace, and revolution. This chapter takes up the topics of love and community and compares Barth's treatment of them in *Romans* II and the *Dogmatics* in order to discover whether the continuity in Barth's conception of ethics is borne out in relation to particular ethical questions. Chapter 7 continues this task of comparison in relation to war, peace, and revolution.

This chapter proceeds in four parts. The first follows two dialectical themes from *Romans* II into the *Dogmatics*: the relationship between divine and human action in human love, and the bipolar nature of love as harsh/yielding, sweet/bitter, and so on. The second part of the chapter examines the relationship between the two love commandments in the *Dogmatics*, to which Barth gives repeated attention. In the third part of the chapter, I examine Barth's description of eros and agape in the *Dogmatics*, and the relationship between them. Finally, in the fourth part of the chapter I compare Barth's difficulty with identifying who should be included as the objects of agape with his emphasis on otherness as the basis of community in *Romans* II.

The Status and Nature of Love

We saw at the beginning of Chapter 2 that the primary and controlling insight in Barth's treatment of love in *Romans* II is that love for God is altogether the gift of God, and not a human possession, expressed primarily in worship and secondarily in love for the neighbour. With regard to the question of how far love is a human action, Barth retains in the *Dogmatics* a strong commitment to the position that Christian love has its origin in God. The fact that we love 'is no less a gift and work of God, a virgin birth ... than is the human existence of the eternal Son of God' and the Bible knows nothing 'of a natural love to God which is proper to us apart from divine revelation, or of a natural capacity for love which is prior to revelation'.[1] It is God's love that is creative in establishing fellowship between God and humankind: God's love always 'throws a bridge over a crevasse' and is always 'the light shining out of darkness'.[2] Yet Barth is also consistently aware that Christian love must not be merely a divine reality: 'On the other hand, we must insist that the love of the children of God does become an event in an act or acts of human self-determination: it is a creaturely

---

1   *CD* I/2, 373 (410).
2   *CD* II/1, 278 (312).

reality.'³ Barth is critical of Luther and Nygren, who depict Christians as pipes or channels for God's love, asking 'Have we been released from eros only to say the more pietistically about agape that which effaces all clear contours and destroys all healthy distances?'⁴ It is clear that human love is not simply an extension of divine love, Barth notes, from 'the great frailty of that which emerges as love in the life of even the best Christians. If it were merely identical with the flowing of the stream of divine love into human life … it could not and would not be so weak and puny.'⁵

Human love is a truly human action that has its basis in God's love: it is the human response to the love of God. The Christian loves 'as one who is called and impelled by God to do so by the fact that He has disclosed Himself and is known as the One who first loves, and first loves [the Christian], in the glory and majesty of His divine essence'.⁶ Love is analogous to faith in this respect: just as 'Christian faith is the human response to God's justifying sentence, so Christian love is the human response to His direction'.⁷ Jesus Christ was the demonstration of God's love for the world; 'Christian love is the active human recognition of this proof of the love of God. It recognizes it by following it, imitating it, modelling itself upon it'.⁸ It cannot precede the divine love, since it is the response of the individual confronted by God's action, but '[i]ts dependence on this action does not violate its character as a spontaneous and responsible human action'. The Creator and the creature 'do not exist on the same level', so '[t]here is no rivalry between the divine freedom and the human action'.⁹ Barth insists 'we have to describe love quite unequivocally as a free act', an act in which 'man is at work, not as God's puppet, but with his own heart and soul and strength, as an independent subject who encounters and replies to God and is responsible to Him as His partner'.¹⁰

In *Romans* II we saw that Barth held up agape as the great positive ethical possibility, but his assertion that human love was wholly the gift of God made its nature as a real human action uncertain. In the *Dogmatics,* Barth sets out his position more carefully and more extensively. He recognizes the importance of demarcating a creaturely sphere in which free independent human action is possible, and is particularly concerned to achieve this in relation to love. This is one area of his ethical thought where there seems to be a move away from dialectic in the transition from *Romans* II to the *Dogmatics*: the opposition of human love as wholly God's work but demanded of the individual becomes a coherent account of how human love cannot precede divine love but is a free human response to it.¹¹

---

3   *CD* I/2, 373 (410).
4   *CD* IV/2, 752 (854).
5   *CD* IV/2, 785 (891).
6   *CD* IV/2, 752 (854).
7   *CD* IV/1, 102 (110).
8   *CD* IV/1, 103 (111).
9   *CD* IV/2, 752 (855).
10   *CD* IV/2, 785–6 (890–1).
11   It is interesting to compare Barth's treatment of divine and human agency in human love, with his

The second dialectical element of Barth's treatment of love in *Romans* II identified in Chapter 2 was the polarized nature of love as sweet/bitter, yielding/harsh, peaceful/conflictual, forgetting/knowing, forgiving/punishing, receiving/rejecting. This dialectic is not only present in the *Dogmatics*, but is developed and expanded in Barth's exposition of the perfections of God.

In his treatment of love, Barth follows his methodology throughout the *Dogmatics* in asserting that to understand human love, we cannot begin from a master concept of love, or from a phenomenological study, but must begin with God's love for us:

> To know what love is, we have first to ask concerning the unique love of God for us. What our love is will necessarily appear when we ask about our response to this love of God for us and the confirmation and acknowledgement which we owe it. Only then, and by means of the standard which is given to us in that way, can we assess the rightness or wrongness of a concept of love which is otherwise completely arbitrary.[12]

In order to understand Barth's account of love in the *Dogmatics*, then, we must begin at the beginning with his treatment of God's love, which he summarizes in identifying God as 'the One who loves in freedom'.[13] God loves as God wills fellowship with us for its own sake, without reference to our aptitude, as an end in itself, and as a necessity of God's being.[14] But God remains free in this loving, which Barth expounds in terms of God's aseity and absoluteness. God's aseity means God is God's own basis, and 'free from all origination, conditioning or determination from without, by that which is not Himself'.[15] God's absoluteness 'means noetically that God cannot be classified or included in the same category with anything that He is not'[16] and ontically, 'that He is distinct from everything, that He is self-sufficient and independent in relation to it, and that He is so in a peculiar and pre-eminent fashion – as no created being confronts any other'.[17]

This dialectical structure of loving in freedom determines the framework for Barth's discussion of the divine attributes of God, which he discusses under the heading of God's perfections. The perfections are grouped in pairs, the meaning of each constrained by the dialectical opposition of its second term. Thus grace is a mode of God's being 'in so far as it seeks and creates fellowship by its own free inclination

---

treatment of the relationship in the proclamation of God's Word. In his discussion of the Word of God, Barth describes the relationship between human and divine agency in the same action as dialectical. God's action in speaking is no less God's action because it is also a human action: 'even though it is a human act too, it is sharply distinguished from all human acts by the fact that it is not affected by the *sic et non* of that dialectic' (*CD* I/1, 157 (162)).

12   *CD* I/2, 376 (413).
13   *CD* II/1, 257 (288).
14   *CD* II/1, 276–80 (310–15).
15   *CD* II/1, 307 (346).
16   *CD* II/1, 310 (348).
17   *CD* II/1, 311 (350).

and favour, unconditioned by any merit or claim in the beloved',[18] but God's loving is distinctive in that it is also holy: 'As holy, it is characterised by the fact that God, as He seeks and creates fellowship, is always the Lord. He therefore distinguishes and maintains His own will as against every other will. He condemns, excludes and annihilates all contradiction and resistance to it.'[19] The character of God's loving as holy means that this love will not be soft or sentimental. God 'does not relax His wrath' in loving, and while it never fails, Barth concludes from a study of Old Testament texts that 'it burns and shrivels and destroys where it is ignored and meets with no response'.[20] Barth emphasizes the importance of the tension between the perfections of grace and holiness:

> Only in this opposition is God known in His being as love and grace. For only in this relationship of opposition does He actually create and maintain fellowship between Himself and us, and turn towards us. Only in this tension, as we experience and recognise it as such, and subject ourselves to it, do we truly believe in Him and yield to Him the right which He has against us and over us: the right in which we can then place our confidence. If He is not present to us in this tension, He is not present to us at all.[21]

Similarly, God's mercy 'lies in His readiness to share in sympathy the distress of another, a readiness which springs from His inmost nature and stamps all His being and doing',[22] but it is conditioned by God's righteousness, which 'springs from the fact that when God wills and creates the possibility of fellowship with man He does that which is worthy of Himself, and therefore in this fellowship He asserts His worth in spite of all contradiction and resistance, and therefore in this fellowship He causes only His own worth to prevail and rule'.[23] The third and final pairing of perfections under the divine loving is God's patience, which is 'His will, deep-rooted in His essence and constituting His divine being and action, to allow another – for the sake of His own grace and mercy and in the affirmation of His holiness and justice – space and time for the development of its own existence, thus conceding to this existence a reality side by side with His own',[24] and God's wisdom, expressed in so far as 'His whole activity, as willed by Him, is also thought out by Him, and thought out by Him from the very outset with correctness and completeness, so that it is an intelligent and to that extent a reliable and liberating activity'.[25]

These perfections of the divine loving are followed by the perfections of the divine freedom, also expressed in dialectical pairs: God's unity and omnipresence,

---

18   *CD* II/1, 353 (398).
19   *CD* II/1, 359 (403).
20   *CD* IV/2, 775 (879).
21   *CD* II/1, 362 (406–7).
22   *CD* II/1, 369 (415).
23   *CD* II/1, 376 (423).
24   *CD* II/1, 409 (461).
25   *CD* II/1, 425–6 (479).

constancy and omnipotence, and eternity and glory. We can see that Barth's account of the being of God in action, and therefore his account of divine love, is intrinsically dialectical. It is only in the opposition between love and freedom, and the resultant tensions between each pair of the divine perfections, that the uniqueness of God's love can be understood. Since according to Barth we can understand human love only in relation to the way in which God loves humanity, love for God and the neighbour must share this dialectical structure.[26]

The Two Love Commandments

One of the aspects of the discussion of love in the *Dogmatics* where this twofold structure is apparent is Barth's ongoing treatment of the relationship between the commandments to love God and to love the neighbour, which he touches on in each of its four volumes. The *Romans* II left this topic problematic: if love of God is expressed primarily in worship and secondarily in love of the neighbour, there is no place for direct love of God and love of the neighbour is justified only indirectly as part of our love of God. At one point in the *Dogmatics*, Barth explicitly corrects his earlier work, noting that he may have contributed to the attitude that there can be no direct Christian love for God.[27] The close identification between God and the neighbour in *Romans* II also makes the relationship between the two loves less clear: we saw in Chapter 2 that Barth asserts that everything depends on whether or not we find God in the other. In the *Dogmatics*, Barth remains committed to the view that

---

26   Barth does not specify the relationship between God's love and human love further in the *Dogmatics*, which leaves many open questions. There are relevant differences in divine and human love that mean we should not aspire to love in the way that God does. In his theological anthropology, Barth explicitly addresses our similarities to and differences from the person of Jesus Christ and the implications of these similarities and differences for Christological ethics (*CD* III/2, 222ff. (264ff)). For a discussion of the question of how far it is appropriate to use imitation of Christ as a model for Christian ethics, see Gene Outka, 'Following at a Distance: Ethics and the Identity of Jesus', in *Scriptural Authority and Narrative Interpretation*, ed. Garrett Green (Philadelphia: Fortress Press, 1987), 144–60.

27   'In his bitter fight for agape against eros A. Nygren ... has even decreed that there can be no question of a spontaneous love of man for God ... Since in my earlier period I myself made some direct and indirect contribution to this attitude, I think it only right to state my present views on the matter ... Christian love, especially in its form as love for God and for Jesus, is continually exposed to transformation into its erotico-religious opposite ... It was this that we had in view some forty years ago ... [I]t was a time when we had to deal with Neo-Protestantism, and since in the investigation of its origins we rightly came on Mysticism and Pietism it was natural that we should be sharp-sighted and rather severe in this respect ... But were we not on the point of subscribing to a no less dubious antithesis ... according to which the work of the Holy Spirit must be reduced to the management of an eternal working-day, and with the abolition of a true and direct love for God and Jesus there is basically no place for prayer? There was scope for better instruction on this point' (*CD* IV/2, 795 (902)).

there is a very close relationship between love for God and for the neighbour. In the New Testament sense of love, 'it is not possible either to love one's neighbour without first loving God, or to love God without then loving one's neighbour'.[28] He is also committed, however, to the distinctiveness of the commands.

Barth sets out three possibilities for how the two love commandments could be related: they could be two absolute demands, they could be identical expressions of one absolute command, or the second command could be a subordinate command. He rejects the first possibility because we are commanded to love God with totality and exclusiveness, and the same cannot be demanded in relation to the neighbour, unless we make the neighbour a second God. Second, the commands cannot be identical, because this would require the ascription of an autonomous inherent value to the neighbour, whereas Scripture sees the individual as having no inherent dignity apart from in relationship with God. The third possibility of a subordinate command is better, but the biblical text does not treat the command to love the neighbour as a lower level of commanding, and in any case it is not clear that we can conceive of a command of God that is relative rather than absolute.[29] Barth's solution is to remind us that the children of God live 'in the space between the resurrection and the ascension of Jesus ... in two times and two worlds'. The two commands are two different demands:

> The first one, the commandment to love God, is intended for the child of God in his completed existence in Jesus Christ as the heavenly Head of His earthly members. The second commandment, to love the neighbour, is intended for the child of God in his not yet completed walk and activity as an earthly member of this heavenly Head. It is the same God speaking to the same man. He speaks to him in two ways, because he exists in two ways.[30]

In his discussion of the observance of the Sabbath, Barth is again concerned to show that the two commands should be seen as distinct. There is no reason, he notes, to disapprove of the distinction made by ethicists between duties towards God and duties to the neighbour or oneself. We cannot withdraw from our obligations to our neighbours by 'fleeing to a special religious sphere', yet 'only on the basis of a very strained exegesis of Mk. 12 29 f. and its parallels could we say that the commandment to love our neighbour in some sense absorbs that to love God and takes away its independent quality'. Instead of two existences, Barth here construes the duality of the two loves as two spheres of activity:

> the double command to love points us to two different spheres of activity which are relatively – no more, but very clearly so – distinct. Alongside work there is also prayer; alongside practical love for one's brother there is also divine service

---

28   *CD* II/2, 616 (685).
29   *CD* I/2, 402–8 (442–50).
30   *CD* I/2, 409 (451).

in the narrower sense; alongside activity in state and community there is also that in the congregation; alongside the other sciences there is also theology.[31]

Barth returns again to the two love commandments in the doctrine of reconciliation, where he characterizes the two loves as two dimensions, again distinct but closely related. As the communion in which Jesus Christ brings all persons together is known,

> it is at once and necessarily evident that there is a solidarity of all men in the fellowship with God in which they have all been placed in Jesus Christ, and a special solidarity of those who are aware of the fact, the fellowship of those who believe in Him, the Christian community. In this horizontal dimension Christian love is love to the neighbour or the brother. This must be distinguished from love to God which is Christian love in the vertical dimension. It will not take place without love to God. And there would be no love to God if it did not take place. But while it can only follow, and must follow, this prior love, it is an autonomous loving, for God in heaven and the neighbour on earth are two and not one. Love to others cannot exhaust itself in love to God, nor can love to God exhaust itself in love to others.[32]

The alternate images of two existences, spheres of activity, or dimensions, of human loving are complementary, each groping to express both the distinctiveness and the interrelatedness of the two love commandments. The movement from *Romans* II to the *Dogmatics* on this topic is from unity to duality: Barth recognized that the complexity of the love to which we are called could not be reduced to the requirement to love God, but must reflect the duality of our twofold existence between Jesus' resurrection and ascension.

Eros and Agape

One decidedly non-dialectical theme in Barth's discussion of love in *Romans* II is the opposition he describes between eros and agape. The two are simply opposed to each other, separated by 'the flaming sword of death and eternity'. Eros is the form of the world – agape is protest and enmity against it; eros deceives – agape is without dissimulation; eros is slavery – agape is of God; eros lusts – agape never fails.[33] In the *Dogmatics*, Barth's view of the relation between eros and agape is more complex. Some of this complexity is unintentional and unfortunate: as Gene Outka observes,

---

31   *CD* III/4, 49 (53). Barth adds an interesting note here about the eventual disappearance of the ethical problem: 'That Rev. 21:22 says there is no temple in the heavenly Jerusalem is certainly true; but it is bound up with the fact that the ethical problem will then cease to be a problem at all, since even from man's side the relationship between God and man will then be finally ordered and ruled.'

32   *CD* IV/1, 105–6 (114).

33   *Romans* II, 320 (331), 451 (475), 467 (491), 496 (522).

Barth means different things by eros at different points in the work.[34] Eros is used to refer to human creativity in general, sexual desire, the eros of Greek religion, the 'sanctified eros' of Christian marriage, or simply as self-love.[35] What Barth is clear about, is that it is wrong to see a simple duality between eros and agape. Agape has then been 'far too unthinkingly accepted merely as an antithesis to Greek eros and thus unconsciously depicted and extolled in the contours and colours of the original' and we have to ask seriously 'whether what is called agape is not really a spiritualised, idealised, sublimated, and pious form of eros'.[36]

While Barth believes that eros is 'the direct opposite of Christian love', he also recognizes three reasons to be careful in criticizing it. The first is that 'in a crude or subtle form (and perhaps both)' all Christians love in this way too; the second, that 'this other love can claim some of the greatest figures in the history of the human spirit'; the third that we all 'exist in a world which in its best and finest as well as its most basic phenomena is for the most part built upon this other rather than Christian love'.[37] Barth is consistent in stressing the importance of not forming 'too impoverished a conception' of eros, or seeking it only in degenerate forms. It is a human phenomenon reaching back to the beginnings of history, its power evident in the way it 'invaded Christian thought' in caritas. 'As long as men love', Barth observes, 'even though they are Christians they will always live within the framework of eros'.[38] Despite this high view of eros, however, Barth insists that Christian love and eros are 'two movements in opposite directions' so that there can only be conflict between them.

Barth is aware of the difficulty of all Christians loving in the way of eros, yet it being the opposite of Christian love and in conflict with it:

> Man loves either in one way or the other, and he has to choose whether it is to be in the one way or the other. If in fact he loves in both ways at the same time, as is often the case even with the Christian, this can only be with the disruption, the 'falling out', which we had occasion to discuss in relation to 'conversion'.[39]

In his treatment of conversion, Barth describes this 'falling out' – he laments the lack of an English or French term to translate *Auseinandersetzung* – as resulting from the

---

34   Gene Outka, *Agape: An Ethical Analysis* (New Haven, Connecticut: Yale University Press, 1972), 222–4. Outka identifies three different senses of eros in the *Dogmatics*: a glad being with the other found in Greek eros, love between man and woman, and the acquisitive love contrasted with agape in IV/2.

35   See *CD* I/2, 192 (210); *CD* III/1, 313 (359); *CD* III/2, 279 (336–7); *CD* III/4, 219–20 (246); *CD* IV/2, 734–5 (832–3). For a more detailed survey of these texts, see David Clough, '*Eros* and *Agape* in Karl Barth's *Church Dogmatics*', *International Journal of Systematic Theology*, 2:2 (2000), 189–203.

36   *CD* III/2, 280 (337–8).

37   *CD* IV/2, 735 (833–4).

38   *CD* IV/2, 737 (836–7).

39   *CD* IV/2, 736 (835).

individual being under a twofold determination, 'simul (totus) iustus, simul (totus) peccator'.[40] Barth stresses the impossibility of any sort of coexistence between these two determinations: 'In the twofold determination of the man engaged in conversion we have to do with two total men who cannot be united but are necessarily in extreme contradiction. We are confronted with mutually exclusive determinations.'[41] The situation is untenable:

> Its whole will and movement and impulse is to fall out or to fall apart, and to do so in the direction unequivocally characterised by the radically different content of this twofold determination; not dualistically in a division or re-stabilised co-existence of an old man and a new, a sinner and saint; but monistically in the passing and death and definitive end and destruction of the one in favour of the development and life and exclusive, uncompromised and inviolable existence of the other.[42]

Applying this back to the relationship between eros and agape makes Barth's intentions here very much clearer. The two loves stand in a dialectical relationship in the Christian, who at once loves wholly with eros and wholly with agape, but for whom this existence is no easy accommodation, but an experience of being totally at odds with herself. Eros is how the world loves: it is creative and achieves greatness; in the Greeks it gave insight into human nature as glad fellow-humanity; in its form as sexual desire it is familiar and dangerous; it is capable of superlative heights of wondrous love of God, but is always finally a melancholy love of self. Agape is not merely the antithesis of this worldly love, but is a new thing, a joyful giving of ourselves, thereby a renouncing of the idea that we belong to ourselves, and an exaltation that we may love as God loves. The Christian loves in both these ways, but this is an unhappy and unstable tension that must be resolved in the end of eros in the death of the sinner, and the exclusive existence of agape in the life of the saint.[43]

The Object of Agape

The central insight in Barth's discussion of community I identified in Chapter 2 was that fellowship means 'an encountering of the *other* in the full existentiality of

---

40 *CD* IV/2, 572 (646).
41 *CD* IV/2, 571 (646).
42 *CD* IV/2, 573–4 (648–9).
43 Outka notes Barth's conflicting claims that human actions are governed either by agape or eros, and that human actions are governed by both, and concludes that 'nothing very definite is forthcoming about how these claims might conceivably connect' (Outka, *Agape*, 228). My contention here is that the comparison with Barth's account of conversion provides this connection in recognizing both the 'simul … simul' existence of eros and agape and their mutual exclusivity that forces a resolution of this 'both/and' in the direction of one.

his utter otherness'[44] and, far from blurring this otherness, it requires it and makes sense of it. It cannot be based on any positive human possession, such as 'religious temperament, moral consciousness, humanitarianism', Barth argued, because they distinguish persons from one another. Genuine fellowship is grounded on what we lack: it is when we recognize ourselves as sinners that we see we are sisters and brothers.[45] Barth also made a connection between the otherness of the neighbour and of God: 'the "other" – the neighbour – who stands at the side of each one of us is the uplifted finger which by its "otherness" reminds us of the *wholly* other'.[46] The importance of recognizing the otherness of the other is still a theme in the *Dogmatics*, and Barth still sees the connection between God and the neighbour in this respect:

> The decisive element … is that love is love for another. Of course this element is real only in love to God, and in the love to the neighbour which it includes and posits. All other loving is compromised as such by the uncertainty of the objectivity or otherness of the one who is loved, by the possibility that the one who supposedly loves is perhaps alone. Where there is no otherness of the one who is loved, where the one who loves is alone, he does not really love.[47]

Barth argues that love for God that respects God's otherness means confessing that we are different from the object of our love: we love as sinners.[48] Later, in his Christological anthropology, Barth portrays Jesus as determined completely by the otherness of his fellows: 'Jesus has to let His being, Himself, be prescribed and dictated and determined by an alien human being (that of His more near and distant fellows), and by the need and infinite peril of this being.'[49]

The larger weight of material in the *Dogmatics*, however, emphasizes sameness over otherness as a basis for fellowship. Jesus is alien to his fellows, but Barth expresses the encounter between two human beings as 'I am as Thou art'.[50] He is careful to indicate that the two persons do not become one another, that they remain distinguished with their own validity and history. Their encounter is based on what is shared between them, however, fellow creatures of the same God. It is their sameness that is the basis for their fellowship, not their difference.

Barth's treatment of agape follows this direction of basing fellowship on what is shared. Here it is one's location in salvation history that must be in common between the lover and the loved, thus restricting the operation of agape to within the Christian

---

44   *Romans* II, 443 (466). I have followed the italic emphasis of the German text in this and the following passages, rather than reproducing Hoskyns's use of capitalization for emphasis.

45   *Romans* II, 100–101 (82).

46   *Romans* II, 444 (468). The 'uplifted finger' recalls Barth's fascination with John the Baptist pointing to Christ in Matthias Grünewald's Crucifixion, which he had above the desk in his study. See, for example, *CD* I/1, 112 (115).

47   *CD* I/2, 386–7 (425–6).

48   *CD* I/2, 390 (429).

49   *CD* III/2, 214–15 (256).

50   'Ich bin, indem Du bist' (*CD* III/2, 248 (298)).

community. Love for other persons, Barth argues, 'presupposes that the one or many who are loved stand in a certain proximity to the one who loves – a proximity in which others do not find themselves'.[51] The Bible certainly speaks of relationships with others beyond this proximity, but not in terms of love. The issue is then who is in this proximate relationship and who is not: the question of who is my neighbour. Barth addressed this question in the first volume of the *Dogmatics*, with an exegetical treatment of the parable of the Good Samaritan. The meaning of the parable is clear, he notes, 'though obstinately surrounded by traditional exposition'.[52] The parable is told in response to the lawyer asking who his neighbour is, and he answers Jesus' question at the end of the parable by identifying the neighbour to the wounded man as the one who showed compassion to him.[53] Barth draws the conclusion that clearly follows but that is nonetheless surprising. The neighbour is the one who shows compassion to us: the true form of the neighbour is 'the bearer and representative of the divine compassion'.[54] The neighbour 'proclaims and shows forth Jesus Christ within this world',[55] and through my neighbour, 'I am referred to the order in which I can and should offer to God ... the absolutely necessary praise which is meet and acceptable to Him'.[56] This means that not everyone is my neighbour: not everyone stands in this relationship to me. Yet it is not only members of the Church who can be neighbours:

> As the Bible sees it, service of the compassionate neighbour is certainly not restricted to the life of the Church in itself and as such. It is not restricted to those members of the Church who are already called and recognizable as such. Humanity as a whole can take part in this service. The Samaritan in the parable shows us incontestably that even those who do not know that they are doing so, or what they are doing, can assume and exercise the function of a compassionate neighbour.[57]

It is impossible to be 'absolutely outside the Church', Barth maintains here, since everyone exists with the Church 'in the space between the ascension and the parousia of Jesus Christ'. Therefore simply as a fellow human being, any person can be a neighbour to me.[58]

In the fourth volume of the *Dogmatics*, Barth is inconsistent regarding who should be the objects of Christian love. In IV/1, when he turns from the vertical dimension of Christian love to the horizontal, he clearly means that Christians and non-Christians

---

51   *CD* IV/2, 803 (910).
52   *CD* I/2, 418 (461).
53   Luke 10:29–37.
54   *CD* I/2, 416 (459).
55   *CD* I/2, 421 (464).
56   *CD* I/2, 420 (463).
57   *CD* I/2, 422 (465–6).
58   *CD* I/2, 423 (466).

should be loved: the love of Jesus Christ is the coming together of all persons with one another, and 'there is a solidarity of all persons in the fellowship with God in which they have all been placed in Jesus Christ, and a special solidarity of those who are aware of the fact, the fellowship of those who believe in God, the Christian community'.[59] In this passage, Barth calls love towards all persons love to the 'neighbour', and love towards other Christians love to the 'brother'. Confusingly, however, further down the paragraph Barth refers to Matthew 25:31–40: Jesus' teaching that what persons do to the least of his brothers, they do to him. Barth is clear that both Christians and non-Christians belong in the category of Jesus' 'brothers'. They represent Jesus Christ

> as the neighbour, as the one who fell among thieves, and as the Good Samaritan ... They are not identical with Him. But He cannot be had without them, nor can reconciliation with Him nor conversion to Him. He cannot be had without gratitude for their witness and a willingness to be witnesses to them, without love to them, without their indispensability to each one whom God loves, without that one seriously setting out and never ceasing to seek and find them, both in the community and therefore in the world as well, Christian and also non-Christian neighbours.[60]

In IV/2, however, Barth gives a different account of who the neighbour is, which does not fit easily with the Good Samaritan: 'the one who apart from God is loved in the act of Christian love, being necessarily loved together with God, is the fellow human being who stands in a definite historical relationship to the Christian who loves.'[61] This historical relationship is salvation history, so it is only 'those with whom we find ourselves in this context of the history of salvation' who can be the objects of Christian love.[62] Barth is quick to say there should be no 'restriction in principle' to this group, as our knowledge of who are neighbours are in this sense is never complete. Nonetheless, there is a proper 'practical and provisional' restriction of Christian love to the circle of sisters and brothers in Christ.[63] Barth has clearly come a long way from the emphasis in the first volume on the otherness of the one loved as a criterion for genuine love.

This ambiguity regarding the identity of the Christian's neighbour is the result of Barth's commitment to affirm the special status of the Church in relation to the rest of the world:

---

59   *CD* IV/1, 105 (114). I have revised the translation here: the use of 'men' is especially unfortunate when the solidarity of all humanity is being emphasized. The repeated use of 'brother' in the passage which follows is also distracting, but is less easy to avoid.

60   *CD* IV/1, 106 (115).

61   *CD* IV/2, 802 (910); translation revised. It is clear that Barth means to identify the neighbour here from the beginning of the excursus that follows this passage: 'What we have been attempting is a general and formal description of the important biblical concept of the "neighbour"' (803 (911)).

62   *CD* IV/2, 806–7 (914–15).

63   *CD* IV/2, 807–8 (915–17).

It is here in this people that Jesus Christ has His body, the earthly-historical form of His existence. It is here that God speaks with humanity and is heard by them … His purpose is for all persons, and He addresses Himself to the whole world. But – without prejudice to His fatherly providence over all creaturely happening – He does so here and only here. For it is here that His love is active as an electing, renewing and creative basis of the response of human love.[64]

God's love in this community must elicit a response in love that is not found outside it, and since the neighbour we are called to love is someone in proximity to us, it seems the object as well as the subject of this love must be within the Church. Yet in the two places cited above where Barth introduces the parable of the Good Samaritan, he is forced by the text to conclude that our neighbour may be foreign to us: the otherness of the Samaritan is an inescapable aspect of the parable. This is the cause of the ambiguity we find here in response to the question of who my neighbour is. The resolution in the context of the *Dogmatics* is straightforward: we simply need to reintroduce the theme we saw in the first volume in this context, that everyone exists with the Church between the ascension and parousia of Christ. We can then say that while we might expect to see the fullest expression of Christian love among those who know themselves to be called into fellowship by Jesus Christ, the Good Samaritan makes clear that we will both find others loving as Christians are called to do, and be called ourselves to love the stranger wounded at the side of the road. The latter part of this interpretation is not contrary to Barth's account here: he does not want Christians to avoid love for the stranger. Barth states that Christians 'must be ready and on the way to love for all', and notes that it is love between Christians that is his theme here. However, his stress on the importance of a common history with the neighbour makes his account ambiguous without the additional interpretation I have outlined.[65]

In concluding as to the relationship between Barth's treatments of love in *Romans* II and the *Dogmatics*, we must strike two notes. The first, and predominant, is that the dialectical elements in the account of love in the *Dogmatics* place it in strong continuity with *Romans* II. Barth's discussion of God's love is characterized throughout by its fundamental dialectical structure, a dialectical model of two contemporaneous existences best explains the relationship between the two love commandments, and it is the dialectical '*simul iustus, simul peccator*' that makes sense of the relationship between eros and agape in the life of the Christian. In two of these cases, we have seen that in the *Dogmatics* Barth is more consistent with the dialectical structure of *Romans* II than he was in *Romans* II itself: in the relationship

---

64   *CD* IV/2, 806 (914).

65   *CD* IV/2, 809 (917). Outka identifies a different ambiguity regarding Barth's treatment of agape in IV/2, and suggests that the most probable reading is that Barth has attached two meanings to the same word: a love for the neighbour independent of her attractiveness, and a particular mutuality within the Christian community (Outka, *Agape*, 213–14). My reading of Barth in this section is that even the neighbour love independent of attractiveness is only to be directed towards those with whom we find ourselves in salvation history, and that among this community, such love should be mutual and reciprocal. Barth intends Christian love to incorporate both aspects.

between the love commandments he moves from a simple unity to an appreciation of their distinct but interrelated character; and in the relationship between eros and agape, he moves from a simple opposition to a recognition of their simultaneity as well as their exclusiveness. There is also a second note, however, softer than the first but discordant with it. With the exceptions I have noted, Barth moves from an emphasis on the dialectical relationship between fellowship and otherness in *Romans* II, to a stipulation of sameness as the criterion of love for the neighbour in the *Dogmatics*. This would tend to support the interpretation I have been arguing against, that the *Dogmatics* escapes from the negatively weighted dialectic of *Romans* II. My survey shows, however, that this is a note of discord, rather than the keynote of Barth's discussion here. The dominant tone in Barth's account of love in the *Dogmatics* is in harmony with the earlier work, and therefore provides a further evidence that Barth's ethical thought in the *Dogmatics* retains the unresolved dialectical structuring of *Romans* II.

CHAPTER 7

War, Peace, and Revolution
in the *Dogmatics*

In the preceding chapters I have demonstrated strong continuities in Barth's ethical thought between *Romans* II and the *Dogmatics* in relation to his metaethics and his treatment of the themes of love and community. My third and final point of comparison is the second set of ethical themes in *Romans* II that I identified in Chapter 2: war, peace, and revolution.

War and Peace

In *Romans* II, Barth described war ironically as natural and understandable: our fellow human beings clearly have no right to peace because they are 'unattractive, crotchety, impenitent' and they irritate us.[1] This natural activity, then, is the natural activity of men making themselves God. Yet God is the boundary of human possibility, so the possibility that we will have to fight cannot be ruled out entirely. Even in the exceptional case, we cannot fight in good conscience, because there is no such thing as a good conscience in any circumstances. The Church must keep itself free from militarism, 'but it will also with a friendly gesture rebuff the attentions of pacifism'.[2] In the *Dogmatics*, Barth treats pacifism and warfare in volume III/4. He completed it in 1951, 29 years after the publication of the second edition of *Romans* II. This period of European history gave Barth ample opportunity both to reflect on the proper attitude of the Church to war, and to act on the result of his convictions. He vigorously supported the war against Hitler, and wrote to Christians in England, France, the United States, and elsewhere to urge them to do so.[3] Following the experience of the Second World War Barth's position in the *Dogmatics* has shifted from that of *Romans* II. The framework remains the same: the Church must not finally ally itself either with the militarists or the pacifists. Yet Barth has moved closer to

---

1 *Romans* II, 469 (494).
2 *Romans* II, 471 (496).
3 Barth's wartime letters are available in Karl Barth, *Eine Schweitzer Stimme, 1938–1945* (Zurich: Evangelischer Verlag, 1945), and Will Herberg provides a short survey of a few of the letters in 'The Social Philosophy of Karl Barth', in *Community, State, and Church: Three Essays*, ed. Karl Barth (New York: Anchor, 1968), 11–67. Yoder includes a critique of Herberg's essay in John H. Yoder, *Karl Barth and the Problem of War* (Nashville: Abingdon Press, 1970), 119–31.

pacifism: the pacifist position 'has almost infinite arguments in its favour and is almost overpoweringly strong'.[4]

John Howard Yoder has identified an important difficulty with Barth's treatment of warfare in the *Dogmatics*, which we cannot avoid considering in order to compare it with the discussion in *Romans* II. For while Barth moves closer to embracing pacifism in the *Dogmatics*, he is also more explicit about the circumstances in which the Church may hear God's command to fight. To find a way through the problems Yoder identifies, we will have to attend in this section to some interpretative issues that are internal to Barth's account of war in the *Dogmatics*.

Barth treats the issue of warfare under the heading of 'The Protection of Life', which he describes as the elucidation of the commandment 'Thou shalt not kill'. All human life belongs to God, so respect and protection is demanded for it. The commandment to protect it, however, has its horizon in the will of God the Creator, so the protection of life is limited and not absolute. To think otherwise would be to treat human life as 'a kind of second God'.[5] Barth notes that the main theme of the section on the protection of life is the exceptional case (*Grenzfall*) where 'the Lord of life may further its protection even in the strange form of its conclusion and termination'.[6] He discusses the possibility of this *Grenzfall* in relation to suicide, abortion, euthanasia, killing in self-defence, capital punishment, and tyrannicide before turning to a consideration of killing in warfare.

Barth's first words on warfare call for an unflinching realism about the nature of modern national conflict. He identifies three illusions that we can no longer entertain. First, there are no longer uncommitted spectators in a nation at war. All members of a nation are now military personnel and therefore belligerents, directly or indirectly: no longer is war fought by small armies from the 'military classes'.[7] Second, it is

---

4   *CD* III/4, 455 (520).
5   *CD* III/4, 398 (453).
6   *CD* III/4, 398 (454).
7   It would be fruitful to examine how relevant the three illusions Barth identifies here remain in the context of the developments in warfare since the Second World War. In relation to the first illusion, that there is a meaningful category of noncombatants, the evidence is mixed. Contemporary military techniques reduce the need for large-scale conscription, so there has been a movement back to smaller professional armies, but the recent increase in smaller-scale civil wars, such as those in the former USSR, the former Yugoslavia, Rwanda, and Liberia have made combatants of significant proportions of the population. The military-industrial complex continues to require the daily involvement of many citizens in preparations for wars by their own nation, or by others via the lucrative trade in armaments. In addition, the sizeable proportion of tax revenues devoted to military spending by most governments involves virtually all members of society in war preparations at a different level. Barth's observations here remain relevant, then, though we should note the problems in both justifying war and weakening the limitations on its practice, such as this distinction between combatants and noncombatants. For a reassessment of the trajectory of Barth's thought in the context of nuclear weapons, see Rowan Williams, 'Barth, War and the State', in *Reckoning with Barth: Essays in Commemoration of the Centenary of Karl Barth's Birth*, ed. Nigel Biggar (London: Mowbray, 1988), 170–90.

now clear that the issue in modern warfare is economic power: 'the struggle for coal, potash, ore, oil and rubber, for markets and communications, for more stable frontiers and spheres of influence as bases from which to deploy power for the acquisition of more power'. In the past, it was easier to believe that wars were fought for more noble motives, such as honour, justice, freedom, and other supreme values, but it is now difficult to believe this sincerely. The armaments industry, with its close links to science and industry, 'imperiously demands that war should break out from time to time to use up existing stocks and create the demand for new ones'. Barth amends the Roman proverb 'if you want peace, prepare for war' to 'if you do not want war, prepare for peace', but claims that the way in which we are possessed by economic power means that neither of these is applicable. We want a form of war even in peacetime, so our mobilization for war, and the outbreak of war, are 'inevitable'.[8] The third illusion Barth identifies is that war requires anything other than 'quite nakedly and brutally the killing of as many as possible of the men who make up the opposing forces'.[9] Previously, it was easier to focus on the skill, courage, and readiness for self-sacrifice that war demanded of the individual, and to believe that the individual confronted by an individual enemy was in an unavoidable position of self-defence.

> To-day, however, the increasing scientific objectivity of military killing, the development, appalling effectiveness and dreadful nature of the methods, instruments and machines employed, and the extension of the conflict to the civilian population, have made it quite clear that war does in fact mean no more and no less than killing, with neither glory, dignity nor chivalry, with neither restraint nor consideration in any respect ... Much is already gained if only we do at last soberly admit that, whatever may be the purpose or possible justice of a war, it now means that, without disguise or shame, not only individuals or even armies, but whole nations are out to destroy one another by every possible means. It only needed the atom and hydrogen bomb to complete the self-disclosure of war in this regard.[10]

Following this blunt assessment of contemporary warfare, Barth observes that the *Grenzfall* in relation to warfare must be stated with even stricter reserve than in the other cases of killing he considered previously. This is so for three reasons: first, war involves a whole nation in killing, making everyone responsible for whether this is commanded killing or forbidden murder; second, it involves killing those who are

---

8   *CD* III/4, 451–2 (516–17). The issue of the real motives for waging war obviously continues to be relevant, as exemplified by the debate in relation to the recent wars of the US and UK against Iraq.

9   *CD* III/4, 452 (518).

10   *CD* III/4, 453 (518–19). Recent charges of genocide in Rwanda, the former Yugoslavia, and the Sudan, make clear the continuing relevance of Barth's concept of total war here. In relation to the war in Kosovo, total war seems applicable in different ways to the activity of both sides: the displacement, rape, and murder of Kosovars by the Serbs, and the crippling of the economy of Serbia by NATO, with the inevitable Kosovar and Serbian civilian casualties. On NATO's side, this is in spite of rhetoric that champions discrimination in choice of targets.

only enemies in the sense that they are fighting for their country; and third, war demands almost everything that God has forbidden be done by millions on a broad scale: 'To kill effectively, and in connexion therewith, must not those who wage war steal, rob, commit arson, lie, deceive, slander, and unfortunately to a large extent fornicate, not to speak of the almost inevitable repression of all the finer and weightier forms of obedience?'[11] All affirmative answers to the question of whether war can be commanded by God 'are wrong if they do not start with the assumption that the inflexible negative of pacifism has almost infinite arguments in its favour and is almost overpoweringly strong'.[12] Barth agrees with those who lament the Church's change of political theology after Constantine: 'in a kind of panic at all costs to give the emperor or other ruler his due there has been a complete surrender of the wholesome detachment from this imperial or national undertaking which the early Church had been able in its own way and for good reasons to maintain.'[13] For Barth the mistake here is in eschatology: the Church's justification of war is an indication that 'the realities and laws of this passing aeon … have come to be rated more highly than the passing of this world and the coming of the Lord. The criterion has thus been lost without the application of which there can be no controlling Christian will and action within this passing aeon'. We have lost a sense of the 'unheard-of and extraordinary' idea of killing for the state: the primary task of Christian ethics in this context is 'to recover and manifest a distinctive horror of war and aloofness from it'.[14]

The exercise of power is an *opus alienum* for the state, Barth claims: the state possesses power and is able to exercise it, but Christian ethics must always challenge the state with the question of whether the exercise of power is necessary. The normal task of the state is 'to fashion peace in such a way that life is served and war kept at bay':[15] it is when a state does not pursue this normal task that it is compelled to take up the abnormal task of war. It 'requires no great faith, insight nor courage' to condemn war absolutely, or to 'howl with the wolves that unfortunately war belongs no less to the present world order, historical life and the nature of the state than does peace'.

> What does require Christian faith, insight and courage – and the Christian Church and Christian ethics are there to show them – is to tell nations and governments that peace is the real emergency to which all our time, powers and ability must be devoted from the very outset in order that men may live and live properly, so that no refuge need be sought in war, nor need there be expected in it what peace has denied. Pacifists and militarists are usually agreed in the fact that for them the fashioning of peace as the fashioning of the state for democracy, and

---

11   *CD* III/4, 454 (519–20).
12   *CD* III/4, 455 (520).
13   *CD* III/4, 456 (521).
14   *CD* III/4, 456 (521–2).
15   *CD* III/4, 456 (524).

of democracy for social democracy, is a secondary concern as compared with rearmament or disarmament. It is for this reason that Christian ethics must be opposed to both.[16]

Pacifists and militarists share an obsession with armament levels that the Church must forswear, focusing its attention instead on building institutions capable of sustaining peace. Barth suggests that 'the cogent element of truth in the pacifist position' will benefit if it is not presented as the total truth 'but is deliberately qualified, perhaps at the expense of logical consistency'. The consistency of theological ethics 'may for once differ from that of logic'.[17]

After this description of the horror of war, and the Church's responsibility for building peace, Barth moves on to characterize briefly the *Grenzfall* in which war may be commanded by God. The first criterion he provides to identify this possibility is that the existence or autonomy of a state must be attacked, so that a nation finds itself forced to choose to surrender or assert itself. Barth then asks why this possibility should be allowed, and responds 'that there may well be bound up with the independent life of a nation the responsibility for the whole physical, intellectual and spiritual life of the people comprising it, and therefore their relationship to God'. He continues:

> It may well be that they are forbidden by God to renounce the independent status of their nation, and that they must therefore defend it without considering either their own lives or the lives of those who threaten it. Christian ethics cannot possibly deny that this case may sometimes occur. The divine command itself posits and presents it as a case of extreme urgency.
> I may remark in passing that I myself should see it as such a case if there were any attack on the independence, neutrality and territorial integrity of the Swiss Confederation, and I should speak and act accordingly.[18]

Barth makes three further brief points about this exceptional case in the three pages he devotes to it. First, he suggests that a nation may be called to go to war to help a weaker neighbour, as well as if its own existence is threatened. Second, he recognizes that, if a state is to be ready to go to war in these cases, it must prepare itself to do so even in peacetime, and arm itself accordingly. Third, Barth claims that the 'distinctively Christian note in the acceptance of this demand is that it is quite unconditional. That is to say, it is independent of the success or failure of the enterprise, and therefore of the strength of one's own forces in comparison with those of the enemy.' If war 'is ventured in obedience and therefore with a good conscience, it is also ventured in faith and therefore with joyous and reckless determination'.[19]

---

16   *CD* III/4, 459 (525–6).
17   *CD* III/4, 461 (527).
18   *CD* III/4, 462 (528–9).
19   *CD* III/4, 463 (530). The contrast between Barth's account and Just War Theory is at its greatest at this point: Barth sets aside the criteria of proportionality and likelihood of success.

Barth's final word on the subject of war in this volume is in relation to conscientious objection: he supports conscientious objection so long as it is in relation to particular wars, rather than to warfare in general, and calls on the Church to guide individuals in these decisions, which may require the Church to counsel individuals not to fight for the state.[20]

John H. Yoder has provided the most extensive and careful criticism of Barth's treatment of war in the *Dogmatics*. His contention is that Barth's use of the category of *Grenzfall* is mistaken, and the mistake is particularly evident in the 'non-Barthian' way Barth uses extra-biblical categories to resolve the question of whether war could be commanded by God. Yoder questions the need for the attention Barth gives to exceptional cases in ethics: 'Why should it not be possible for a general statement in Christian ethics to have the same validity as a general statement within some other realm of Christian dogmatics?'[21] The concept of the *Grenzfall* means Barth expects exceptions in advance; the *Grenzfall* 'does not emerge unpredicted at a point where concrete problems turn out on inspection to be otherwise insoluble; the concrete cases are, rather, found to fit the place prepared for them by the systematic exposition'.[22] Barth is wrong that pacifists are less free to obey God: 'the pacifist who in his ethics claims to be bound to the general line of God's revelation without being able or authorized to predict exceptions is no less free for obedience than the theologian who in dogmatics is also bound to the general line of God's revelation in an affirmation about the nature of Christ or about the essence of the Church'.[23] Yoder asserts that if human finitude means it is impossible to affirm with complete certainty that God has always forbidden all killing, it must be even less possible to affirm that there are places where God will affirm killing.[24] This leads him to conclude that

> the *Grenzfall* is not a formal concept with validity in the discipline of ethics. It is simply the label which Barth has seen fit to attach to the fact that, in some situations, he considers himself obliged to make a choice which runs against what all the formal concepts of his own ethics would seem to require. Barth has not constructed in the *Grenzfall* a reliable method of theological ethics in which it would be possible to found either logically or with relation to the revelation of God in Christ the advocacy of certain deviant ways of acting, such as killing when killing is otherwise forbidden. He has simply found a name for the fact that in certain contexts he is convinced of the necessity of not acting according to the way God seems to have spoken in Christ.[25]

Yoder substantiates this charge in his consideration of Barth's delimitation of the exceptional case of warfare commanded by God. Barth's claim that a nation may be

20   *CD* III/4, 464–9 (531–9).
21   Yoder, *Karl Barth*, 61.
22   Ibid., 65.
23   Ibid., 62.
24   Ibid., 72–3.
25   Ibid., 73.

commanded to fight to ensure its survival is very surprising to Yoder. It reintroduces the idea of a *Volk*, with an independent moral value and a special relationship to God which Barth rejected strongly earlier in the *Dogmatics*.[26] Yoder also argues that the consequences of admitting the possibility of warfare are disproportionate to its status as an exceptional case. In particular, 'to say that the state should be constantly prepared for war is like saying that an honest man should always be prepared for lying or a faithful husband for divorce; it confuses an extreme eventuality with normality, thus demonstrating the inadequacy of the *Grenzfall* as a tool for straight thinking'.[27] Respect for life itself, Yoder argues, is a philosophical abstraction from the biblical texts, which Barth then uses to justify the destruction of life.[28]

Yoder's conclusion is that 'between Barth and an integral Christian pacifism the only differences lie at points where Barth did not finish working out the implications of his originality'.[29] Two pieces of evidence support Yoder's view. First, in volume IV/2 of the *Dogmatics*, Barth briefly revisits the topic of the use of force in his consideration of Jesus' directions to his disciples. Here he observes that Jesus attests to the kingdom of God 'as the end of the fixed idea of the necessity and beneficial value of force'. The kingdom 'invalidates the whole friend–foe relationship' in its call for love of the enemy. There can be no question of a general rule here, but

> for the one whom Jesus, in His call to discipleship, places under this particular command and prohibition, there is a concrete and incontestable direction which has to be carried out exactly as given. In conformity with the New Testament one cannot be pacifist in principle, only practically. But let everyone give heed whether, being called to discipleship, it is either possible for him to avoid, or permissible for him to neglect becoming practically pacifist![30]

The second piece of evidence that Barth's treatment of warfare in III/4 might not have represented his definitive view is from a comment Barth made in 1962 concerning it:

> Of course that was all written in 1951 … I cannot yet completely reject it even now. Nevertheless I would say, that it is perhaps not one of the most felicitous passages in the Kirchliche Dogmatik … I first spoke 99 per cent against war and the military. I hope this impressed you!

---

26 Ibid., 80. Barth wrote: 'In this connexion we must consider one of the most curious and tragic events in the whole history of Protestant theology. It took place in Germany in the years between the two world wars. I refer to the novel elevation on a wide front, if with varying emphases, of the term "people" to the front rank of theological and ethical concepts, and the underlying assertion and teaching that in the national determination of man we have an order of creation no less than in the relationship of man and woman and parents and children' (*CD* III/4, 305 (345)).

27 Yoder, *Karl Barth*, 107.

28 Ibid., 112.

29 Ibid., 118.

30 *CD* IV/2, 530 (622), incorporating Yoder's revised translation (Yoder, *Karl Barth*, 116–17).

In the same interview, he condemned the mischievous use of the text by some German politicians to prove the possibility of a modern just war.[31]

There are two aspects to Yoder's criticism of Barth here: first, a general criticism of the structure of Barth's ethics, centred on the concept of *Grenzfall*, and, second, a specific criticism of Barth's discussion of warfare. I agree with the specific criticism, but dispute the general one. A general defence of Barth's ethical methodology will have to wait for the next chapter, but it is immediately clear that Barth's use of the *Grenzfall* here is different from the way he uses it in discussing other cases of the protection of life. In each of the accounts of suicide, abortion, euthanasia, killing in self-defence, capital punishment, and tyrannicide, Barth emphasizes the reasons why the command of God will almost always require the protection of life, but he finally allows the possibility of rare exceptions. The openness to these borderline cases does not threaten the line of argument up to that point, and Barth does not call for deliberate preparation for the exceptional case. Yet in the case of war, the *Grenzfall* overturns and negates Barth's argument that in 99 per cent of cases the command of God forbids warfare.

Comparison with Barth's treatment of killing in self-defence is particularly instructive. Barth argues that self-defence is 'almost entirely excluded' by Pauline texts and the Sermon on the Mount. The latter puts the attacker in the same category as the beggar and the person who seeks a loan. Self-defence may be natural, but is forbidden to the Christian except in rare cases. Where Christians have been 'strictly disciplined', 'thoroughly disarmed', and 'clearly pointed to peace' it is then possible that they may hear the exceptional command to defend a third party or themselves.[32] If we were to follow the pattern of Barth's discussion of warfare, we would then go on to spell out the consequences of this exceptional case. If we are to be free to defend others and ourselves when we receive the *Grenzfall* command here, then we must be appropriately prepared. Training in self-defence will clearly be required, and our readiness for self-defence would be further enhanced if we ensured that we were armed at all times and regularly devoted time to training in the use of firearms. Barth does not follow this path in the case of killing in self-defence because it is so obviously counter-productive. The command of God will almost always be to refrain from self-defence, so the preparation we require is to learn how to keep ourselves from following our instincts to strike back and how to resolve conflicts peacefully. Spending time in self-defence training and always carrying a firearm to be ready for the exceptional case where a forceful response is commanded by God would make it difficult or impossible to retain a commitment to not resisting one's attacker. Careful preparation for the exceptional case threatens to make it unexceptional.

---

31 Cited by Yoder, *Karl Barth*, 117 n. Incidentally, Yoder claims on this page that III/4 makes no reference to atomic weapons. This is incorrect (see *CD* III/4, 453 (519)), although Barth acknowledges in the *Stimme* interview that he could have made more of this to suggest that atomic weapons were incompatible with just warfare.

32 *CD* III/4, 427–37 (488–99).

This example is unfortunately not the caricature it seems to be. Barth's treatment of the *Grenzfall* case in discussing warfare is exactly analogous to training and carrying weapons for personal self-defence. He rejects retaining standing armies as a national policy, but requires preparation for war in peacetime if a country has decided only to go to war when commanded by God in an emergency.[33] This is in spite of Barth's earlier harsh criticism of national preparations for war in peacetime and its connection with the military-industrial complex, and his statement that the task of the Christian Church and Christian ethics 'is to tell nations and governments that peace is the real emergency to which all our time, powers and ability must be devoted from the very outset'.[34] We cannot devote all our powers to the emergency of peace, and at the same time devote some of our powers to making sure we are in a position to win a war if peace fails. The great economic and human resources such preparations for war demand is one of the most powerful arguments in favour of a national policy of pacifism. According to Barth's discussion, the exceptional case in which we are called to war implies an exceptionless norm that requires us to expend substantial resources on war preparations. Yoder's comparison with an honest person preparing to lie, or a faithful spouse for divorce – or, better, infidelity – is precisely to the point. Barth's treatment of the exceptional case here overturns and renders irrelevant the 99 per cent he intended to speak against war and the military. His recommendation of routine preparation for war means that Barth cannot support his contention that war is an *opus alienum* of the state: it has clearly become the *opus proprium* he rejected.

One way of resolving these difficulties in Barth's account of war would be to work back from this de facto acceptance of war preparations and weaken his earlier commitment to the insights of pacifism and the importance of preparations for peace. This option would clearly be against the major line of argument of this passage. Only 3 of the 20 pages on war in the English translation of III/4 are devoted to explicating the exceptional case: the other 17 emphasize the horror of war, the importance of building institutions for peace, and the role of conscientious objection. The recommendation of practical pacifism in IV/2 and the interview Yoder cites from *Stimme* provide further evidence against this line of interpretation. A second alternative in interpreting Barth here is that offered by Yoder: reject the concept of *Grenzfall* and embrace the absolute ethical demand of pacifism. This option is counter to Barth's deepest metaethical commitments. All ethical absolutism is idolatrous, according to Barth: Christians must be obediently open to whatever God's command may require of them.

The difficulty I have identified with Barth's account of war in the *Dogmatics* is not with his treatment of pacifism, or the structure of his metaethics, but with his treatment of the exceptional case in relation to warfare. A more promising interpretation of Barth's thought here addresses this issue directly. Barth must allow

---

33   Switzerland required and still requires national service of all its male citizens, with regular firearms training throughout adult life.

34   *CD* III/4, 459 (525).

the possibility of the use of force in response to God's command; he need not treat this possible scenario as he does. Returning to the example of self-defence, we have seen that Barth allows that self-defence may be commanded in the *Grenzfall* case, but he does not recommend preparations for this eventuality. In the context of warfare, Barth stipulates that the exception is harder to justify because of the scale of the evil war creates, which means that preparations in this case would be for a possibility even rarer than self-defence. If we add to this that Barth considers that in peacetime we must devote all our energy to peacemaking, and that preparation for war demands substantial human and economic resources, we have a persuasive case that Christians cannot support preparations for the exceptional case in which they may be called upon to go to war: they are too busy with the emergency of peace to prepare for the distant and unlikely prospect of war, and know that war preparations are incompatible with serious attempts to build a peaceful order. This means there is no mandate to prepare for war. There remains the almost unthinkable possibility that God will call Christians to engage in large-scale killing of their fellows, but this *Grenzfall* case no longer transforms the rest of the existence of the Christian. It is true that a nation governed on this basis will be less likely to succeed in war if it is ever called upon to fight, but the Christian vocation is to peacemaking, not to amassing state-of-the-art tools for mass killing and destruction, and consigning a significant section of society to full-time training in using these weapons without qualms. This interpretation of Barth's treatment of war in the *Dogmatics* results in a consistent account in which his view of the nature of modern warfare and the insights of pacifism are respected, and the *Grenzfall* case is restored to its position at the extreme border, rather than the centre, of his thought. The interpretation is in accordance with his suggestion of a position of 'practical pacifism' in IV/2, and with the evidence from the *Stimme* interview that he intended to write 99 per cent against war and the military. It also facilitates the task Barth assigns to Christian ethics here: 'to recover and manifest a distinctive horror of war and aloofness from it'.[35]

Revolution

In Chapter 2, I showed that Barth considered the revolution of God to be one of the central messages of Romans. This revolution is the true dissolution of state, church, law, and society, and relativizes human attempts at reaction or revolution. Revolutionaries are right in their critiques of secular government, but being closer to the truth makes them more dangerous than the forces of legitimism. Human revolution is understandable, just as conflict with one's enemies is, but it cannot avoid being overcome with evil, and the revolutionary emulates the state in usurping God's authority. Barth's treatment of revolution in the second edition of *Romans* II, then,

---

35   *CD* III/4, 456 (521–2).

is characteristic of the work as a whole: human action is destabilized by reference to the action of God. This is not a rejection of the need for action, but a dialectical affirmation of its importance, qualified by a recognition of its limited human status. Barth's account of revolution in the *Dogmatics* is entirely consistent with that of *Romans* II and retains its dialectical character. I will demonstrate this by showing that Barth is committed in the *Dogmatics* to three key assertions: that God's action is revolutionary, that God's revolution relativizes the importance of human reaction and revolution, and that the church is nonetheless called to a revolutionary witness that includes political activism.

There is no shortage of evidence that Barth considers revolution to be a characteristic of God's activity in the *Dogmatics*, particularly in volume IV. It is God as Creator that Barth first characterizes as revolutionary, however: the absolute newness of the new life brought by Jesus Christ shows that the Creator is in Him, since 'a mere creature cannot be so revolutionary in relation to another'.[36] In relation to judgement, Barth observes that if we do not recognize judgement as total, we 'are not dealing with the revolution of God … which is our current concern'.[37] In characterizing the work of Christ under the heading of 'The Royal Man', Barth argues that the conformity of Jesus with God 'consists actively in what we can only call the pronouncedly revolutionary character of His relationship to the orders of life and value current in the world around Him'.[38] The freedom of God in Jesus Christ made Him 'a revolutionary far more radical than any that came either before or after Him'.[39] Jesus deals with all the orders of life and value by breaking all bonds asunder in a way 'all the more revolutionary' than addressing them in principle or in the execution of a programme.[40] He accomplished a revolution in the juridical and political sphere, and must be seen 'as the poor man who if He blessed and befriended any blessed and befriended the poor and not the rich, the incomparable revolutionary who laid the axe at the root of the trees'.[41] The word and work of Jesus were a matter of 'the one great revolution' in which everything was at stake.[42]

Later in IV/2 Barth maintains that in His death Jesus Christ proved His likeness to the God 'who is so unassuming in the world but so revolutionary in relation to it'.[43] The existence of Jesus proclaims and accomplishes the revolution of God, which breaks ties with possessions, worldly honour, family, and religion where little human revolutions cannot even limit them.[44] In IV/3 Barth asserts that 'all intellectual, moral, artistic, social or political revolutions, all wars and world wars' are but 'limited,

---

36 *CD* III/1, 32 (34).
37 *CD* IV/1, 546 (609).
38 *CD* IV/2, 172 (191).
39 *CD* IV/2, 172 (192).
40 *CD* IV/2, 173 (193).
41 *CD* IV/2, 178–9 (199–200).
42 *CD* IV/2, 261 (289).
43 *CD* IV/2, 291 (323).
44 *CD* IV/2, 543–4 (614–15).

particular and passing domestic squabblings compared with the revolution and conflict' accomplished in Christ.[45] Barth describes both encounter with Jesus Christ, and God's love as revolutionary,[46] and the Christian as the one who points to the 'revolutionary alteration of the whole reality of the world' in Christ.[47] Finally, in the IV/4 fragment, Barth states that the grace of God 'comes with revolutionary force into the life' of every person.[48] Clearly, the action of God remains revolutionary for Barth in the *Dogmatics*.

Human revolutions, however, are still for the most part viewed negatively or equivocally. Barth states that all the sorts of evolutions and revolutions in the Church are signs of decay.[49] Revolution is one of the human afflictions the meaning of which 'is revealed in its true frightfulness only on Good Friday'.[50] A framework of parental judgements prevent a child becoming 'an unbalanced young revolutionary';[51] a lust for superabundance gives rise to 'revolutions of empty and inordinate desires'.[52] Volume IV provides the most material for this perspective on revolution, as it did for the first. Evil is 'the nihilist revolution which can only result in the annihilation of all creatures'.[53] God's judgement shows the true nature of human 'crises and catastrophes and revolutions and their relative and limited killing and making alive, with their relative and limited certainty'.[54] Barth frequently treats reaction and revolution as fundamentally alike. They 'have always drawn their nourishment from the same source, the one in fear, the other in desire, and both in godlessness'.[55] Christian ethics has always wavered 'between the attractions of conservatism and those of revolution (or perhaps only Bohemianism)'.[56] Stupidity loves to make itself out to be 'either the pillar of society or the sacred force of revolutionary renewal'.[57] Christians cannot count on the support of revolutionaries, because they will never give their complete allegiance to self-evident things, but will not command their complete negation.[58] The people of God 'can yield neither to reactionary spasms on the one hand nor to revolutionary on the other, because in relation to the reality of history already present in Jesus Christ it knows how provisional and improper is all the construction and destruction of man'.[59] Barth remains committed in the

---

45   *CD* IV/3.1, 242 (277–8).
46   *CD* IV/3.1, 441 (508), 444 (511).
47   *CD* IV/3.2, 511 (712–13).
48   *CD* IV/4, 21 (22–3).
49   *CD* I/2, 584 (650).
50   *CD* II/2, 395 (444).
51   *CD* III/4, 254 (284).
52   *CD* III/4, 538 (617).
53   *CD* IV/1, 411 (456).
54   *CD* IV/1, 562 (627).
55   *CD* II/1, 468 (526).
56   *CD* IV/1, 690 (771).
57   *CD* IV/2, 414 (466).
58   *CD* IV/2, 610 (691).
59   *CD* IV/3.2, 717 (821).

Dogmatics, then, to the view that God's revolution puts all human reaction and revolution in question.

This ambivalence between reaction and revolution seems to make action or inaction equally problematic. Barth gives a compelling description of such an existence:

> Life involves an unceasing dialectic, in which [the Christian] is pushed and rocked backwards and forwards by an alien, irresistible movement, being caught up in a constant change and alteration, in sheer ambiguities, in a relativity and convertibility of all antitheses, which make pointless any will to abide, indeed, any will at all and therefore any consistent action ... Can we seriously try to be conservative or progressive? Reaction always provokes revolution and revolution reaction. In this antithesis, and all the other alternatives, is there a wise mean, a neutral abstention from choice? Yes, but only at the cost of surrendering activity to inactivity, in which everything perhaps calls for even more clear and active decision. Only at the cost perhaps of declining responsibility in the most important questions and thus becoming even more useless than the most useless demagogues and zealots on the right hand and the left. Is not all contending for the rights and freedom of the individual burdened by the fact that it does violence to fellowship, and all contending for fellowship by the fact that it does violence to the rights and freedom of the individual? Is there any faithfulness on the one side without the reverse of open or secret unfaithfulness on the other?[60]

This state is dire indeed, but its direness is unsurprising, since it is part of Barth's depiction of the false situation of the Christian under the threat of damnation. We may be sure that he does not intend his dialectical account of revolution to result in this indeterminism and resultant despair for the redeemed children of God. We find, in fact, that he is prepared to recommend two types of revolutionary activity to the Church, in its witness to Christ, and in its political engagement.

The confession that Jesus is the one Lord has revolutionary force,[61] and '[n]o sentence is more dangerous or revolutionary than that God is One and there is no other like Him'.[62] The message of the Church secretly revolutionizes the world around it,[63] and is revolutionary enough for it to be menaced from without.[64] Barth argues that Jesus 'has founded and established in the existence of His community an element of provisional peace and order', but notes that even as conservative a saying as Titus 2:12, that we should live sober, righteous and godly lives 'continues in very revolutionary fashion' with reference to the passing of the world and the coming of the Lord.[65] The revolutionary activity of the Church is not restricted to its witness to the word of Christ. Barth criticizes the Church for doing nothing to counter the rise

---

60 *CD* IV/3.1, 471–2 (543).
61 *CD* IV/3.1, 88 (98).
62 *CD* II/1, 444 (500).
63 *CD* IV/3.2, 852 (977).
64 *CD* IV/2, 662 (749).
65 *CD* III/4, 263 (295).

of historical materialism, noting that it has always stood on the side of the 'ruling classes'.[66] In his treatment of warfare, Barth states that the conscientious objector 'must act honestly and consistently as a revolutionary, prepared to pay the price of his action' and that the Church must be prepared to face threats or suffering for its 'revolutionary loyalty' when it advises individuals not to fight in a national conflict.[67] In political life, the witness of the Church will sometimes have to be surprisingly conservative, but at other times 'extremely revolutionary'.[68] More definitely,

> it has to be said that the command of God, to the extent that it can and will be heard, is self-evidently and in all circumstances a call for counter-movements on behalf of humanity and against its denial in any form, and therefore a call for the championing of the weak against every kind of encroachment on the part of the strong.[69]

The Church cannot escape part of the responsibility for the development of modern capitalism, and must always 'keep to the "left" in opposition to its champions, i.e., to confess that it is fundamentally on the side of the victims of this disorder and to espouse their cause'.[70] Barth affirms this engagement while acknowledging at the same time that 'the relativity of even the most radical attempt at reform in the guise of "revolution" simply proves again that whatever can be done by men or said by Christians in the direction of such attempts can have only relative significance and force'.[71] The Church must continue to act politically, then, even while acknowledging the limited significance of its activity.

Barth's treatment of the themes of war, peace, and revolution in the *Dogmatics* is a third substantial piece of evidence that there is strong continuity between the ethical thought of *Romans* II and the *Dogmatics*, adding to the results of the previous chapters documenting the congruity of the two works in relation to the role of ethics and to the theme of love and community. It is clear that in the *Dogmatics* Barth intends to steer the path of opposition to both militarism and absolutist pacifism that he navigated in *Romans* II. He is closer to pacifism in the *Dogmatics* than *Romans* II, but he is not able to rule out the possibility that Christians may have to fight. While revolution does not play the same prominent role in the *Dogmatics* that it did in *Romans* II, I have shown that Barth remains committed to three central theses: the revolutionary nature of God's activity, the relativizing impact this has on human reaction and revolution, and the call to the Church to revolutionary witness including

---

66   *CD* III/2, 389–90 (467).
67   *CD* III/4, 468–9 (536–8).
68   *CD* III/4, 511 (586).
69   *CD* III/4, 544 (624).
70   *CD* III/4, 544 (624–5).
71   *CD* III/4, 544–5 (625).

political action. In relation to both these topics, the dialectical shape of Barth's ethical thought in the *Dogmatics* is apparent once again: we must be committed to peace, yet not give our final allegiance to pacifism; we must be committed to political action, yet recognize that in relation to God's revolutionary power all human reaction and revolution is put in question.

III
RE-READING BARTH'S ETHICS

CHAPTER 8

Interpreting Barth's Ethics

The preceding chapters have shown that there is strong continuity in Barth's thought between the second edition of *Romans* II and the *Church Dogmatics*, a continuity most evident in the importance of dialectic in the structure of each. Part I mined the ethical seams of the 1922 *Romans* II for its metaethics and its treatment of ethical themes, and Part II surveyed Barth's use of dialectic between the two works, before comparing the results of the *Romans* II excavation with those of corresponding locations in the *Dogmatics*. In this chapter, I summarize the results of this comparative work, and then draw out their implications for the interpretation of Barth's ethics. The following chapter concludes by situating the reading of Barth's ethics that emerges in the context of contemporary Christian ethics.

Reading *Romans* II Alongside the *Dogmatics*

My strategy for comparing the ethics of *Romans* II and the *Dogmatics* has been to take the three dominant elements I identified in the ethics of *Romans* II – metaethics; love and community; war, peace, and revolution – and place them beside Barth's discussion of the same issues in the *Dogmatics*. As I noted at the beginning of Chapter 5, this methodology does not result in a complete record of the differences in Barth's ethics in the two works, since I do not treat the many ethical topics Barth attends to in the *Dogmatics* that did not receive attention in *Romans* II. As the previous chapters have shown, however, the ethical content of *Romans* II is sufficiently substantive to make the comparison meaningful and fruitful: the role and character of Christian ethics is specified fully enough to compare with the metaethics of the *Dogmatics*, and the two topical themes of love and war are outlined in *Romans* II with sufficient detail to discuss them in relation to the corresponding themes in the *Dogmatics*.

In Chapter 5, I examined the metaethics of the two works. I showed first that Barth sees ethics and dogmatics in the same integral relationship in *Romans* II and the *Dogmatics*, and that he accords an important role to 'the ethical question' in both. The central metaphor of crisis in the Romans commentary seems initially to be absent in the later work, but I demonstrated that its impact, though not its name, remains important. The use of 'command' to characterize the relationship between God and the Christian is, conversely, much more widespread in the *Dogmatics*, but Barth uses the term to express ethical commitments already present in *Romans* II, and his criticism of casuistry in the *Dogmatics* echoes the call in *Romans* II to break off our thinking that it may be a thinking about God. Finally, the ethics of the *Dogmatics* retains the dialectical contours of *Romans* II, although, again, the language has changed: the tension between the 'No' and the 'Yes' of God in *Romans* II remains present in the *Dogmatics* in the tensions between our approach to the command in openness and/or with experience, the nature of the command as universal and/or particular, and the possibility and/or impossibility of knowing what God will command.

It is important not to gloss over the discontinuities in Barth's metaethics my survey has also uncovered. Reading the *Dogmatics* engenders a different experience than the assault *Romans* II makes on the reader. The desolate and cratered wastelands of Romans have given way to a more habitable environment in the *Dogmatics*. Barth's decision to use the concept of command as a unifying theme in the latter work is a significant development, even given that this choice is based on commitments already present in the former. Most importantly, perhaps, while the crisis is still evident in the *Dogmatics*, Barth also sets out the alternative possibility of claiming our place as God's covenant partners and being freed for life within the affirmation of God's 'Yes' to humankind. In *Romans* II this confidence was hinted at in Barth's glimpses beyond the realm of opposition and affirmation of 'God for us', but in such proximity to the crisis, Barth was constrained to 'break off' from the attempt to specify what this realm beyond might look like.

In Chapter 6, I took up the first of the ethical themes in *Romans* II identified in Chapter 2: Barth's treatment of love and community. Comparing Barth's treatment of the theme in *Romans* II and the *Dogmatics* made clear that here, too, there are strong continuities between the two works, especially with regard to the central role of dialectic in each. In the *Dogmatics* Barth retains his commitment in *Romans* II that Christian love originates in God, and he characterizes the relationship between human and divine agency in the same action as dialectical, following *Romans* II. The earlier text describes love in a plethora of dialectical pairs as sweet/bitter, yielding/harsh, peaceful/conflictual, forgetting/knowing, forgiving/punishing, receiving/rejecting. The *Dogmatics* extends and develops this dialectic by structuring the perfections of God in dialectical tension between love and freedom, and breaks down this loving in freedom into grace/holiness, mercy/righteousness, and patience/wisdom.

Unexpectedly, two of the discontinuities between Barth's accounts of love in *Romans* II and the *Dogmatics* are where the role of dialectic has increased in the latter. First, Barth notes in the *Dogmatics* that he may have contributed to the wrong notion that there can be no direct love of God in his earlier work, and emphasizes the importance of two distinct commandments to love God and the neighbour. He set out three alternative models for the relationship between the two love commandments in different places in the *Dogmatics*: as the two existences of the children of God before and after the parousia; as two spheres of activity oriented towards God and fellow human beings; and as two dimensions of Christian love, vertical and horizontal. The elements in these pairs coexist, so that there is an inescapable duality in the existence of the Christian, where in *Romans* II there was only the unity of love for God, expressed in worship and love of the neighbour. Second, where *Romans* II sets out an undialectical simple opposition between eros and agape, the account of the two in the *Dogmatics* is much more complex. Attending to Barth's description of conversion shows that he sees the relationship between eros and agape as a dialectical mutual exclusivity/co-existence in the life of the Christian, who is '*simul justus, simul peccator*'.

Two other discontinuities relax dialectical tensions established in *Romans* II. While Barth continues to recognize the duality of any human action as arising from both divine and human agency, he devotes more care to attempting to specify a genuine creaturely sphere in which Christians are able to respond freely to the love of God, contrary to Luther and Nygren's image of human beings as merely 'pipes' for God's love. More significantly, in the *Dogmatics* Barth moves decisively away from the claim in *Romans* II that fellowship depends on a recognition of the otherness of the other, to the repeated claim that the fellowship of the Church depends on the sameness of what the neighbour and I have in common.

Chapter 7 compared the material on war and revolution in *Romans* II with that in the *Dogmatics*. Barth's treatment of war is more extensive in the *Dogmatics*, and I argued that a serious problem with his discussion of the *Grenzfall* case must be solved before we can compare his understanding with that of *Romans* II. The solution I proposed as most persuasive avoided this problem without going against either the 99 per cent Barth said he intended to speak against war, or his wider metaethical commitments. This interpretation of Barth places him in continuity with the framework set up in *Romans* II: a powerful critique of militarism, but also a recognition that to express opposition to war in the form of absolute pacifism would be to idolize an ethical norm and place boundaries on the obedience we are willing to offer God. Within this framework my interpretation of Barth's position suggests it has shifted closer to pacifism in the *Dogmatics*, but Barth continues to insist that the Church must work for different aims than those of either militarists or pacifists. Finally, I showed that Barth is committed in both *Romans* II and the *Dogmatics* to three key theses in relation to revolution: that God's action is revolutionary, that this action relativizes the importance of human forces of reaction and revolution, and that nonetheless the Church is called to a revolutionary witness that will include political activism. The *Dogmatics* retains *Romans* II's dialectical affirmation of the importance of activism, qualified by a recognition of its limited human status.

This survey of the comparative work of Part II allows us to conclude that there is strong continuity between Barth's ethical thought in *Romans* II and the *Dogmatics*. We can note developments in Barth's ethics between the two works – most notably, the *Dogmatics* can clearly give more comprehensive and nuanced attention to ethical themes, Barth's ethics are affected by the change to a less fraught and embattled atmosphere in the *Dogmatics*, and there is a marked shift from a concept of fellowship predicated on otherness in *Romans* II, to an emphasis on community based on what is common to its members in the *Dogmatics* – yet we can pick out these developments precisely because the central commitments of Barth's metaethics, and the key points of his accounts of love, community, war, peace, and revolution, remain unchanged.

The foremost element of this commonality between *Romans* II and the *Dogmatics* is the prominence of dialectic as a structural element in both works. It is not a novel finding that dialectic is important in *Romans* II, but the significance of dialectic for the interpretation of the ethics of the *Dogmatics* has not been previously recognized.

Barth on Barth

I noted in the Introduction that one possible reason for setting aside Barth's early work was that he himself had done so in his later commentary. In the preface to the fifth edition of *Romans* in 1926, Barth worried about the success of the book, when he 'had set out to please none but the very few'. He comments on the difficulty of living with its legacy:

> In his 'Reminiscences' Admiral Tirpitz says that, whereas it is easy to hoist your flag, it is difficult to strike it honourably. I would add that it is even more difficult – at any rate when there is no question of hauling it down – to continue to fly it honourably. And this is my situation. As it becomes more and more clear how much there remained to be done after the book was written, I often wish that I had never written it.[1]

In the preface to the next edition two years later, he feels the need to say:

> were I to set to work again upon the exposition of the Epistle, and were I determined to repeat the same thing, I should certainly have to express it quite differently. I have, in the meantime, learnt that in Paul there is on the one hand a far greater variety and on the other hand a far greater monotony than I had then attributed to him. Much would therefore have to be drastically curtailed, and much expanded. Much would have to be expressed more carefully and with greater reserve; much, however, with greater clarity and more emphatically. A great deal of the scaffolding of the book was due to my own particular situation at the time and also to the general situation. This would have to be pulled down. Many threads, on the other hand, which I had not then noticed in the Epistle, would now have to be brought to light. Those who read the book must also bear in mind the quite simple fact that I am now seven years older, and that all our exercise books obviously need correcting. Moreover, since the appearance of the fifth edition, I have embarked on the publication of my *Prolegomena to Christian Dogmatics*. This means that a certain weight has been lifted from the earlier book, inasmuch as any serious criticism of it has at least to take also into consideration what is said in the second and more comprehensive book, where I have attempted a greater breadth of treatment and also greater precision.[2]

Barth's verbosity on this issue makes clear his sensitivity to criticism. He asserts that the context gave rise to much of the book's scaffolding, and that his readers

---

1   *Romans* II, 22–3 (XXXIV–XXXV).
2   *Romans* II, 25 (XXXVII).

should look to his next work – later abandoned – for a more complete statement of his views.

A third reference point for Barth's own view of *Romans* II is from an excursus at the end of *Church Dogmatics* II/1, in which he identifies weaknesses in the eschatological view of the 1922 *Romans*. After quoting from a passage in which he stressed God's promise as pertaining to the future, he comments 'Well roared, lion!' Barth maintains that there is nothing wrong with the words he used, but that they were hazardous

> because to be legitimate exposition of the Bible they needed others no less sharp and direct to compensate and therefore to substantiate their total claim. But these were lacking. If we claim to have too perfect an understanding of the Gospel, we at once lose understanding. In our exposition we cannot claim to be wholly right over against others, or we are at once in the wrong. At that time we had not sufficiently considered the pre-temporality of God which Neo-Protestants of all shades had put in such a distorted way at the centre. Hence we had not seen the biblical conception of eternity in its fullness. The result was that we could not speak about the post-temporality of God in such a way as to make it clear that we actually meant to speak of God and not of a general ideal of limit and crisis.[3]

What is particularly striking about this passage is that Barth is correcting the lack of balance between emphasis between the positive and negative elements of the dialectic of God's presence and absence. His account in *Church Dogmatics* II/1 more fully recognizes the need to do justice to both poles, and so is more consistently dialectical in shape than the original version. We should also note the danger he identifies of speaking of limit and crisis, rather than God. The crisis I have described is that of our struggle to speak about God in the face of the living Word that disturbs our speech. As I suggest in the next chapter, the reality of this crisis cannot be an excuse for not engaging in faithful seeking after God's will.

Barth's worries about how he presented his thought in *Romans* II are not grounds for setting aside the conclusion that his ethical thought retained its dialectical shape from 1922 onwards. While he came to express some concepts in different ways, we have seen that the structure of a theological ethic caught between what it must be and what it could not be remained.[4]

---

3   *CD* II/1, 635 (715–16).

4   We should also note in this context McCormack's comment in relation to Barth's review of the changes between the first and second editions of *Romans*: 'Barth was not always a reliable guide for interpreting his earlier works – particularly those which he wished his readers to leave behind' (Bruce L. McCormack, *Karl Barth's Critically Realistic Dialectical Theology: Its Genesis and Development, 1909–1936* (Oxford: Clarendon Press, 1995)), 182.

Barth's Dialectical Ethics

The discovery of this continuity between the ethical content of the 1922 *Romans* II and the *Dogmatics* is surprising because, from von Balthasar's study of Barth's theology[5] until Bruce McCormack's work of 1995,[6] it was the orthodoxy in Barth scholarship to divide his work after his break with liberalism in 1915 into two periods, the juncture between them commonly placed at Barth's 1931 book on Anselm.[7] The earlier period, including both editions of *Romans*, but also many occasional writings and Barth's lectures in Göttingen and Münster, was characterized as 'dialectical'; the Anselm book is seen as the answer Barth found that allowed him to escape from his dialectical period.[8] I have chosen a primarily systematic approach rather than von Balthasar's historical one, but my conclusion that there is substantial continuity in Barth's ethics between the second edition of *Romans* II and the *Dogmatics* clearly runs counter to the view that confines the influence of dialectic in Barth's thought to an early period, and is in line with McCormack's position. The 1922 *Romans* is a particularly good point of comparison to demonstrate the continuity between Barth's theology of the 1920s and the years of the *Church Dogmatics*, because it is taken to be the most thoroughgoing statement of Barth's supposed 'dialectical period'. If Barth's ethics in the *Dogmatics* remain dialectical in structure and similar in conclusions to those of the second edition of *Romans* II, there is no intellectual revolution to account for – at least in relation to ethics – and it is no longer possible to maintain that dialectic is not an important element in the *Dogmatics*.[9]

---

5   Hans Urs von Balthasar, *The Theology of Karl Barth: Exposition and Interpretation*, trans. Edward T. Oakes (San Francisco: Communio Books, Ignatius Press, 1992). The work first appeared in English in 1971.

6   McCormack, *Karl Barth's Theology*.

7   Karl Barth, *Anselm: Fides Quaerens Intellectum: Anselm's Proof of the Existence of God in the Context of His Theological Scheme*, trans. Ian W. Robertson (London: SCM Press, 1960) (Karl Barth, *Fides Quaerens Intellectum: Anselms Beweis der Existenz Gottes im Zusammenhang Seines Theologischen Programms*, ed. Eberhard Jüngel and Ingolf Ulrich Dalferth (Zurich: Theologischer Verlag, 1981)).

8   In addition to von Balthasar, Hans Frei and T.F. Torrance also opted for this reading of Barth's theological development. See McCormack, *Karl Barth's Theology*, 1–28, for a survey.

9   In his detailed historical treatment of the developments in Barth's thought until 1936, Bruce McCormack argues that the von Balthasar thesis is misleading and has led to the assessment of Barth as 'neo-orthodox' in the English-speaking world, whereas in German, studies by Marquardt, and more recently by Ingrid Spieckermann and Michael Beintker, have shown that this categorization is mistaken (McCormack, *Karl Barth's Theology*, 23–8). McCormack's analysis does not extend to the *Dogmatics*, and does not focus on ethics (though see 274–82 for a discussion of the ethics of *Romans* II). It does, however, support my contention that Barth did not abandon dialectic as a structure for his theology after 1931. John Webster's 'Life from the Third Dimension' surveys Barth's theory of human action in four of Barth's early works and concludes that the roots of Barth's account of human agency in the Dogmatics are already visible in the period 1919–22 (John Webster, '"Life from the Third Dimension": Human Action in Barth's Early Ethics', in *Barth's Moral Theology* (Edinburgh: T. & T. Clark, 1998), 11–39). This supports my argument that there is more continuity in Barth's

While the conclusion is striking that Barth's ethics in the *Dogmatics* has strong continuities with the ethics of *Romans* II, my prime interest is the significance this continuity has for the interpretation of Barth's ethical thought. If it were correct that Barth made a radical break with his earlier thought around 1931, *Romans* II would be largely irrelevant to an understanding of Barth's ethics in the *Dogmatics*. Since the ethics of the *Dogmatics* is largely continuous with the ethics of *Romans* II, however, we should expect to be able to gain additional insight into the later work by reading it alongside the former. My argument has shown that this continuity does exist, and that reading *Romans* II alongside the *Dogmatics* draws attention to the fact that dialectical tensions are a key part of the structure of Barth's ethics in the *Dogmatics*. According to Barth in the *Dogmatics*, we seek out God's will bringing all our previous moral experience to bear on an issue, yet must be absolutely open to what God is calling us to do. We cannot know in advance what God's command for us will be, yet we have a responsibility to anticipate as closely as we can what we will be called to. Our ultimate responsibility is to live in accordance with God's word to us, yet there is no single place we can turn to find it, and no definitive methodology to follow. The command is universal, yet particular to each person and each moment in time. We exist in the completed kingdom of God where we are commanded to love God, yet we also exist as those on the way to the kingdom who are commanded to love our neighbour. We are justified and love with agape, yet are sinners and love with eros. We know we are called to be peacemakers, yet cannot make pacifism a final absolute. We are called to action on the side of the victims of capitalism, yet we know human forces of reaction and revolution are irrelevant in the face of the revolution of God. In the light of *Romans* II, it is clear that these oppositional tensions remain a fundamental feature of Barth's ethical thought in the *Dogmatics*.

If it could be shown that Barth's adoption of this structure was a short-lived phenomenon, or that there were fewer of these dialectical oppositions in the ethics of the *Dogmatics*, we could perhaps conclude that these tensions were unintended inconsistencies in Barth's thought. I have shown, however, that Barth used dialectic in his ethics extensively throughout his writings from 1920 onwards: in the 1922 *Romans*, in his writings between *Romans* II and the *Dogmatics*, and in the 30-year period of the composition of the *Dogmatics*. It is clear, then, that Barth deliberately chose to incorporate these unresolved oppositions in his ethical thought. My question in the rest of this chapter is what implications this choice has for our understanding of Barth's ethics.

The first consequence of recognizing the central function of dialectic in Barth's ethics is to show the limits of critiques that take account of only one pole in any of

---

early and later ethical thought than has been previously recognized. Graham Ward interprets Barth very differently to McCormack, but agrees that dialectic remains important to Barth in the *Dogmatics* (see Graham Ward, *Barth, Derrida and the Language of Theology* (Cambridge: Cambridge University Press, 1995) and McCormack's critical review: Bruce L. McCormack, 'Graham Ward's *Barth, Derrida and the Language of Theology*', *Scottish Journal of Theology*, 49:1 (1996), 97–109).

these oppositional pairs. It is legitimate to question whether Barth's strategy of juxtaposing these elements is successful – evaluating this critique is the task of the remainder of this chapter – but it is misleading to criticize one element of a bipolar opposition without recognizing its dialectical context. Since the importance of dialectic in the ethics of the *Dogmatics* has not been appreciated, however, many critics of Barth's ethics have drawn these one-sided conclusions. Most frequently, the criticism is of the elements in which Barth emphasizes the nature of the command as an event without context, an immediate hearing with no human discernment or reflection. For example, Willis claims that Barth's interpretation of the command 'amounts to nothing less than a total exclusion of the necessity of deliberation in ethics' and that 'it is impossible that man could contribute anything to the ethical situation'.[10] Similarly, Gustafson, while sympathetic to some aspects of Barth's ethics, criticizes Barth's emphasis on the uniqueness of the ethical event.[11] These criticisms miss the significance of what Barth opposes to these claims. He does stress the character of the command as unique event rather than the culmination of human deliberation, yet he also stresses both the twofold continuity – on God's side and on the side of humankind – in which the command takes place, and the importance of our moral learning in the school of the divine command.[12] The importance of appreciating the dialectical structure of Barth's ethics in the *Dogmatics* is clear here: criticisms of one pole or another in isolation fail to come to grips with the 'both/and' Barth is attempting. We should also note that Barth's refusal to specify exactly how we hear the divine command, or how far it is possible to delimit the command in advance, are not topics he forgot to address, as critical accounts sometimes imply, but areas in which to set down theses and principles would be to resolve the oppositional tensions in Barth's ethical thought, close up the openings to the divine command they create, and enact the system he rejects.

The second consequence of appreciating Barth's choice to structure the ethics of the *Dogmatics* dialectically is to make clear the appropriate response to the charge that his ethics are unsystematic. Nigel Biggar cites Robin Lovin's view that Barth 'appears to rule out the predictability and universality that systematic thinking in ethics requires' and Biggar himself agrees that:

---

10   Robert E. Willis, *The Ethics of Karl Barth* (Leiden: E.J. Brill, 1971), 183.

11   James M. Gustafson, *Protestant and Roman Catholic Ethics* (Chicago: University of Chicago, 1978), 71. Gustafson is a careful reader of Barth, and so cannot be unaware of the passages emphasizing the context in which the command is heard, but he seems to ignore them in his critique. Nigel Biggar includes these and other critics in his survey of critical responses to Barth's ethical thought: see Nigel Biggar, *The Hastening That Waits: Karl Barth's Ethics* (Oxford: Clarendon Press, 1993), 18–25.

12   Stephen Webb is an example of a critic who picks on the opposite pole to criticize Barth's later theology, concluding that Barth moved from rhetoric in *Romans* II to the 'limited' and 'unimaginative' style of realism in the *Dogmatics* (Stephen H. Webb, *Refiguring Theology* (New York: State University of New York Press, 1991), 167). This analysis misses the tropes Barth employs in the *Dogmatics*: what Webb terms Barth's realism is only one half of what Barth says in the *Dogmatics*.

if the content of God's command cannot be expressed in terms of moral principles or rules that are always applicable to appropriate cases, if its meaning cannot be specified in terms of kinds of acts, if it has no intelligible constancy, then there can be no way of charting one's way through moral complexity by distinguishing good and bad acts in terms of their characteristic features.[13]

Biggar is particularly concerned by Barth's rejection of casuistry. He argues that Barth succumbs to a Protestant prejudice against it, seeing casuistry as the 'epitome of ethical rationalism, as a necessarily closed logical system'. In fact, Biggar suggests, casuistry 'has not always, or perhaps even usually, pretended to provide an absolute method of deciding what is right' and has seldom 'imagined that it could capture cases by the inexorable movement of deductive logic, by the mere application of a technique'. More often it has been open and dialectical, ready to adapt when coming upon unfamiliar cases. Biggar is not only concerned to clear the name of casuistical ethics, however – he also believes Barth's ethics suffers from a failure to acknowledge what it shares with casuistry:

> The elements of this dialectical kind of casuistry are all present in Barth's ethical thought. But his persistent identification of casuistry as the epitome of ethical rationalism prevented him from bringing them to the fore, and so robbed him of part of what is required for an explicit and coherent account of the relationship between systematic ethical deliberation about right action and the hearing of a command of God.[14]

Biggar's argument is that Barth's criticism of ethical system was insufficiently nuanced: he should have restricted his concerns to closed systems, since his own ethics at its best points towards the sort of coherent system of dialectical casuistry we require. This argument combines the descriptive claim that Barth's ethics is more systematic than his metaethics provides for, and the normative claim that this deviation from the course his metaethics charted is good, since the open system of dialectical casuistry is what we need from ethics. My comparison of the ethics of *Romans* II and the *Dogmatics* has shown that Barth's concerns about ethical system were an abiding feature of his thought throughout his career, so it is clear that he would not agree with Biggar's normative claim that we need systematic ethical deliberation based on casuistry. Casuistry assumes that we are in possession of reliable working knowledge of God's will: Barth was always concerned to alert us to the danger of complacency in such an easy confidence.

Yoder's criticism of Barth's ethical methodology is also rooted in a concern that it is unsystematic. In the previous chapter, we saw that Yoder criticizes Barth's use of

---

13 Biggar, *Hastening*, 21–2, citing Robin Lovin, *Christian Faith and Public Choices* (Philadelphia: Fortress Press, 1984), 40. Interestingly, Lovin here observes continuity between the ethics of *Romans* and the *Dogmatics*, claiming that both rule out this necessary predictability.

14 Biggar, *Hastening*, 41. See also Nigel Biggar, 'A Case for Casuistry in the Church', *Modern Theology*, 6:1 (1989), 29–51.

Grenzfall as 'not a formal concept with validity in the discipline of ethics' but simply 'a name for the fact that in certain contexts he is convinced of the necessity of not acting according to the way God seems to have spoken in Christ'.[15] Both Biggar and Yoder are sympathetic to Barth's project and would like to find ways to mitigate the problems they find with it. For Yoder, this means dispensing with the concept of *Grenzfall* entirely, as well as developing Barth's account of the state. Biggar's first strategy is a reinterpretation of Barth, rather than a wholesale revision, and aims to respond to those critics who reject Barth's ethics as unredeemably unsystematic. Biggar argues that Barth's special ethics in III/4 of the *Dogmatics* show a systematic quality beyond what we would expect from II/2, that Barth engages in the casuistry he rejects in name, and that Barth in fact espouses 'what could reasonably be called a version of natural law'.[16] Beyond this point Biggar concludes we must go beyond Barth in the direction of a more systematic approach to ethics, by revising how we use Christ as a moral source, using a wider range of ethical sources, and taking more account of empirical data.[17]

In the previous chapter, I argued that Yoder's diagnosis of the methodological problem with Barth's ethics is based on an extrapolation from Barth's atypical application of the *Grenzfall* in the case of war. The answer to Yoder's criticism is therefore to re-examine Barth's treatment of war, rather than to revise his metaethics. Biggar, in contrast, is addressing a substantive issue in the interpretation of Barth's ethical method: the tension between Barth's emphasis on the divine command as unique, contextless event, and as a decision for which we can prepare ourselves and approach in confidence of continuity of the nature of God as Creator, Reconciler, and Redeemer, and of ourselves as creatures, redeemed sinners, and children of God. Biggar focuses attention on the texts in which Barth stresses the continuity over the disruption of the divine command, and on the systematic characteristics of Barth's special ethics. This technique is successful in defending Barth against the charge of being unsystematic, but in effect replaces the one-sided reading of Barth's critics, who concentrate on the discontinuity texts, with a one-sided reading that makes the continuity texts prominent. In addition, Biggar's cure for the disease Barth's critics diagnose leaves its patient in many respects worse off than he was without treatment. Squeezing Barth's vigorous and provocative ethical thought into the confines of natural law and casuistry deprives it of many of its most compelling qualities: the lion's roar becomes muted and the lion tame.[18]

---

15   John H. Yoder, *Karl Barth and the Problem of War* (Nashville: Abingdon Press, 1970), 73.

16   Biggar, *Hastening*, 164.

17   Ibid., 167–8. In an earlier essay, he also suggests that we need not go far beyond Barth to reach a use of casuistry that remains open to correction, so long as we restrict the *Grenzfall* to correcting normative ethics, rather than allowing it to be a sheer exception to the results of rational reflection (Nigel Biggar, 'Hearing God's Command and Thinking About What's Right: With and Beyond Barth', in *Reckoning with Barth: Essays in Commemoration of the Centenary of Karl Barth's Birth*, ed. Nigel Biggar (London: Mowbray, 1988), 115).

18   In 'Hearing God's Command' Biggar lists five virtues he finds in Barth's ethics: first, it contradicts

An appreciation of the dialectical character of Barth's ethics makes possible a different response to the charge that Barth's ethics are problematically unsystematic. This response will not prove as satisfying to some of those critics as Biggar's, since it does not push Barth so far in the direction of systematization, but it represents a more balanced reading retaining the characteristic energy and challenge of Barth's ethical thought. Barth makes twofold claims here: we must be absolutely open to the command of God, and we bring our previous moral experience to the decision; we cannot know what God will command, and we must try to give as precise a directive as we can to what the command will be. Barth does address ethical topics systematically, as Biggar notes, but Barth also makes clear that all such human attempts are put in question by the event of the divine command, which always has the potential of contradicting what we thought we knew. Barth believes that we cannot escape the responsibility of serious moral reflection, but that we must always recognize that this is a listening for God's command, which will sometimes be a surprise to us. We cannot choose just one element from each of these pairs of claims and remain faithful to Barth's intentions for his ethical thought: he means to say both things at once, holding the claims in dialectical tension. The use of dialectic allows Barth to avoid making the command of God a component of a human ethical system while retaining an ethic with substance and with a role for responsible human decision-making.

Therefore the answer to the criticism that system is essential to Christian ethics, and that Barth's ethics are unsystematic, is twofold. First, we affirm that Barth is prepared to use a systematic approach in his ethics, as Biggar has shown.[19] The fundamental feature of Barth's approach is to treat ethical issues under a Trinitarian framework, but there are also many examples of smaller-scale systems he employs. Second, we note that such systems are only legitimate for Barth if they are recognized to be limited in their scope and tentative in their results. Our systems are not expressions of God's nature and cannot substitute for God's judgement. We cannot reach heaven with even the most sturdy and carefully constructed tower of human reasoning, and the attempt to do ethics in this way coincides exactly with the conception of sin, according to Barth.[20] If the advocates of system in ethics require a grander scheme than Barth allows, the question becomes whether Christian ethics can legitimately embrace the systems they count as a requirement for ethics. Barth makes a powerful case that Christian ethics cannot aim at independence from the final uncertainty of the divine command and remain obedient to God. We can make use of

theories that present moral reflection as merely textual interpretation; second, it forces us to acknowledge our status as sinful creatures as a condition for gaining ethical insight; third, it brings worship and prayer into the heart of Christian ethics; fourth, it demands a constant openness to hear something new; and fifth, it precludes ethical elitism (Biggar, 'Hearing', 104–6). This is some of what draws me to Barth's ethics, too. Pushing Barth towards natural law and casuistry threatens these virtues.

19   Biggar, *Hastening*, 30–32.
20   *CD* II/2, 518 (574).

systems in ethics – Barth is not prepared to take a wholly negative view of hedonism, utilitarianism, or eudaemonism[21] – but they must be employed under the authority of the divine command and in its service, rather than in place of it. A dialectical framework enables Barth both to employ and affirm an appropriate system in his ethics, and to insist that such systems will never succeed in making God's will incarnate in human form.

Recognizing the dialectical structure of Barth's ethics is therefore of significant help in responding to critiques of his ethical thought. Once we have appreciated that Barth is almost always engaged in the attempt to hold two contradictory insights in tension, in order to avoid pre-empting God's Word to us, the old debates about whether he is irresponsibly occasionalist can be seen to miss the point entirely. In his ethics – as in his theology – Barth attempts to be as precise and as definite as possible, while respecting the intrinsic limitations of theology as done by creatures like us. The proper question at issue between Barth and his critics is not whether we *should* be more systematic in our ethics, but whether we *may* be: whether on this side of the eschaton more is possible than the struggle to discern where we may encounter God's command, recognizing that our attempts will always be incomplete, faltering, and in need of correction. Barth's dialectical vision of theology and ethics arises directly from his view of the relationship between Creator and creature, Reconciler and sinner, Redeemer and child of God, and this is where debates about his ethics must begin. Acknowledging the key role of dialectic in his ethics is therefore invaluable in correctly locating the substantive points at issue between Barth and his critics.

There is much more at stake in recognizing the dialectical shape of Barth's ethics, however, than facilitating such a defensive strategy. The real fruit of this new insight is the way it shows Barth's ethical thought to be a compelling resource for contemporary Christian ethics, which I explore in the final chapter.

---

21   *CD* II/2, 650 (724).

CHAPTER 9

Barth's Ethics Today

Crisis? What Crisis?

> Going about our daily affairs ... we live in and act in the company of [an] apparently endless multitude of other human beings, seen or guessed, known and unknown, whose life and actions depend on what we do and in turn influence what we do, what we can do and what we ought to do – and all this in ways we neither understand or are able to presage. In such life, we need moral knowledge and skills more often, and more poignantly, than either knowledge of the 'laws of nature' or technical skills. Yet we do not know where we can get them; and when (if) they are offered, we are seldom sure we can trust them unswervingly ... It is, essentially, this discrepancy between demand and supply that has been recently described as the 'ethical crisis of postmodernity'.[1]

This is Zymunt Bauman's diagnosis of the crisis confronting our attempts to live morally at the turn of the twenty-first century. Unprecedented freedom of choice together with a lack of trust in authority leave individuals burdened with the 'haunting responsibility' of making decisions without any clear grounds for doing so.[2] As the charting of a significant sociological shift in attitudes to morality and authority, Bauman's theories are persuasive, at least in European and North American contexts. We are familiar with the sense of restless moral uncertainty, with ethical thinking struggling to keep pace with the possibilities that technology thrusts before it, and with moral norms themselves being questioned, modified or discarded at a rapid pace.

Churches sometimes like to think that they sit serenely above such sociological change, compassionately surveying it without being themselves directly impacted. If this were true, the crisis Bauman describes would be of comparatively little concern, and might even be an opportunity to highlight the role of the church as a reliable beacon in a world adrift from its moral moorings. The situation of churches is less rosy and more complex than this for two reasons. First, they are among the institutions in which people have lost confidence, whether because they proclaim a message many no longer find credible, or because they have been shown in their practice to have fallen short of the ideals they preach. Second, church members are also members of wider society and are therefore far from immune to changes in it. Along with everyone else, they find themselves struggling to orient themselves in a world where almost everything is up for question. There is no safe haven for the churches, then, in

---

1   Zygmunt Bauman, *Postmodern Ethics* (Oxford: Blackwell, 1993), 16–17.

2   Ibid., 21.

which they can shelter from the crisis Bauman describes, though, as I note below, they can opt to respond to it in different ways.

Bauman offers not only a diagnosis of the postmodern ethical condition, but also a remedy for its ailments. The answer is to embrace the ambivalence of a morality without foundations:

> Human reality is messy and ambiguous – and so moral decisions, unlike abstract ethical principles, are ambivalent. It is in this sort of world that we must live; and yet, as if defying the philosophers who cannot conceive of an 'unprincipled' morality, a morality without foundations, we demonstrate day by day that we can live, or learn to live, or manage to live in such a world, though few of us would be ready to spell out, if asked, what the principles that guide us are, and fewer still would have heard about the 'foundations' which we allegedly cannot do without to be good and kind to each other.[3]

Knowing this to be the truth about life Bauman terms 'modernity without illusions', and the 'postmodern re-enchantment of the world' it allows 'carries a chance of facing human moral capacity point-blank, as it truly is, undisguised and undeformed; to readmit it to the human world from its modern exile; to restore it to its rights and its dignity; to efface the memory of defamation, the stigma left by modern mistrust'.[4]

If we were forced to choose between the crisis Bauman describes and the solution he offers, there would be very good reason to prefer the crisis. With the long wisdom of the tradition it draws on, theology knows better than to imagine we can return to some pristine and pure vision of morality. There is no way back into the Garden of Eden; we cannot share Bauman's aspirations for starting our moral thinking all over again. And even if we were to forget for a moment the unwise character of the search for an undefiled morality, we would not begin our quest for it in the direction Bauman takes. His picture of a new ambivalent morality without principles or foundations, in which we are all good and kind to each other without further guidance, has the touching naivety of the conclusion to Philip Pullman's *His Dark Materials* trilogy. On the final page of *The Amber Spyglass*, Lyra, the heroine, explains that the kingdom of heaven is over: 'We shouldn't live as if it mattered more than this life in this world, because where we are is always the most important place'. Lyra and her beloved Will are called to a new building project, which means they could not have remained in the same world:

> But then we wouldn't have been able to build it. No one could, if they put themselves first. We have to be all those difficult things like cheerful and kind and curious and brave and patient, and we've got to study and think, and work hard, all of us, in all our different worlds, and then we'll build ... the republic of heaven.[5]

---

3   Ibid., 32.
4   Ibid., 34.
5   Philip Pullman, *His Dark Materials: Northern Lights; The Subtle Knife; The Amber Spyglass* (London: Scholastic, 2000), 1015–16.

Pullman shares with Bauman both an exaggerated sense of the possibilities of starting again, and a simple moral remedy for what will make things better next time, though within the constraints of his make-believe world, he perhaps has more excuse. If this were all we needed to get morality right, it would be remarkable if no one had thought of it before. In fact, of course, they have: such vague and optimistic moralizing is a commonplace, discarded the next time we are confronted with the reality that real people, child and adult, are often not good and not kind. For all the demerits of the tradition morality Bauman rejects – and in truth they are many – it does not make the mistake of forgetting such basic truths about its subjects.

If I am right that we cannot ignore the crisis Bauman diagnoses, but cannot adopt the response to it he recommends, we need an alternative theological strategy for engaging with it. My proposal is that we may learn from Barth's theological response to the crisis of German theology at the beginning of the twentieth century, and the ongoing crisis of the very possibility of theology at all. The crisis Barth addressed in the 1922 edition of his commentary on Romans was that God and humanity, religion and culture, church and nation had become theologically confused, so that they were mistaken for one another in an unholy way. The crisis was one of speaking too freely in the name of God, clothing earthly reality with a mantle of fake divinity, and calling sacred the vilest profanity. A 1931 passage by Heinrich Weinel, cited by Barth in the *Church Dogmatics*, illustrates the fruition of theological errors he was concerned about:

> Christianity does not repudiate the 'people's movement', but willingly allows itself to be summoned by it to help to maintain and ennoble more fully and consciously than ever before nationality and race. This is the more necessary today when we are subjected to an international wave of forces destructive of nationality and morality. Theology must be fully aware of this, and express in dogmatics a Christianity which has taken up into itself the values of nationality and race. Ethics must emphasise more than ever nationality, country and community. The theological historian must teach mediaeval and modern history more radically as the history of German religion. Religious instruction must take the form of Church history and moral teaching, and give prominence to our German prophets rather than to the Old Testament (in hymn-books, text-books and reading). In its festivals the practical life of the Church must consciously associate itself with national customs and ennoble them. So far as is possible, it must support all efforts to preserve a healthy race. Christianity is not international, but supranational. It honours and sanctifies nationality as a creation of God.[6]

Barth's response was to witness to the Wholly Other God, whose 'No!' brought an end to such cosy and dangerous mixing of divinity and humanity. As I have shown, however, Barth saw that the stress on God's 'No' had to find a place in tension with the 'Yes' to humankind that was the other part of the truth of God's dealings with us. We

---

6   Heinrich Weinel, *Die Religion in Geschichte und Gegenwart*, vol. 2; cited in *CD* III/4, 308–9 (349).

now face a new crisis in our speaking about God's relationship with the world. The crisis is not now that we are generally over-familiar in our perception of God's work in the world, but that we have lost confidence that God can be spoken of at all in a meaningful way. Underlying both crises, however, is the deeper one that Barth recognized as characterizing all theology: our talk about God cannot do justice to its object, and yet we must talk about God. In 1922, the problem was that the first part of this dialectic had been forgotten; for us it is the second. In each situation the danger of reaction is significant: in 1922 to opt simply for the Wholly Other God would have been as problematic as now to opt simply for a God who can be spoken of without difficulty. What was needed then, and what we need now, is a dialectical theology and ethics that can do justice to both aspects of the crisis in our speaking about God.

At the end of Part I, I cited Alan Richardson's critique of Barth's theology and its relevance outside its own time and place. 'We cannot see the world through dialectical spectacles' he commented because 'we live in a different world' and can dismiss Barthianism as a 'passing post-war neurosis' leaving our complacency undisturbed.[7] The question of whether Richardson is right about this is for me the most important concern of this book. Of course, there is merit in understanding Barth's theology rightly, and I am convinced that recognizing the dialectical shape of his ethical thought, as I have argued we must, is a major step forward in this endeavour. I confess, however, that what interests me more is whether there are aspects of Barth's account of Christian ethics that are relevant for how we engage in this task today. If Richardson is right and the crisis Barth confronted in the 1922 edition of *Romans* was merely a local and temporary phenomenon, then we may safely leave Barth's ethics of crisis – and this account of it – to the historians. If Richardson is wrong, however, if the world we live in and the place of theology in it is similar in some respects to the one Barth inhabited, then it may be that the dialectical spectacles Barth provides may be a valuable aid to our vision too.

This study has suggested that Barth's dialectical approach to theological ethics was not a short-term strategy for a local context, but was a fundamental insight about how theology and ethics must be done that he remained committed to from 1922 to the end of his theological writing. Even on the summary evidence of the events leading up to the 1922 *Romans* presented in Chapter 1, there can be no doubt that Barth was a theologian alert to events in the world and concerned that theology should inform and be informed by them, and to ignore this context is to fail to appreciate much of the significance in his work.[8] To consider the relevance of his thought as wholly bound by this context, however, is at least as serious a miscalculation. For Barth, dialectical theology was a response to crisis, but this crisis was not particular to German theology

---

7   Alan Richardson, 'Review of Cornelius Van Til, *The New Foundations of Modernism*', *Theology*, 51:331 (1948), 30.

8   Timothy Gorringe makes this point well in Timothy Gorringe, *Karl Barth: Against Hegemony*, Christian Theology in Context (Oxford and New York: Clarendon Press: Oxford University Press, 1999).

in the first part of the twentieth century. Rather, the failure of the theology of his day struck him as an example of a crisis that is the everyday and ongoing situation of theology: in its speech about God the language of theology is inadequate to express its object. The familiar story – that Barth's theology went through a stage of 'crisis theology' in response to contemporary events but later, the crisis over, developed in a crisis-free mode – is superficially attractive, has utility for orthodox and postmodern theologians alike, and – as I have shown in relation to ethics – is demonstrably false. Instead we must recognize that Barth's theology in its entirety is a theology in crisis, an insight that is neatly summarized in Barth's own words: 'It is not as if I had found any way *out* of this critical situation. *Exactly not that*. But this critical situation itself became to me an explanation of the character of all theology.'[9] My claim is that this was true not only when Barth wrote it in 1922, but that it remained true to the end of his theological career. Barth did not find a way out of the crisis he made manifest in *Romans* II: '*exactly not that*'. In all its variety, the whole of Barth's theology following *Romans* II addressed the problematic of how to do theology given the existence of the crisis.

In responding to the crisis that Barth announced, we are presented with the same three options Barth set out in October of 1922: dogmatism, self-criticism, and dialectic.[10] Dogmatism proceeds as if there were no crisis, as if theology were adequate to its object. It quashes the human question about God with its own monolithic answer; its static formulations stand between human beings and the revealing God. Self-criticism is the way of negative theology: the denial that anything can be attributed to God. This addresses the weakness of dogmatism by acknowledging the crisis in which human beings are confronted by God, but there is no way forward: 'the cross is erected, but the resurrection is not preached; and therefore it cannot be really the cross of Christ.'[11]

It is not difficult to locate in contemporary Christian ethics the modern analogues of dogmatism and self-criticism. The heirs to dogmatism are the various absolutist visions from Protestant and Roman Catholic church traditions that claim as the possession of the church, or of a few within it, a certain and comprehensive knowledge of God's will for how human beings are to live. It may be the Bible that is claimed to provide unmediated knowledge of the mind of God, or the tradition of the church, or particular kinds of religious experience. In each case, judgements on the content and interpretation of this knowledge are usually reserved for those holding positions of authority in the church. There is no crisis obstructing our ability to gain this knowledge, according to this view, and no danger in claiming it. This view of ethics is attractive and popular. It offers simple answers to complex questions. The

---

9   Karl Barth, *The Word of God and the Word of Man*, trans. Douglas Horton (London: Hodder & Stoughton, 1929), 101 (Karl Barth, *Das Wort Gottes und die Theologie* (Munich: Chr. Kaiser Verlag, 1929), 102).
10   Ibid., 200 (167).
11   Ibid., 205 (171).

standard of behaviour required by absolutist views may be demanding, but adherence to the standard promises a quiet conscience. Like dogmatism, however, absolutism in theological ethics attains this apparent calm and simplicity by quashing all human questions as unfaithful prevarication, and interposing new, humanly-scribed tablets of law between God and God's people, and thereby negating the challenge, threat, and promise of encounter with the living Word. Absolutism in ethics is unsustainable because Richardson is wrong: the crisis that Barth addressed in *Romans* II and that sets the parameters for all his subsequent theology was not some local, temporary phenomenon of purely historical interest. The crisis Barth proclaimed is 'an explanation of the character of all theology', the limiting parameters within which all theology must be done. This crisis means that the absolute knowledge absolutism claims is not possible this side of the eschaton. The certainty it offers is that of an astrologer's prediction; the simplicity it offers, that of a Disneyfied fairy tale; the peace it offers, that of a neatly kept grave.

Heirs to the approach of self-criticism that Barth identified are those relativistic approaches to theological ethics that stress the difficulty, complexity and indeterminacy of the discipline. Far from denying the crisis Barth identified, as the absolutists do, the relativists acknowledge and embrace it. No one can be sure what God wants of human beings in a relativist framework, so we have two choices: either look for other sources of moral knowledge and attempt to construct a reasonable code of conduct to make up for the lack of divine guidance, or just revel in the delightful postmodern ethical free-for-all that results. In either case, relativistic approaches effectively deny the relevance of theology for ethics, and so the ethics they generate is frequently unrecognizable as theological at all. Relativism recognizes the crisis, but throws up its hands at the possibility of continuing theology within it.

Much less evident in contemporary debates is a modern ethical successor to the dialectical approach to theology that Barth describes, which can affirm with absolutists the urgent need for human beings to attend to the will of God for their lives but can also affirm with relativists the significant obstacles in the path of knowing right and wrong as God does. A dialectical approach to ethics has the potential to avoid, on the one side, the idolatry that claims God's will as a human possession and, on the other side, the apostasy that gives up on the struggle to discern God's will. Barth pictures the possibility of theological ethics as poised in unstable equilibrium, on the edge of a knife, between the necessity and impossibility of knowledge of God's will. Absolutist and relativist approaches are unable to maintain this precarious balance, and fall, one on each side, prematurely resolving the tension of the dialectic by claiming half-truths as final answers.

The crisis Barth announced in the 1922 *Romans* as underlying the crisis of German theology is the same crisis that confronts us now. With Bauman, we recognize that the institutions that people looked to for guidance no longer command their trust, and yet the need for ethical guidance is at least as great as ever. In the face of this challenge the churches can resort neither to dogmatism, which merely exacerbates the problem, nor to self-criticism, which denies the possibility of faithful action. We cannot hold the living Word of God captive in any human construct, yet without such a construct to represent God's will to us we are unable to pattern our lives as disciples of Christ. It is futile to deny this crisis, and fruitless to despair over it. Barth recognizes the crisis as setting the conditions for all theology, but also remains committed to attempting a constructive account of theological ethics in the midst of this crisis. The dialectical shape of this *ethics in crisis* is a significant resource for contemporary Christian ethics that shows a way beyond the impasse of absolutism and relativism. By acknowledging with Barth that the crisis he proclaimed is ours too, but, like him, refusing to give up on the demanding task of theological ethics within this crisis, we open the way for an account of theological ethics that is faithful in the attempt to provide guidance for living according to God's will and wise in its awareness of its own shortcomings.

Ethics as Command

For some, this crucial dialectical element in Barth's ethics may be overlooked as a resource for constructive accounts of Christian ethics because of its association with the language of divine command. Contemporary Christian ethicists describe themselves commonly as exponents of narrative ethics, virtue ethics, or natural law ethics – few identify themselves with an ethics of divine command. As I noted in the Introduction, we need to be very cautious about identifying Barth with the tradition of divine command ethics, because while he adopts the language, his interpretation of command turns almost everything about the tradition upside down. This will become clear in a brief survey of the objections commonly advanced against divine command ethics.[12]

If divine command ethics is currently discussed at all, it is as an example of how not to do ethics, usually using Plato's *Euthyphro* to reveal its supposed critical flaw. The relevant transposition of the dilemma Socrates poses in the *Euthyphro* is whether an action is good because God commands it, or whether God commands an action because it is good. If we take the first horn of the dilemma – that God's command is what makes an action good – God could command anything and it would be good by definition, whether it were rape, torture, child abuse or genocide. If we take the second horn – that God enjoins actions the goodness of which is independent of God's command – God seems superfluous to morality, or necessary only as messenger. Some theists have been content to take one horn or the other but most have attempted to find a way to avoid this discomfort. A Thomist, for example, could argue that the

---

12 For an overview of the general issues raised by divine command ethics, see Janine Marie Idziak, *Divine Command Morality: Historical and Contemporary Readings* (New York: Mellen Press, 1979); Paul Helm, *Divine Commands and Morality* (Oxford and New York: Oxford University Press, 1981); and Richard J. Mouw, *The God Who Commands: A Study in Divine Command Ethics* (Notre Dame, Indiana: University of Notre Dame Press, 1990).

will and wisdom of God are unified in a way that makes the choice posed by the dilemma a false one.[13]

One Barthian response to the *Euthyphro* dilemma is to take the first horn, but make it more comfortable. Since the covenant in which God promises to be 'for humanity' precedes even creation for Barth, we can be sure that God will not command actions that are contrary to God's faithful loving-kindness. Robert Adams has developed a version of this strategy, and suggests that, if we had reason to believe God had commanded an action incompatible with our belief that God is loving towards us, we could not say whether it was right or wrong to obey: instead, our entire concept of ethical wrongness would break down.[14] In Barth's terms, the scenario Adams depicts would be coming to the belief that God had broken the covenant with humankind, in which case losing our ethical bearing would be the least of our concerns. Barth's ethics are not vulnerable to the *Euthyphro* objection because, unlike the classical defenders of divine command morality such as William of Ockham, Barth has no interest in defending God's unqualified sovereignty. For Barth, there is nothing divine in power in itself:

> Not even the omnipotence of God – indeed, this least of all – is power of this kind, power over all things and everything. Only the evil impotence which is an attribute of nothingness, chaos, falsehood and its 'powers' is indefinite power, power over all things and everything. Unqualified power is *per se* the power of negation, destruction and dissolution.[15]

If God's commanding is embedded in the promises of the covenant, we do not have to be fearful of the arbitrary and threatening diktats that are the potential consequence of allowing no qualifications on God's exercise of power. We can rely on God's commands being in accordance with the commitments made by God before creation to be for us. Barth's ethics cannot, therefore, be dismissed simply by invocation of the *Euthyphro*.

My judgement, however, is that current disinterest in divine command theory is not primarily because of the philosophical objection from the *Euthyphro*, or even because of the criticisms that Barth's ethics are unsystematic or hard to communicate to a secular world, discussed in the previous chapter. Divine command ethics are dismissed most frequently because they simply seem implausible for one of three reasons.

---

13   For a discussion of this tactic, see Oliver O'Donovan, *Resurrection and Moral Order: An Outline for Evangelical Ethics* (Leicester: Apollos, 1994) and Brian Stiltner, 'Who Can Understand Abraham? The Relation of God and Morality in Kierkegaard and Aquinas', *Journal of Religious Ethics*, 21:2 (1993), 401–25.

14   See Robert M. Adams, 'A Modified Divine Command Theory of Ethical Wrongness' and 'Divine Command Metaethics Modified Again', both in *The Virtue of Faith* (Oxford: Oxford University Press, 1987).

15   *CD* III/4, 391 (446).

First, we know that we do not hear a voice in our head telling us what to do, and if we were to, we consider the rational response would not be to obey it, but to seek psychiatric help. If Barth were advocating this kind of divine intuitionism in his ethics of divine command, his ethical thought would be of little interest. Yet Barth does not believe we learn God's will from a voice in our head: God's command is always clothed in a mundane claim on us: the claim of an object, idea, person, or situation.[16] Barth uses the language of command in order to make clear that ethics is reflection on *responsible* action: action in response to the grace God has shown to humankind. Characterizing ethics as helping Christians to follow God's commands makes clear that it is a secondary enterprise, dependent on God's initiative and as far as is conceivable from a conception of ethics as a self-contained human enterprise, which invents for itself what to consider to be right and wrong.[17]

The second reason divine command ethics seems implausible is that we know roughly what work we need to do in order to make a decision in Christian ethics: we research the subject to gather the empirical facts, discover who and what is affected in which ways, reason about how ethical principles and values might apply to the situation, determine the relevance of biblical texts and themes, reflect on what else is at stake theologically in the decision, and discuss the results of our enquiries with others. Divine command ethics seems to deny that any of this activity is relevant to an ethical decision: instead we seem to be required to sit and wait for the answer to be divinely communicated to us. Barth, of course, does not believe we should merely sit and wait for the divine command: if this were his view there would be no need for any ethical reflection at all. The task of ethics is to attempt to anticipate the divine command in order to guide those attempting to find out God's will, and in the special ethics of creation in volume III/4 of the *Dogmatics* Barth does so by engaging in a range of different strategies of ethical reflection, including all of those listed above. We receive God's command as we engage in the attempt to discover how we should act. The crucial difference between Barth's approach to ethics and other approaches is not what ethicists do, but how they characterize their activity and the significance they ascribe to the results of it.

The final reason I believe that an ethics of divine command is dismissed out of hand is that obedience to any form of authority, divine or human, is suspect in a post-Enlightenment context. To be responsible for one's actions means to consider oneself the author of them, and this responsibility cannot be delegated to a superior. The authentic moral life in this context is seeking out for oneself those values and

---

16   '[T]he claim of God's command always wears the garment of another claim ... An object with its question, the compulsion of a necessity of thought, one of those hypotheses or conventions, a higher or more primitive necessity of life, a necessity which in itself seems to be that of a very human wish or very human cleverness, a summons coming from this or that quarter, a call which man directs to himself – all these can actually be the command of God veiled in this form, and therefore genuinely participate in the corresponding authority and dignity' (*CD* II/2, 584–5 (649); translation revised).

17   For an example of the opposite approach, see J.L. Mackie, *Ethics: Inventing Right and Wrong* (London: Penguin Books, 1977).

principles to which one will give allegiance. Following the commands of God, in contrast, looks morally suspect, if not infantile.[18] This critique misses the mark of Barth's ethics, however, in at least three ways. First, it is no longer tenable to assert that the ideal moral agent remains aloof from all commitments in order to evaluate the merits of all positions on an equal basis. In this notional 'view from nowhere' there are no criteria whatever;[19] in order to make judgements one needs already to be placed in a particular position and to judge on the basis of its values, principles, or stories. Given that all moral agents must be situated in this way, the allegiance of those who profess faith in God is in the first instance no more suspect than those who profess secular liberalism. Second, as I showed in response to the *Euthyphro* dilemma, following the will of God need not be unthinking or uncritical. It is possible to give a coherent account of one's reasons for living according to the will of God, and of the circumstances in which one would have to reexamine this commitment. Giving one's allegiance to God can therefore be a commitment that is rationally defensible.

The third way the critique of obedience misses the target of Barth's ethics is that for him God's command is not adequately characterized simply as a heteronomous event, confronting us from the outside. The distinctive feature of God's command in contrast to all other command is that it is a permission, 'the granting of a freedom', setting us free. It does not compel, but 'bursts open the door of the compulsion' under which an individual is living and is against us 'only insofar as we are against ourselves'.[20] Barth acknowledges that God's command also says 'Do this and do not do that':

> But in the mouth of God this means something different. Do this – not because an outer or inner voice now requires this of you, not because it must be so in virtue of any necessity rooted in the nature and structure of the cosmos or of humankind, but: Do this, because in so doing you may make it true that your rejection has been rejected in the death of Jesus on the cross, that for His sake your sin has been forgiven. Do this, because in Jesus Christ you have been born anew in the image of God. Do it in the freedom to which you have been chosen and called, because in this freedom you may do this, and can do only this. For this, and not for any other reason, do this. You may do it. And: Do not do this – not because you hear an inner or outer voice which seeks to make it doubtful or dreadful for you, not because there is any power in heaven or on earth to prevent or spoil or for some reason forbid it. No, but: Do not do this, because it would be a continuation of the fall of Adam, because it would not correspond to the grace addressed to you but contradict it, because you would have to do it as the captive which you certainly are not, because you, the free person, are exempted from the necessity of doing

---

18   For a critique of theological ethics on this basis, see Patrick Nowell-Smith, 'Morality: Religious and Secular', in *Christian Ethics and Contemporary Moral Philosophy*, ed. I.T. Ramsey (London: SCM Press Ltd, 1966).

19   See Thomas Nagel, *The View from Nowhere* (Oxford: Oxford University Press, 1986).

20   *CD* II/2, 585–95 (648–61).

it – really exempted by the fact that you have been made righteous and glorious in the resurrection of Jesus Christ, that you have actually been cut off by Him from this very possibility. This is how the command of God speaks.[21]

Following God's command as Barth conceives it, then, cannot be conceived as irresponsible or immature or limiting. Barth's insistence that the command is also a permission transforms the tradition of divine command ethics, replacing a slavish obedience to the whim of a divine autocrat with the joyous discovery of our liberation from all the compulsions and drives that we thought were inescapable. We are freed from the arbitrary supermarket selection of this or that action, and freed for the determination of becoming the person we were meant to be. In seeking to follow God's command we are not giving up our own will for that of a superior, but discovering the way in which we can be most fully our true selves in Christ and fulfil our highest calling. This is freedom indeed.

Barth's ethical thought, then, does not share the implausibility of the standard caricature of divine command theory. Its plausibility depends on whether one is prepared to accept two central claims, the dialectical tension between which structures the entirety of Barth's ethical thought. The first claim is that God has a will for how human lives are lived, and the task of ethics is to attempt to determine what it is. God wills Christians to live in a particular way, to be a particular people, to make particular decisions. God seeks to communicate this will to us, and ethics provides a guide to the content of this communication. If God has a will for our lives and we may know it, it is clearly a Christian responsibility to seek out what that will is and attempt to live in accordance with it. If there were no continuity in God's will, this would be a difficult and frustrating process, but God's covenanted faithfulness means that God's will for us is not haphazard or arbitrary. This continuity makes it possible to try to anticipate God's will in particular spheres by reflecting on our understanding of God's revealed will. Ethics is only genuine and useful insofar as it can 'indicate with increasing urgency and compulsion the divine command and the human action corresponding to it'.[22] If we leave the language of command aside, I take it that the claim that God wills Christians to live in particular ways, seeks to communicate this will, and calls Christians to attempt to discern it, would obtain broad consent among Christian ethicists. It is not completely uncontroversial – some would see the relationship between divine will and human action as more remote, so that God wills our flourishing, say, but is indifferent to how we achieve it, or prefers to leave the decisions to us – but most adherents of narrative, virtue, and natural law ethics would affirm the claim.

The second central claim structuring Barth's ethical thought is in tension with the first. It states that we cannot capture the will of God in human concepts and systems of thought. No principle, rule, law, value, theory, understanding of the good, or

---

21   *CD* II/2, 587 (652); translation revised.
22   *CD* III/4, 31 (33).

reflection on past experience is identical with the will of God.[23] To claim otherwise is to make an idol of ethics, substituting an earthly dead artifice for a divine living reality. In attempting to determine the will of God, therefore, ethicists must take great care to avoid either saying more than they can properly say, or claiming a status for their conclusions that is illegitimate. The conclusions of Christian ethics can only be approximations to the divine will, and Christian ethicists must always retain an awareness of the tentative character of the results of their work. Barth is not driven to make this second claim by an over-zealous concern for the freedom of God. For Barth, God is not absolutely free in relation to God's creation, because God has chosen to live by the covenant made with humanity before the world was created. Barth insists on this second claim that we cannot capture the will of God because he is impressed above all by the need for Christians to be open to the Word of God. If we find a specific rule or principle that we believe perfectly encapsulates the will of God, we have no further need to listen for God's word to us: we have effectively stopped up our ears on this matter to any future divine communication. This second central claim ensures that we never stop seeking out God's word to us, because we recognize each ethical insight we gain as provisional and in need of further elucidation or correction. This second claim is more controversial than the first. It is straightforward to concede the point that ethicists do not speak with the voice of God, and so may make errors in their method or conclusions. It is harder to let go of an ambition for Christian ethics to develop solid and reliable principles and values that will in turn generate conclusions that can be depended upon. Barth maintains in this second claim that Christian ethics must not aim so high. We must free ourselves of the temptation 'to win clear of the occurrence, the freedom and the peril of this event, to reach dry land, as it were, and to stand there like God, knowing good and evil'.[24]

Barth's ethical thought exists within and is characterized by the tension created by the juxtaposition of these two claims – the task of Christian ethics is to seek out God's will, yet God's will cannot be captured in human thought and system. Each of the three dialectical pairs I identified in the metaethics of the *Dogmatics* – our approach to the command with experience and/or in openness, the nature of the command as universal and/or particular, and the possibility and/or impossibility of knowing what God will command – has its basis in this central dialectic between what ethics must attempt and what it cannot achieve.

Barth's commitment to the first claim, that ethics must attempt to specify as narrowly as possible what God will command, has not been appreciated by all interpreters of his ethics. William Johnson believes that Barth's ethics imposes 'a radical and purely formal regard for the "other" '[25] and 'does not indicate what being

---

23   Cf. *CD* II/2, 646 (719–20).
24   *CD* III/4, 11 (10).
25   William Stacy Johnson, *The Mystery of God: Karl Barth and the Postmodern Foundations of Theology* (Louisville, Kentucky: Westminster John Knox Press, 1997), 161.

"for" the other might mean in any given situation'[26] so that '[a]nyone looking to Barth for detailed ethical admonitions will surely be disappointed'.[27] Johnson admits that he is more concerned with what Barth should have said than what he actually did say,[28] but it is much harder for postmodern theologians such as Johnson to appropriate Barth's ethics than they appear to appreciate. As we have seen, Barth demands that ethicists go beyond formal statements to specify as closely as possible what God will command. Johnson notes that Barth's treatment of gender relations does not accord with his interpretation,[29] but fails to appreciate that the whole of Barth's special ethics in III/4 and IV/4 are examples of his concern to go far beyond the formal regard Johnson celebrates for its nonfoundational indeterminacy. A faithful interpretation of Barth's ethics cannot avoid the recognition that ethics has the responsibility of attempting to determine what God will command with as much detail as possible.

If Barth's commitment to the first claim is what motivates him to attempt special ethics, it is his commitment to the second claim – that God's will cannot be captured in human systems of thought – that motivates him to choose an ethic of divine command for his ethical thought, rather than natural law or some other ethical theory. It is at this point that there is an opportunity for a fruitful interchange between Barth's ethic of divine command and other approaches to Christian ethics. The key question is to what extent we can reliably conclude what is God's will for humankind. Barth believes that God's will is not as open and available to us through reason and reflection on the created order as advocates of most versions of natural law maintain. He also considers that we cannot derive God's will for us from the Bible or its stories in as straightforward a way as some biblical ethicists and narrative ethicists believe: we must recognize that the Bible witnesses to commands given to other people at another time. These approaches deny that theological ethics can only be done in the context of the crisis that confronts all human attempts at theology: they believe we can aspire to clear and reliable knowledge of God's will. Barth believes we cannot aim so high: the decision to base his ethics on the command of God arises from the danger he sees in asserting that we know more than we can know of what God wills for us.

One of Barth's key contributions to contemporary Christian ethics is to remind us of the space in which Christian ethics must exist: between the requirement for Christian ethics to render as close an approximation as possible to the will of God, and the recognition that ethics can never become a substitute for seeking after God's will, that its conclusions always remain tentative and provisional, awaiting refinement or correction. An ethic of divine command, appropriately specified, seemed to him, and seems to me, the best theoretical structure to fill out this space, but, even for those who adopt other approaches, Barth's dialectical ethical thought is a valuable reminder of what Christian ethics must be and what it cannot be. Whatever our starting point for

---

26   Ibid., 162.
27   Ibid., 154.
28   Ibid., 9.
29   Ibid., 164–5.

theological ethics – be it Scripture, or natural law, or the teaching of the church, or the development of Christian virtue and character, or a seeking after God's will through all of these means – we must pursue our ethical thought and action with faithful confidence that we may know of God's will for how we should live, but with the humble recognition that we are always on the way to such an understanding, rather than in full and final possession of it.

Ethics in Public

There are definite difficulties in Barth's dialectical ethical methodology. It is designed to resist systematization, so if we follow Barth we will not be able to construct a reliable scheme of principles and values that will lead us to ethical answers we can count on. We will develop ways to approach ethical problems, and will learn from the successes and failures of ourselves and of others, but there will always be a tentative, ad hoc quality to our search for ethical guidance. This account of ethics is also poorly suited to apologetics: divine command theory is certain to be less persuasive in the context of government enquiries, for instance, than cost-benefit analysis, but will also be less convincing than approaches that identify universal characteristics of human nature and argue for ethical conclusions based on them.[30] Barth certainly intends that ethical decisions should be justifiable to other Christians,[31] but the translation of this justification to a wider society will always be a secondary process with no guarantee of success. These are both real difficulties in comparison with other accounts of ethics: we need an ethical theory that is readily applicable to contemporary problems and Barth's political activism makes clear that he intended his ethics to play a role in shaping society beyond the Christian community.

We cannot simply find our way around these difficulties. They are consequences of Barth's deliberate choice to make ethics open to God's command: to set out a method for finding right answers in ethics that was accessible and persuasive in secular terms would substitute the authority of a human system for the authority of God's command. The only reason for adopting Barth's approach to ethics in spite of these difficulties is that one is convinced by his arguments that ethics is not possible for the Christian in any other way. If Barth is right, there is no legitimate alternative account of Christian ethics that is without these difficulties. If it were possible and permissible to construct a systematic way of telling right from wrong as God does, this would clearly be preferable to the theory Barth outlines. In fact, an ethical system cannot

---

30 For examples of the latter category, see John Finnis, *Natural Law and Natural Rights* (Oxford: Clarendon Press, 1980) or Grisez's more theological version, Germain Grisez, *The Way of the Lord Jesus*, vol. I (Chicago: Franciscan Herald Press, 1983).

31 See Nigel Biggar, 'Hearing God's Command and Thinking About What's Right: With and Beyond Barth', in *Reckoning with Barth: Essays in Commemoration of the Centenary of Karl Barth's Birth*, ed. Nigel Biggar (London: Mowbray, 1988), 108–11.

make this possible any more than the fruit of the tree of the knowledge of good and evil could, and the claim that an ethical system could play this role is as false as the snake's. In the absence of a method that can accurately map the will of God onto a human conceptual framework, we must continue to attempt systematic thinking in ethics – Barth's critics are right that ethics requires systematic thought – but we must also continually remind ourselves that the temptation to believe that we hold in our hands the power to know as God knows is the oldest temptation of all. The dialectical structure of Barth's ethical thought enables this necessary human venture of ethics yet never lets us forget that its results stand in the shadow of the judgement of God.

If we cannot circumnavigate these two difficulties – that we do not have a definitive method for reaching ethical conclusions, and that the basis for these conclusions is not persuasive in the public square – it is possible to find a way through them. Barth provides no definitive system for finding answers to ethical problems: to do so would instantiate the fixed and stable knowledge of God's will that he rejects. We know, however, that we prepare ourselves to hear the divine command by reflecting on the consequences for an ethical issue of the relationship of Creator to creature, Reconciler to sinner, and Redeemer to child of God; by considering the biblical witness, the Christian tradition, discussions in the Church, the results of secular ethical theories, relevant empirical data, and as many other sources as we can find.[32] The task of the ethicist is not straightforward, but it is not inconceivable or impossibly involved.

In relation to the difficulty of making Christian ethics heard in political debate, we need to rethink what we want of an ethical theory in this respect. Yoder has made a strong contribution here. He argues that behind all the manoeuvres we use to convince the world of the truth of our message

> there is the fear of vulnerability, a cringing before the danger that we may be told by an audience in that wider world that they do not believe us. We want what we say not only to be understandable, credible, meaningful ... We want people to have to believe us. We hanker for patterns of argument which will not be subject to reasonable doubt. We are impressed by the power to convince which we see exercised by demonstrations in mathematics and logic, in the natural sciences, and in documented history ... and we want our claims about God or morality to be similarly coercive. We think that truth must somehow be made irresistible, because that is the way in which the small world in which we grew up taught us what the rules are, and that is how the larger world we since moved into imposed itself on us. We become 'apologetic', ready to decrease the vigor of our claims, if that will decrease their vulnerability to rejection.[33]

Yoder's rejection of apologetics echoes Barth's identification of the temptation for Christian ethics to embark on apologetic debate: Barth insists that apologetics

---

32   See Nigel Biggar, *The Hastening That Waits: Karl Barth's Ethics* (Oxford: Clarendon Press, 1993), 146–51.

33   John H. Yoder, 'On Not Being Ashamed of the Gospel: Particularity, Pluralism, and Validation', *Faith and Philosophy*, 9:3 (1992), 285–300, 287 (ellipsis points in original).

implies measuring theological ethics against general ethics and can only be justified if we refuse to believe in ethics independent of the grace and command of God.[34] Yoder continues by arguing that Christian statements must be 'specifically or specifiably Christian, i.e. true to kind, authentically representing their species' rather than necessarily distinctive, and claims that '[t]he ground for the transcultural intelligibility of the meaning of Jesus is not an a priori semantic move made by methodologically preoccupied intellectuals (or apologetically concerned missionaries, for that matter). It is a set of first century events, which some of its interpreters call Incarnation'.[35]

The first response to the difficulty of making our Christian ethics heard in a wider world, therefore, is to refuse to allow this broader audience to be a criterion for what we decide to accept as true, and to remember that the Gospel has always been understood by non-Christians, from Pentecost onwards. The second response is to accept that the influence of any ethical theory on public debate is inevitably a political issue. If Christians decide in the light of their beliefs that it is important to convince a wider public that legislation should or should not be enacted, they must enter the political fray, find common ground and make alliances with groups that do not share their presuppositions, and be wise as serpents in their decisions to stand firm or make concessions to achieve political goals. Christians who have reached their conclusions on the basis of natural law reasoning may initially seem to share more presuppositions with non-Christian participants in the debate, but the main part of the negotiation will not concern presuppositions at all, but the positions that the disputants' presuppositions lead them to.[36] Barth's dialectical account of divine command theory will therefore not be significantly disadvantaged in the public square in comparison with other accounts of Christian ethics.

Ethics for Wayfarers

One of the most striking representations of Barth's theological method is that of *theologia viatorum*, a theology of wayfarers, which he first employed in the 1925 address 'Church and Theology', and developed in *Die Christliche Dogmatik*.[37] The angels and saints in heaven are free to engage in *theologia comprehensorum*, comprehensive theology, a theology that sees face to face and is therefore free to proclaim its truths with complete certainty. We, however, during our earthly

---

34   *CD* II/2, 520–21 (577–8).
35   Yoder, 'On Not Being Ashamed', 294–5.
36   I am in agreement here with Rawls's view that adherents of different 'comprehensive doctrines' can reach political agreement. I disagree with his view that public debate must be conducted in the terms of public reason, however: this restricts unacceptably the speech and actions of those with religious comprehensive doctrines, even if the justification he calls them to provide can be after the fact. See John Rawls, *Political Liberalism* (New York: Columbia University Press, 1993).
37   See Chapter 4 for a discussion of these texts.

pilgrimage see as in a mirror darkly, and so our theology must take a different form. The kind of truth available to us is 'truth apprehended, believed and confessed provisionally and in an earthly, human way'.[38] Our theology is an earthly activity in a definite here and now, carried out by human beings journeying, like Adam, towards their own country but not possessing any country of their own.[39] We have to give up on aspirations to know God as the angels and the saints in heaven do, and, for now, must be content with the earthly, time-bound and human, and therefore incomplete, tentative and provisional, theology of wayfarers.

This distinction between the comprehensive theology of the angels and saints, and the wayfaring theology of those on earth has clear implications for ethics. If we cannot pretend to be the possessors of a comprehensive theology, we certainly cannot pretend to possess a comprehensive theological ethics. A comprehensive account of theological ethics would only be possible if there were no crisis, if our knowledge of good and evil were unimpeded and there were no spiritual dangers in our grasping after it. What, then, would be the distinctive features of theological ethics that recognized the need to renounce a claim to comprehensiveness in this sense? In conclusion, I offer a sketch of an account of theological ethics drawing on the dialectical shape of Barth's ethics in crisis: an ethics for wayfarers as faithful, humble, and active.

First, a wayfarers' ethic must be *faithful*: committed to the task of seeking out God's will for God's people. Recognizing that theological ethics cannot be based on the comprehensive theology of the angels and saints in heaven does not free us from the requirement that we strive to attain as sure and full knowledge of God's will for us as is possible. The pilgrimage that the church makes on earth has a direction and a final destination; it is not an idle wandering. The task of ethics on this journey is to erect signposts to show which of the paths that immediately confront the church leads towards its ultimate destination. How are the churches of the wealthy to further God's mission in a global context where the most basic needs of many are ignored to provide luxuries for the few? How is human and non-human life to be valued as part of God's good creation in the face of modern technology that may threaten or promote it? How is the church to discern the appropriate place of human sexual expression at a time when it has had to learn so much from those outside its doors about sex as a profound gift of God, but also at a time when western cultures question and throw aside taboo after taboo? A wayfaring ethic must be faithful in facing these and many other questions that confront the church in the expectation that God's call may be heard. To be faithful means to maintain this expectation in the face of doubts that there is no way

---

38   Karl Barth, *Die Christliche Dogmatik im Entwurf. 1. Bd.: Die Lehre vom Worte Gottes. Prolegomena zur Christlichen Dogmatik, München 1927*, Karl Barth-Gesamtausgabe (Zurich: Gerhard Sauter, 1982), 162.

39   Karl Barth, *Theology and Church: Shorter Writings 1920–1928*, trans. Louise Pettibone Smith (New York and Evanston: Harper & Row, 1962), 298 (Karl Barth, *Die Theologie und die Kirche*, Gesammelte Vortrag, vol. 2 (Munich: Evangelischer Verlag AG, 1928), 318).

ahead, that no path is better than any other, or that no guidance from God is available so a path must be chosen on some other basis. It is this faithfulness that distinguishes a dialectical approach to theological ethics from the apostasy of relativism, which recognizes the demands of doing ethics in the context of the crisis Barth announced, and gives up on the attempt of knowing God's will at all.

Second, a wayfarers' ethic must be *humble*: prepared to acknowledge the obstacles that stand in the way of knowing God's will. This is a crucial element in recognizing that ethics is based on the theology of wayfarers, rather than the comprehensive theology of the angels and saints in heaven, and exists in the context of the crisis that confronts all theology with its inability to speak of its object. A humble ethic knows itself to be human, not divine; earthly, not heavenly; of this time and place, not eternal nor universal; partial, not complete; provisional, not final; open to hearing anew, not closed in self-righteous isolation. This does not mean it is plagued by self-doubt, hesitant, or self-effacing. To be humble means being honest about the crisis that impacts ethics and the consequent status of its conclusions. To be humble means recognizing the task of ethics to be one of mapping the territory and pointing the way, rather than route-marching the people of God under armed guard. To be humble means admitting that one may be wrong even as one makes a bold clarion call to a church set on what seems to be the wrong road. It is this humility that distinguishes a dialectical wayfaring ethic from the idolatry of absolutism that falsely claims to be in possession of the certain knowledge that will only be ours at the eschaton.

Third, a wayfarers' ethic must be *active*: engaged in the struggle to chart the way ahead. Once one has realized the scale and significance for theology of the crisis Barth diagnosed, and appreciated what is at stake in renouncing the certain foundation of a comprehensive theology, it is tempting to ponder on the demands of the ethical task in this new context in preference to setting about it. This makes the crisis an excuse for a lethargic moral torpor, indolence in the face of theological complexity. For Barth, the demands of the world, its 'pressing practical duties', the 'wickedness in the streets' and the daily papers[40] made clear that theology could not luxuriate in such self-referential musings. It is 'the need of making decisions of will, the need for action, the world as it is' that drives theology.[41] We cannot avoid the ethical question: what we are to do today, and tomorrow, and beyond. To opt for inaction is itself a moral choice – and only infrequently the right one. We must decide what to do and what not to do, so the question is on what basis we make these decisions: using the insights that theological ethics can provide; giving up on seeking God's will and using some other basis; or making the decisions on whim, with no basis at all. The fact that theological ethics remains within the crisis Barth made known, that it can only be based on the provisional theology of wayfarers, makes no difference at all to our need for the guidance it provides. For theology to give up on

---

40   *Romans* II, 438 (461–2).
41   *Romans* II, 427 (450).

this wrestling with the needs of the world would not be humility, but another form of faithlessness.

The ethics of Barth's *Church Dogmatics* are strikingly consistent with those of the second edition of *Romans* II, and the most notable feature of this continuity is the importance of dialectic as a structure for the ethics of both works. Appreciating this key role of dialectic is significant for interpreting Barth's ethical thought: it shows up the weakness of one-sided criticisms of Barth's ethics, and makes clear his attitude to system in ethics. Most importantly, recognizing the dialectical character of Barth's ethical thought in response to the crisis he announced in 1922 shows us a way of pursuing Christian ethics that recognizes both the necessity of the endeavour and its inescapably problematic character: we cannot be spared the responsibility of serious reflection on how we should live, but all such reflection can only be a working guide to where we, individually and collectively, may encounter God's will for our lives in the form of the divine command. We need more from ethics than a postmodern contentless norm, providing no power to identify injustice and no shape for our obedience, but we need less from ethics than a system that stands in the way of our listening for the Word of God by convincing us we already know what it will be. Barth's dialectical ethical thought, his vision for how to do ethics in the crisis of encounter with God's living Word, points the way to an understanding of Christian ethics with critical power, substantive guidance, and openness to the unexpected grace of God.

Bibliography

Works by Karl Barth

English translations, where available, are cited first, with the German edition in parentheses.

Anselm: Fides Quaerens Intellectum: Anselm's Proof of the Existence of God in the Context of His Theological Scheme. Translated by Ian W. Robertson. London: SCM. Press, 1960. (*Fides Quaerens Intellectum: Anselms Beweis der Existenz Gottes im Zusammenhang Seines Theologischen Programms.* Edited by Eberhard Jüngel and Ingolf Ulrich Dalferth. Zurich: Theologischer Verlag, 1981.)
Church Dogmatics, 4 volumes, 13 part-volumes. Edited by G.W. Bromiley and T.F. Torrance. Edinburgh: T. & T. Clark, 1936–77. (*Kirchliche Dogmatik.* Zurich: Theologischer Verlag, 1986–93.)
Die Christliche Dogmatik im Entwurf. 1. Bd.: Die Lehre vom Worte Gottes. Prolegomena zur Christlichen Dogmatik, München 1927. Karl Barth-Gesamtausgabe. Zurich: Gerhard Sauter, 1982.
Eine Schweitzer Stimme, 1938–1945. Zurich: Evangelischer Verlag, 1945.
The Epistle to the Romans. Translated by Edwyn C. Hoskyns. Oxford: Oxford University Press, 1968. (*Der Römerbrief (Zweite Fassung) 1922.* Zurich: Theologischer Verlag, 1989.)
The Göttingen Dogmatics: Instruction in the Christian Religion. Translated by Geoffrey W. Bromiley. Edited by Hannelotte Reiffen. Vol. I. Grand Rapids, Michigan: Eerdmans, 1991. (*Unterricht in der Christlichen Religion, Erster Band: Prolegomena, 1924.* Edited by Hannelotte Reiffen. Karl Barth-Gesamtausgabe. Zurich: Theologischer Verlag, 1985.)
How I Changed My Mind. Richmond, Virginia: John Knox Press, 1966.
Theology and Church: Shorter Writings 1920–1928. Translated by Louise Pettibone Smith. New York and Evanston: Harper & Row, 1962. (*Die Theologie und die Kirche.* Gesammelte Vortrag. Vol. 2. Munich: Evangelischer Verlag AG, Zollikon-Zurich, 1928.)
The Theology of Schleiermacher. Edited by Dietrich Ritschl. Translated by G.W. Bromiley. Edinburgh: T. & T. Clark, 1982. (*Die Theologie Schleiemachers 1923/4.* Karl Barth-Gesamtausgabe. Zurich: Theologischer Verlag, 1978.)
The Word of God and the Word of Man. Translated by Douglas Horton. London: Hodder & Stoughton, 1929. (*Das Wort Gottes und die Theologie.* Munich: Chr. Kaiser Verlag, 1929.)

Other Works

Adams, Robert M. 'A Modified Divine Command Theory of Ethical Wrongness'. In *The Virtue of Faith*, 97–122. Oxford: Oxford University Press, 1987.
———. 'Divine Command Metaethics Modified Again'. In *The Virtue of Faith*, 128–43. Oxford: Oxford University Press, 1987.
Bauman, Zygmunt. *Postmodern Ethics.* Oxford: Blackwell, 1993.
Beintker, Michael. *Die Dialektik in der 'Dialektischen Theologie' Karl Barths.* Munich: Chr. Kaiser Verlag, 1987.
Biggar, Nigel, 'A Case for Casuistry in the Church', *Modern Theology*, 6:1 (1989), 29–51.
———. *The Hastening That Waits: Karl Barth's Ethics.* Oxford: Clarendon Press, 1993.

————. 'Hearing God's Command and Thinking About What's Right: With and Beyond Barth'. In *Reckoning with Barth: Essays in Commemoration of the Centenary of Karl Barth's Birth*, edited by Nigel Biggar, 108–11. London: Mowbray, 1988.

Boff, Leonardo. *Ecology and Liberation: A New Paradigm*. Ecology and Justice Series. Maryknoll, New York: Orbis Books, 1995.

Bonhoeffer, Dietrich. *Ethics*. Translated by Neville Horton Smith. Edited by Eberhard Bethge. London: Collins, 1964.

Bouillard, Henri. *Genèse et Evolution de la Théologie Dialectique*. Paris: Aubier, 1957.

Busch, Eberhard. *Karl Barth: His Life from Letters and Autobiographical Texts*. Translated by John Bowden. Philadelphia: Fortress Press, 1976.

Clough, David, '*Eros* and *Agape* in Karl Barth's *Church Dogmatics*', *International Journal of Systematic Theology*, 2:2 (2000), 189–203.

————. 'Fighting at the Command of God: Assessing the Borderline Case in Karl Barth's Account of War in the *Church Dogmatics*'. In *Conversing with Barth*, edited by John McDowell and Mike Higton, 214–26. Aldershot: Ashgate, 2004.

Cullberg, John. *Das Problem der Ethik in der Dialektischen Theologie*. Vol. 1. Uppsala: A.-B. Lundequistska Bokhandeln, 1938.

Finnis, John. *Natural Law and Natural Rights*. Oxford: Clarendon Press, 1980.

Ford, Ford Maddox. *The Good Soldier*. London: Penguin Books, 1946.

Gill, Theodore Alexander. *Protestant Political Theory: The Political Problem in Some New Reformation Theology*. Zurich: University of Zurich, 1953.

Gorringe, Timothy. *Karl Barth: Against Hegemony*. Christian Theology in Context. Oxford; New York: Clarendon Press: Oxford University Press, 1999.

Grisez, Germain. *The Way of the Lord Jesus*. Vol. I. Chicago: Franciscan Herald Press, 1983.

Gustafson, James M. *Ethics from a Theocentric Perspective*. Vol. 2. Chicago: University of Chicago, 1984.

————. *Protestant and Roman Catholic Ethics*. Chicago: University of Chicago, 1978.

Helm, Paul. *Divine Commands and Morality*. Oxford and New York: Oxford University Press, 1981.

Henry, Martin. *Franz Overbeck: Theologian? Religion and History in the Thought of Franz Overbeck*. European University Studies Series 23: Theology. Frankfurt: Peter Lang, 1995.

Herberg, Will. 'The Social Philosophy of Karl Barth'. In *Community, State, and Church: Three Essays*, edited by Karl Barth, 11–67. New York: Anchor, 1968.

Hood, Robert E. *Contemporary Political Orders and Christ*. Allison Park, Pennsylvania: Pickwick Publications, 1985.

Hunsinger, George. 'Toward a Radical Barth'. In *Karl Barth and Radical Politics*, edited by George Hunsinger, 181–233. Philadelphia: Westminster Press, 1976.

Idziak, Janine Marie. *Divine Command Morality: Historical and Contemporary Readings*. New York: Mellen Press, 1979.

Johnson, William Stacy. *The Mystery of God: Karl Barth and the Postmodern Foundations of Theology*. Louisville, Kentucky: Westminster John Knox Press, 1997.

Kant, Immanuel. *Groundwork of the Metaphysic of Morals*. Edited by H.J. Paton. London: Hutchinson & Co. Ltd, 1948.

Kierkegaard, Søren. *Fear and Trembling*. Translated by Alasdair Hannay. London: Penguin Books, 1985.

Link, Wilhelm. '"Christliche Ethik" und "Dialektische Theology"'. In *Theologische Aufsätze. Karl Barth Zum 50. Geburtstag*, edited by E. Wolf, 262–74. Munich: Chr. Kaiser Verlag, 1936.

Lovin, Robin. *Christian Faith and Public Choices*. Philadelphia: Fortress Press, 1984.

Lowe, Walter. *Theology and Difference: The Wound of Reason*. Bloomington: Indiana University Press, 1993.

Mackie, J.L. *Ethics: Inventing Right and Wrong*. London: Penguin Books, 1977.

Marquardt, Friedrich-Wilhelm. 'Socialism in the Theology of Karl Barth'. In *Karl Barth and Radical Politics*, edited by George Hunsinger, 47–76. Philadelphia: Westminster Press, 1976.

———. *Theologie und Sozialismus: Das Beispiel Karl Barths*. Munich: Chr. Kaiser Verlag, 1972.

McCormack, Bruce L., 'Graham Ward's *Barth, Derrida and the Language of Theology*', *Scottish Journal of Theology*, 49:1 (Winter 1996), 97–109.

———. *Karl Barth's Critically Realistic Dialectical Theology: Its Genesis and Development, 1909–1936*. Oxford: Clarendon Press, 1995.

McDowell, John and Higton, Mike (eds). *Conversing with Barth*. Aldershot: Ashgate, 2004.

Mouw, Richard J. *The God Who Commands: A Study in Divine Command Ethics*. Notre Dame, Indiana: University of Notre Dame Press, 1990.

Nagel, Thomas. *The View from Nowhere*. Oxford: Oxford University Press, 1986.

Nowell-Smith, Patrick. 'Morality: Religious and Secular'. In *Christian Ethics and Contemporary Moral Philosophy*, edited by I.T. Ramsey, 95–112. London: SCM Press Ltd, 1966.

O'Donovan, Oliver. *Resurrection and Moral Order: An Outline for Evangelical Ethics*. Leicester: Apollos, 1994.

Outka, Gene. *Agape: An Ethical Analysis*. New Haven, Connecticut: Yale University Press, 1972.

———. 'Following at a Distance: Ethics and the Identity of Jesus'. In *Scriptural Authority and Narrative Interpretation*, edited by Garrett Green, 144–60. Philadelphia: Fortress Press, 1987.

Overbeck, Franz. *Christentum und Kultur*. Edited by Carl Albrecht Bernoulli. Basel: Benno & Schwabe & Co., 1919.

Peterson, Erik. *Was Ist Theologie?*. Bonn: Friedrich Cohen, 1925.

Pullman, Philip. *His Dark Materials: Northern Lights; The Subtle Knife; The Amber Spyglass*. London: Scholastic, 2000.

Rawls, John. *Political Liberalism*. New York: Columbia University Press, 1993.

Richardson, Alan, 'Review of Cornelius Van Til, *The New Foundations of Modernism*', *Theology*, 51:331 (1948), 30–31.

Smith, Steven G. *The Argument to the Other: Reason Beyond Reason in the Thought of Karl Barth and Emmanuel Levinas*. Chico, California: Scholars Press, 1983.

Stiltner, Brian, 'Who Can Understand Abraham? The Relation of God and Morality in Kierkegaard and Aquinas', *Journal of Religious Ethics*, 21:2 (1993), 401–25.

Villa-Vicencio, Charles. 'Karl Barth's "Revolution of God": Quietism or Anarchy?' In *On Reading Karl Barth in South Africa*, edited by Charles Villa-Vicencio, 45–58. Grand Rapids, Michigan: Eerdmans, 1988.

von Balthasar, Hans Urs. *The Theology of Karl Barth: Exposition and Interpretation*. Translated by Edward T. Oakes. San Francisco: Communio Books, Ignatius Press, 1992.

Wanamaker, C.A. 'Romans 13: A Hermeneutic for Church and State'. In *On Reading Karl Barth in South Africa*, edited by Charles Villa-Vicencio, 91–104. Grand Rapids, Michigan: William B. Eerdmans, 1988.

Ward, Graham. *Barth, Derrida and the Language of Theology*. Cambridge: Cambridge University Press, 1995.

Webb, Stephen H. *Refiguring Theology*. New York: State University of New York Press, 1991.

Webster, John. '"Life from the Third Dimension": Human Action in Barth's Early Ethics'. In *Barth's Moral Theology*, 11–39. Edinburgh: T. & T. Clark, 1998.

———, 'On the Frontiers of What Is Observable', *Downside Review*, 105 (1987), 169–80.

Williams, Rowan. 'Barth, War and the State'. In *Reckoning with Barth: Essays in Commemoration of the Centenary of Karl Barth's Birth*, edited by Nigel Biggar, 170–90. London: Mowbray, 1988.

Willis, Robert E. *The Ethics of Karl Barth*. Leiden: E.J. Brill, 1971.

Yoder, John H. *Karl Barth and the Problem of War*. Nashville: Abingdon Press, 1970.

————, 'On Not Being Ashamed of the Gospel: Particularity, Pluralism, and Validation', *Faith and Philosophy*, 9:3 (1992), 285–300.

Index